A Comparative Perspective of Women's Economic Empowerment

The need for the creation of an enabling political, legal and economic environment for women within Turkey is rising. A growing concern is shown at the ethnic divisions and local discrimination against women, which have spilled over into the labor market. This book lends a supporting voice to the economic and social empowerment of women globally, focusing on the real causes and the unpredictable nature of the ongoing conflicts surrounding the issue.

The authors bring to the forefront problems of development within various regions and the implementation of projects, which address the state of women, inequality and risks, that are inimical to their participation in the economy. Emphasis is laid on why women should be permitted access to the many opportunities in information technology and exchange, partnership growth and networking in this digital era. The oppressive policies of Turkey are scrutinized to unravel the dangers they pose to the corporate existence of women in the modern world. Furthermore, this book centers on the deliberation on regional politics and issues on gender and women's empowerment in modern Turkey whilst comparing with other countries. The work sheds light on salient issues and possible remedies within target countries and the concerted efforts made to create a reliable structure to discuss gender conflicts. Ample contributions from countries such as the USA, Germany, Serbia, South Africa and United Kingdom are pivotal to comparing and examining the main debates. Addressing several global gender-related examples as well as Turkey's national principles, this book encourages full involvement of women and girls in deciding the fate of their country.

This book serves as the rallying point of an array of informative and mind-expanding works of literature in regional studies, gender studies, migration economy, and area studies in countries like Turkey, USA, Serbia, UK, and India. Experts, students, and readers in the academic sphere may find this work educative and intellectually fulfilling.

Meltem İnce Yenilmez is an associate professor in the Department of Economics, Yasar University, Turkey. Her research interests range from Gender Inequality and Discrimination Policies in Labor Market to Women Empowerment and Female Labor Force. Her works have been published in English and in Turkish in edited volumes and in leading national and international journals. She has taken part in international/national socio-economic projects, and conducted the Jean Monnet Module on "Gender Politics and EU in the Time of Crisis".

Onur Burak Çelik is an assistant professor in the Department of Economics, Yasar University, Turkey. He completed his undergraduate study in Mathematics at Bogazici University and his master's degree in economics at the same university. He went to the USA in 2002 and earned his Ph.D. degree in economics at the University of Connecticut in 2009. In the same year, he joined the Eastern Connecticut State University academic staff. Afterwards, he worked at Quinnipiac University from 2010 to 2013. Currently, his primary research interest is sports economics.

Routledge Studies in Labour Economics

1. Youth and the Crisis
Unemployment, Education and Health in Europe
Edited by Gianluigi Coppola and Niall O'Higgins

2. Workers and the Global Informal Economy
Interdisciplinary Perspectives
Edited by Supriya Routh and Vando Borghi

3. The Political Economy of Employment Relations
Alternative Theory and Practice
Aslihan Aykac

4. The Economics of Trade Unions
A Study of a Research Field and Its Findings
Hristos Doucouliagos, Richard B. Freeman and Patrice Laroche

5. Young People and the Labour Market
A Comparative Perspective
Floro Caroleo, Olga Demidova, Enrico Marelli and Marcello Signorelli

6. Women's Economic Empowerment in Turkey
Edited by Onur Burak Çelik and Meltem İnce Yenilmez

7. A Comparative Perspective of Women's Economic Empowerment
Edited by Meltem İnce Yenilmez and Onur Burak Çelik

For more information about this series, please visit https://www.routledge.com/
Routledge-Studies-in-Labour-Economics/book-series/RSLE

A Comparative Perspective of Women's Economic Empowerment

Edited by
Meltem İnce Yenilmez and
Onur Burak Çelik

LONDON AND NEW YORK

First published 2019
by Routledge
2 Park Square, Milton Park, Abingdon, Oxon OX14 4RN

and by Routledge
605 Third Avenue, New York, NY 10017

First issued in paperback 2020

Routledge is an imprint of the Taylor & Francis Group, an informa business

British Library Cataloguing in Publication Data
A catalogue record for this book is available from the British Library

Library of Congress Cataloging-in-Publication Data
Names: Yenilmez, Meltem Ince, editor. | Celik, Onur Burak, editor.
Title: A comparative perspective of women's economic empowerment /
edited by Meltem Ince Yenilmez and Onur Burak Celik.
Description: 1 Edition. | New York : Routledge, 2019. |
Series: Routledge studies in labour economics
Identifiers: LCCN 2019007300| ISBN 9780367146948 (hardback) |
ISBN 9780429053146 (ebk)
Subjects: LCSH: Women--Employment--Case studies. | Women--Economic
conditions--Case studies. | Women--Social conditions--Case studies.
Classification: LCC HD6053 .C726 2019 | DDC 331.4--dc23
LC record available at https://lccn.loc.gov/2019007300

ISBN 13: 978-0-367-72842-7 (pbk)
ISBN 13: 978-0-367-14694-8 (hbk)

Typeset in Times New Roman
by Taylor & Francis Books

To my dear wife İlkay who gave me strength with her unconditional support, to my daughter Bianca Arya who gave me the energy to go on, to my mother and my primary school teacher Gönül Çelik.

Onur Burak ÇELİK

For my beloved son Bryan Poyraz, for my husband Özgür and my family who always believe in me.

Meltem İNCE YENİLMEZ

Contents

Figures

Tables

Contributors

Sonja ĐJURIČIN is a Research Associate in the Institute of Economic Sciences Belgrade (Republic of Serbia).

Murat Şakir EROĞUL is an Assistant Professor in the Department of Management at Adelphi University, NY (USA).

Gözde ERSÖZ is an Associate Professor in the Department of Physical Education and Sports at Namik Kemal University, Tekirdag (Turkey).

Jörg FREILING is a Professor and Vice Dean, Chair in Small Business & Entrepreneurship at University of Bremen, Bremen (Germany).

Humaira HANSROD is a Doctoral Candidate in the Department of International Development at University of Oxford, Oxford (UK).

Aki HARIMA is a Postdoctoral Researcher in the Chair in Small Business & Entrepreneurship (LEMEX) at University of Bremen, Bremen (Germany).

Mohammed HASHIRU is a Doctoral Candidate in the Department of International Relations at Karadeniz Technical University, Trabzon (Turkey).

Meltem İNCE YENİLMEZ is an Associate Professor in the Department of Economics at Yasar University, Izmir (Turkey).

Ceyhun Çağlar KILINÇ has a B.A. degree in Business from Eastern Mediterranean University (EMU). After graduating from B.A. he gained M.A and Ph. D. degrees from Selcuk University in Business. His research interests are on the topics of marketing, tourism marketing and service quality. He was an Associate Professor of Business in Tourism Faculty of Selcuk University, Konya (Turkey) until February 2019. He is now in the Manavgat Tourism Faculty at Akdeniz University (Turkey). Dr. Kılınç is also a member of some international academic journals worldwide and now is the co-editor of *International Journal of Economic & Management Perspectives*.

Sharon MAYER is a Master Graduate, Chair in Small Business & Entrepreneurship (LEMEX) at University of Bremen, Bremen (Germany).

xiv *Contributors*

Quynh Duong PHUONG is a Research Assistant, Chair in Small Business & Entrepreneurship (LEMEX) at University of Bremen, Bremen (Germany).

Mehmet ŞENGÜR is an Assistant Professor in the Department of Economics at Osmangazi University, Eskisehir (Turkey).

Altın Aslı ŞİMŞEK is an Assistant Professor in the Department of Law at Atilim University, Ankara (Turkey).

Bahar TANER is a Professor in the Department of Tourism Management at Mersin University, Mersin (Turkey).

Viktoria THEOHAVORA is a Master's Degree Graduate, Chair in Small Business & Entrepreneurship (LEMEX) at University of Bremen, Bremen (Germany).

Özgür TÜFEKÇİ is an Assistant Professor in the Department of International Relations at Karadeniz Technical University, Trabzon (Turkey).

Çağla ÜNLÜTÜRK ULUTAŞ is an Associate Professor in the Department of Labour Economics and Industrial Relations at University of Pamukkale, Denizli (Turkey).

Hatice Ahsen UTKU is a Doctoral Candidate in the Department of Political Science at Northeastern University, Boston (USA).

Mehmet Erdem YAYA is a Professor in the Department of Economics at Eastern Michigan University, Michigan (USA).

Gülsün YILDIRIM has a B.A. degree in Tourism Management from Adnan Menderes University and ELT from Pamukkale University. She has an M.A degree from Eskişehir Osmangazi University in Tourism Management and a Ph.D. degree from Selcuk University/Gazi University in Tourism Management. She has been working as a lecturer in Ardesen Vocational School of Recep Tayyip Erdogan University, Rize (Turkey) since 2012.

Preface

A common image of the work women do and the work that men do is that women manage the home and childcare while men earn the family income. Although this image is inaccurate even in developed countries, many find such a division of labor so natural and inevitable that they deplore any deviation from it. However, why does such a stereotype seem so natural? In this set of economics, sociological and feminist articles about women's empowerment from recent issues in the literature, historical and contemporary explanations are presented and evaluated for developed countries.

Once we can see that even a very familiar division of labor is socially constructed rather than inevitable and unchangeable, we can consider a completely new set of questions. What kinds of policies have to be considered to empower women? Who does and who does not benefit from women's empowerment? Is it desirable to change the behavioral patterns of societies – both within and outside the home? If so, what are some of the obstacles to and opportunities for this change?

Not everyone – not even sociologists, economists and feminists – agree on how to answer these questions. This is the first book published that is entirely devoted to the social, economic and political aspects of women's empowerment. The articles in this book draw a number of perspectives – micro and macro, liberal and radical – with different emphases and policy implications. The book brings together the work of a number of people who are applying their minds to the challenges and problems of empowerment issues and a developing field of research. The contributions come from colleagues working in their disciplines of administration and economics. Other disciplines also play an important role, particularly sports, finance, sociology and international studies.

Several authors in the book suggest that we can find answers to our questions only when we develop an understanding of "empowerment" from women's perspective. We present neither a final explanation of why things are as they are, nor a recipe for what to do about them. However, we do provide both theories and facts that students and academics can use to develop their own expectations and make their own decisions. We think this book is valuable for those studying the worlds of empowerment as well as those concerned about the position of women in contemporary Turkish society.

The variety of readings presented here under the title of *A Comparative Perspective of Women's Economic Empowerment* is an interrelated collection and the book is itself a collective effort – not just involving the two editors. Therefore, our last task should be to thank all those who have contributed to this volume for the way in which they have recognized that complex ideas are accessible ideas. It has been a great pleasure to compile this volume and a very important part of that pleasure has been the constant reminder of the depth, the range and the excitement of the study of women's empowerment. In addition, we are grateful to our families for being a constant source of encouragement, support and efficient assistance.

Meltem İNCE YENİLMEZ
Onur Burak ÇELIK

1   Women Empowerment and Emancipation

Meltem İNCE YENİLMEZ

Introduction

It is essential to use all social and financial resources for progress in a globalized and interconnected world. Even though equality among people is seen as a comprehensive guideline and a fundamental human right, women still face discrimination, rejection, and estrangement, regardless of general advances in society. Gender equity, established in human rights, is perceived both as an essential basic advancement on its own and as indispensable to other improvement objectives. Only if women and young girls can completely understand their rights in all areas of life can human development result.

In 1995, instruments like the Beijing Action Platform attended by 189 UN Member States at the Fourth World Conference on Women, and the Millennium Declaration signed by 189 countries in 2000 provided the basic framework for rights. These two dates are important since all UN Member States decided to take action and agreed on the declarations of the meetings. Despite progression in the last decade, an extensive range of challenges to sexual orientation and women's empowerment remain. These consolidate around women having unequal access to money and common resources; social and real exploitation of adult and young women; the uneven weight of unpaid work; and brutality against women. These problems slow down progress for women and also for their families and their different systems. The current situation of sexual orientation uniformity in Turkey is not promising. Turkey is as of now an Upper Middle Income Country (MIC), with strong and progressive monetary improvement, signifying GDP of 10,666 USD per capita in 2016. In 2004, Turkey began the EU accession process with moves towards meeting EU standards, incorporating changes in human rights, value, and reasonable, lawful treatment. Despite these changes, particularly in the Constitution (Ataselim-Yilmaz, 2015), the Civil Code and the Labor Act, the execution and genuine affirmation of these rights is up until now a test, or, in other words, the fundamental improvement markers for women are a long way behind similar MICs and EU member states. The UNECE (2017) Report on achieving the Millennium Development Goals (MDGs) in Europe and Central Asia demonstrates that the objective of reducing gender inequality in essential instruction has nearly been accomplished, in spite of the fact that the extent of young women who are not taking up optional training is significant. The Report includes the present basic problems: especially those related to geological and social sexual preferences that are residual difficulties for the achievement of MDGs. The main gaps are in the findings of women's participation in government and labor force. The presence of women in authoritative positions at the political level is 14.3%, and that of local government is less two than 2%. Women's enthusiasm for work drive is only 32.5%, which puts Turkey behind all other OECD countries and many developing countries around the globe. The World Economic Forum's Global Gender Gap Report benchmarks national gender equality disparities of countries on money related, political, social and prosperity based criteria. In 2016, Turkey was situated 131th among 142 countries in the general document. In the Economic Participation and Opportunity sub-record, Turkey is situated 138th. Closing the sex disparity gap in all locales and drawing in women to take an active role in budgetary life is essential to building strong economies, setting up stable social orders, and achieving all-inclusive goals for development. It is multi-dimensional as it covers:

1   Economic freedom
2   Social mindfulness
3   Political awareness

These components can be listed as financial empowering, social strengthening and political emancipation.

Women's Economic Empowerment

All the poverty relief programs are focused on women as they are financially more hindered than men and as their role in raising children is essential for the financial improvement of a country. Financial strengthening is making women mindful about their job/significance in financial advancement and gives them space for accomplishing financial freedom and records their outstanding commitments to the production procedure. Financial access is just a tools to plan systems concentrating on building credit value and money related autonomy among women by reducing the gender bias that keeps women from accessing their legitimate place in each circle of life. Women living outside cities have less access to assets to create stable earnings. Family unit salary is not divided proportionally between men and women therefore the circulation of amount of wages received inside the family might be unequal.

Different investigations into intra-household division of assets demonstrate that in many regions of the world there exists a solid bias against women, for example, in terms of nourishment, healthcare, training, and inheritance. In terms of progress initiatives, the vast majority of aid programs are intended to help strengthen women's position; they begin with facilitating access to credit and contributions to salary ranges, which are generally acknowledged as being effective measures for financial empowerment. Thus financial strengthening is an important condition for empowering women to have equal access to equal wages because, without financial stability, women are not able to practice their rights and privileges. Without equal payment, individuals need additional options in order to have security or else have to accept the decisions made for them. Without an individual or group voice, the defenceless will remain that way. The cooperative energy created from a collective approach is significantly higher than that from an individual methodology, which prompts the strategy creators and different organizations to embrace a participatory approach to engaging women. The dynamic association/investment of women in energetic gatherings like self-help-groups, neighborhood-groups and so forth empowers them to understand the objective of strengthening. Therefore, Turkish government has realized the power and the potential of a collective self-improvement of women and has begun to constitute training programs. The ongoing investigations into improvement issues show that progress can be made by raising the awareness among poor women and increasing their participation in the training programs.

Social Strengthening of Women

Social emancipation implies a more equitable economic wellbeing for women in the public realm since the main duty of every government is to guarantee equality and rights to all individuals in the society. It is regularly contended that encouraging women's entrance into finance can only be a powerful means for accomplishing women's empowerment if it is connected to different sorts of exercises like drawing attention to the effects of women's subordination, the importance of confidence, and the significance and advantages of enabling women. Achieving gender equality depends on the acknowledgment that all intercessions for women must guarantee a situation free from all types of violence against women and furthermore guarantee the investment and satisfactory portrayal of women in many approaches. One of the proposals of the National Policy on Education (1997) was to advance strengthening of women through the organization of education, and these essential learning opportunities are the starting point to raise women's training. The National Literacy Mission with the coordinated effort of UNESCO is another step forward to solving the problem of the lack of education in the age group of 15–35 years (Mishra, 1998).The generalization of basic education, enrolment, and attendance of young women in schools, expanding the quantity of young women's lodging, women's polytechnics and vocational establishments, informal adult training and distant training programs were some advances made to help women training and promote social strengthening.

The vision of the government's Tenth Plan (2014–2018) is to guarantee that each woman in the nation can achieve her maximum potential and to offer the advantages of development and success through a participatory methodology, which engages women and makes them partners in their development. When women can raise a voice in central leadership, which begins inside the family, they will be in a situation to become actors in alleviating their poor financial state. And they will start to transform gender relations. Thus they should be dealt with as equal partners in central leadership and usage rather than as recipients. Women's expanded investment at the basic leadership level must be seen to prompt their expanded advancement and strengthening if such interest is to empower them to accomplish more noteworthy command over elements of creation, access to assets and the dissemination of advantages. Collective or cooperative processes dependably give help to strengthening as they open individuals to neighborhood systems and this social communication results in mindfulness about local realities which likewise encourages them to overcome the barriers for accessing resources.

Women Strengthening in Politics

Political strengthening is a procedure that empowers women to build their mobility and break their isolation, to build up their confidence and mental self-image, and to set up their public presence whereby they take an interest in central leadership in a growing system of awareness and critical analysis to control and affect development. Equality in politics tries to provide not only equal rights to both genders but also the opportunity to access the institutions that are the centers of power. Investment of women in Turkish institutions is been perceived as a step towards creating balance.

Today, one of the issues of concern is the level of women's participation in political life. Political participation involves the right to vote, right to compete, right to candidacy, and their involvement in the decision making process and appointment of women at all levels of government. The holding of seats by women in political establishments gives them the opportunity to raise their demands and other related individual and social issues formally. The interest of women in the appointive procedure is an indication of their political awareness and their yearning for status improvement. The figures concerning women's common participation have been steadily rising throughout the years through different races as voters and as competitors and in terms of participation in campaigning. The number of women being voted in as a representative has been consistently expanding.

The Accomplishment of Women's Rights by Assuring the Development of Nations

Particular consideration in Turkey has to be given to strengthening the status of women in society and their representation in political decision making by reforming the gender equality policies either at national level or regional level. The Turkish Constitution stipulates equality among women and men. Also, reforms must be accomplished so as to implement the accepted principles into practice and apply them on the ground. As indicated in the Progress Report by the European Commission in November 2006, the legal framework is adequate.

The Penal Code, the Labor Code and the Law on Municipalities have been revised to give better protection to women's rights. Nevertheless, the report observes that further courses of action are required on parental leave, equal pay and access to work, and government oversight on investment funds. Turkey has accomplished significant headway regarding gender equality. However, the situation of women in Turkey remains extremely problematic in three related areas:

1   Brutal acts perpetrated against women
2   Lesser opportunities in the workplace
3   Minimum access to training.

The issues surrounding implementing Women's rights in Turkey remains a huge problem. The situation is even worse within poorer communities. These communities have higher incidences of illiteracy and so, lack of education has made women vulnerable to certain practices (Kaya, 2009). Domestic violence against women is also a critical problem in Turkey, as it is in many other European countries. Most especially, the South East of Turkey is still widely known for its honour killings. Some of these issues were clearly analysed in February 2016 in the ad hoc Parliamentary Committee on custom and honour crimes against women report and some measures to combat the problem outlined. The Prime Minister in July, that same year equally released a circular with regards to measures that could be taken against these acts.

To bridge the gaping gender gap, there must be an immediate transformation in terms of providing skills training and all-round education for these women. Without these measures, it will be harder for these women to enter the labor market, as many basic skills are necessary. However, to achieve significant progress, the administrative arm must be improved. For instance, the Directorate General for the Status of Women remains understaffed and does not have the relevant and much-needed Equality Body. Nevertheless, some measures and initiatives are ongoing. One such is the provision of education on prevention of violence against women to young men on entry into the military service. In addition, Police Schools have also included documentation about women's rights into their curriculum. However, there must be more effort and initiatives in place to effectively combat this menace.

Transforming the Position of Women in the Labor Market

In view of the efforts made towards establishing the equal place of women in society, there is still a lot to be done. Surprisingly, the situation in the labor market has deteriorated rather than improved. Turkey still has one of the lowest participation rates of women in the labor market at 32% in 2018 as against 64% seen in the European Union. Nevertheless, in recent months, the number for female unemployment has risen. There exists a glaring division between genders and this is made worse by the regional, urban and rural divides. The majority of women in the labor market are concentrated in the unpaid employment and agricultural sectors. There should be more initiatives and incentives put in place to attract more women into the labor market. These measures are not generally targeted at increasing the awareness of women's rights but can also help provide sustainable growth and development to the economy of the country. Owing to the fact that over 70 percent of the informal economy is made up of women, such measures can drive general growth in the Turkish economy. They can equally transform the informal economy to a formal one. Therefore more efforts should be made towards accomplishing these milestones and existing initiatives to combat these problems be praised and supported.

To effectively address these issues, there must be a national employment strategy crafted that closely follows the guidelines of the European Employment Strategy (Kaya, 2009). Significant progress can only be achieved if women's rights implementations are mainstreamed. The dynamics of the social economic situation of women and its connections to internal migration and displacement, urbanization and poverty must be critically analysed. This should be a key element addressed by partnership setups between the Turkish authorities and the European Commission. In addition, several strategies must be put in place towards promoting women's activities and combating the many problems faced by women in society. Turkey must also provide adequate support for the mainstreaming of women's organizations.

Acknowledging the Influential Roles Played by Women NGOs and Civil Society

Turkey has in the past few years witnessed significant growth in its civil society. One of the major landmarks used in identifying this progressive growth is the increase in Women NGOs amounting to over 400 active associations in 2019. Many of these organizations are fast gaining voice and have been able to make significant impacts on the social and political spheres in Turkey. The Turkish Government has acknowledged that these women's associations play a major role in society. Therefore in partnerships with the Directorate General for the Status of Woman and the social service units, some initiatives and relevant legislation have been enacted.

Some of these initiatives include the combat against the unregistered economy, implementation of the revised Labor Code and the 2006 Women's employment summit organized by the Turkish Confederation of Employer Associations. To fully combat these problems, partnerships between organizations is essential because it drives success efficiently and seamlessly. An impressive example is the October 2004, "Stop domestic violence| campaign, which came to light through the partnerships of the foundation of Contemporary Education, Office of the Istanbul Governor, and the Daily *Hürriyet*. These campaigns were a huge success and have brought concrete results since their inception. The "Come on Girls Let's Go to School" program is also a successful campaign that has attracted more girl primary education.

Many TV and newspaper outlets have equally extended their support to these campaigns. In addition, through firm connections between organizations within the EU and the Turkish associations, more initiatives and organizations will be created. All of this will further strengthen and promote women participating in all areas of Turkish society.

Financial Support is a Core Element in the Support of Women Empowerment

The European Commission actively supports efforts and reforms made by Turkey through the process of EU accession negotiations. Many women related projects already possess sufficient support through EU funds. The Commission is actively supporting the strengthening of the administrative capacity of the Directorate General for the Status of Women. It is also actively driving the implementation of gender equality legislation and policies on the mainstream level. So far, some improvements have been seen especially because the Commission has partnered with central and local authorities as well as NGOs. Special assistance has also been provided to foster communication among local governments and Women NGOs. It is believed that through communication and joint responsibilities, more improvements will be witnessed across the country.

Some projects implemented promote women entrepreneurship through management training and consultancy services. The Business Development Center in Istanbul was created as one such project. Financial support is also targeted towards promoting girl's literacy and minimizes gender disparity in education. Other targeted programs focus on actively fighting against domestic violence especially through the creation of sustainable counselling centers and shelters.

Micro and small business is also promoted especially as women play an important role in such establishments. A good example of such support initiatives is the provisions of vocational and entrepreneurial training for women in traditional arts (jewellery design, gift box making, traditional Antep embroidery). Administrative capacity and human resource development are equally strengthened through some establishments such as the new Instrument for Pre-Accession Assistance (IPA). However, there is still a lot of work to be done. The European Commission must remain firm in its position and provisions of support especially toward programs and projects focused on women. The Turkish authorities still have a major role to play especially by adopting and creating relevant operational programs. These partnerships between Turkey and the European Commission are important to foster progress and attain success.

Conclusion

In conclusion, women empowerment and the fight against domestic violence remains an enormous challenge. It holds the position of top priority for many democratic states including the USA and other member states in the European

Union. Turkey must implement and build structures towards bridging the gender equality gap in the country. However ongoing industrial urban economy and society transformation will influence the progress of women-related activities. To foster the pre-accession process, women empowerment must be seen as a top priority. Therefore all stakeholders must play a vital role in order to ensure progress especially in terms of the implementation of women's rights. One such measure that can foster progress is the establishment of a permanent Gender Equality Committee in the Parliament as first outlined in 2006 circular issued by the Prime Minister.

Nevertheless, the general public is becoming aware of the issues of women's rights in Turkey. This awareness can be increased through the establishment of debates and media programs towards changing mentalities and fighting stereotypes. It is, without doubt, acknowledged that Turkey holds the position of the vanguard in fighting these problems. This can be verified through the November 2006 organization of the Euro-Mediterranean Partnership Ministerial Conference on women held in Istanbul as well as the further adoption of a common framework that would aid the strengthening of women roles in all spheres and sectors in Turkey.

The European Commission will continue to supervise and offer financial support to Turkish women related projects to ensure genuine improvement. As a historian by background, let me finally quote Atatürk: "Human society is composed of two genders which are men and women; is it possible for one half to catch the sky while the other remains anchored to the land?" Naturally, such a concept is impossible. Therefore Turkish women must be empowered to foster a stronger and better economic climate in Turkey.

References

Ataselim-Yilmaz, S. (2015, June 03). Mind the (Gender) Gap. Retrieved from: https://www.huffingtonpost.com/entry/mind-the-gender-gap_b_6809916.html

Kaya, H. E. (2009). An Overview of Turkish Women's Status in Turkey. *Toplum ve Demokrasi*, 2(5), Ocak-Nisan, 211–219.

MEB (MONE) (1997). İlköğretim Kurumları Yönetmeliği (Regulation for Primary Education Institutions). İstanbul: MEB Basımevi.

Mishra, L. (1998). National Literacy Mission: Retrospect and Prospect. *Economic and Political Weekly*, 33(44), 2807–2815.

Turkish Ministry of Planning (2013). *TURKEY: The Tenth Development Plan 2014-2018*. Turkey. Ministry of Planning. Retrieved from: http://planipolis.iiep.unesco.org/en/2013/tenth-development-plan-2014-2018-turkish-5779

UNECE (2017). *SDGs and Gender Equality: UN Interagency Guidance Note for the Europe and Central Asia Region United Nations Europe and Central Asia Issue-Based Coalition on Gender*. Geneva: UN Publication. Retrieved from: https://undg.org/wp-content/uploads/2017/11/UNFPA-EECARO-SDGs-GENDER-WEB.pdf

2 The Effect of Women Empowerment on National Economies

Challenges and Obstacles that Women Face

Bahar TANER

Introduction

Women have been subject to discrimination throughout the ages. Being more than half of the world population, women's share of the world property and income is negligible, 1% and 10% respectively. One major cause of the unequal status of women compared to men in many countries is the patriarchal system that constrains women to the home instead of allowing them to become active partners in the economic system. The world is full of tragic examples of women – regardless of their potential – at the mercy of men who deny their capacity and freedom of choice. Empowerment of women seems to be a valuable tool in challenging this dilemma and strengthening women in all possible ways.

Although there are many different definitions of empowerment within various contexts, most concentrate on matters of power and control over decisions and resources which influence a person's quality of life. Significant gender differences can also be observed in the causes, types and consequences of gaining or losing power. Women empowerment is defined by UNICEF (2000) as "women's having access, being conscious about the reasons of inequality, capability to manage their personal interests; being able to control and act to remove the obstacles which lead to structural inequality". Likewise, United Nations (UNDP, 1995) emphasizes "unfairness in political and economic participation as well as the power for decision making and control over economic resources". According to the Oxford Dictionary, empowerment can be defined as giving individuals more control over their lives or condition. Another definition of empowerment by the World Bank Group (2018) in a broad context is to provide a person with more control and authority over the decisions and resources that influence that person's life. From the 1990s onwards, the empowerment literature shows some notable points. One of them is the lack of a standard recipe for women empowerment. In other words, empowerment differs from one woman to another. Also, empowerment in one part of a woman's life offers no guarantee of transforming power relations in other parts of her life (Cornwall, 2016).

Women can gain increased control over their lives by exercising real choices which can be examplified as

- having better access to information, rules and procedures,
- enjoying the same education opportunity as men,
- enjoying membership in local women's organizations,
- having a voice in society, reaching political representation,
- getting more share of the country's income and assets,
- increasing their self-confidence and developing negotiating ability.

In this chapter, among the topics elaborated on are the meaning of empowerment, the legal framework and milestones in women empowerment, a model for women empowerment in all areas of life besides economy, the ways of empowering women, the contribution of government, women's rights organizations, and businesses to women empowerment. Successful examples of women empowerment from businesses will be presented. Lastly, the importance of women's labor and women empowerment on a nation's economic development will be discussed.

Legal Framework and Milestones in Women Empowerment and Gender Equality

There is an extensive body of legal documents concerning economic empowerment of women. The major ones are the following.

Beijing Declaration

Commitments in this document are

- To improve women's economic independence, to enable women to have more employment opportunities and revise economic structures to decrease poverty; providing all women access to public services and productive resources, equal to men.
- To achieve women's access to finance, economic resources, technology, land, information, communication, vocational training and markets.
- To eliminate social subordination of women through instituting gender based programs in various sectors.

ILO 2011 Convention – Decent Work for Domestic Workers

This is a compilation of international standards targeted to betterment of the working conditions of domestic workers globally. Most of these workers are women and girls. These documents aim at providing the same fundamental labor rights for both men and women; such as reasonable working hours, minimum weekly rest of one day, enlightening information on working terms and the right to collective bargaining.

ILO Recommendation 2012 – National Bases of Social Protection

This document is an important instrument in gender equality development. It stresses that everyone has the right to social security and that development depends on social security. The following are the key ILO gender equality conventions:

- Convention on Equal Remuneration,
- Convention on Discrimination – Employment and Occupation
- Convention on Workers with Family Responsibilities
- Convention on Maternity Protection.

The first two of these Conventions are among the eight fundamental Conventions of the ILO Declaration on Fundamental Principles and Rights at Work.

Convention on the Elimination of All Forms of Discrimination Against Women (CEDAW)

This document also contains provisions on employment, economic and social benefits, and rural women.

International Covenant on Economic, Social and Cultural Rights

This document stresses equal payment for equal work, fair wages, and in particular women being guaranteed working conditions no less than men.

Milestones in Women Empowerment

At the root of universal efforts to build up empowerment and equality of women, there are several milestones. The formulation of the United Nations Millennium Development Goals that were agreed upon by 191 member states is one of thesemilestones.

Millennium Development Goals

The Millennium Declaration, which was signed in September 2000, is a commitment by world leaders to fight hunger, discrimination, poverty, disease, illiteracy and environmental degradation. The Millennium Development Goals (MDGs), all having specific targets and indicators, are based on this Declaration. The MDGs, which are all interdependent, aim to:

- eliminate hunger and extreme poverty
- make primary education available globally
- promote equality and empowerment of women
- decrease child deaths
- better the health of mothers

- eradicate malaria, AIDS-HIV and other diseases
- secure sustainability of the environment
- organize a global partnership for development.(WHO, 2018)

Sustainable Development Goals

In September 2015 world leaders, building on Millennium Development Goals, , adopted the Sustainable Development Goals (SDGs) to show their commitment to stopping poverty, combatting injusticeand inequality, and striving to solve climatic issues until 2030. The SDGsare to:

1 Eliminate all types of poverty worldwide
2 Eliminate hunger, provide better nutrition, sustainable farming, ensure food security
3 Secure well-being and health for all
4 Provide accessible and quality education, lifelong learning opportunities for both sexes
5 Ensure empowerment of women and girls, achieve gender equality
6 Provide sustainable sanitation and water for everyone
7 Provide sustainable, inexpensive and reliable energy to everyone
8 Provide productive and full job opportunities for everybody
9 Encourage innovation and industrialization, construct strong infrastructure
10 Minimize inequality within and between countries
11 Create safe, sustainable and resilient urban settlements
12 Encourage sustainable production and consumption
13 Take necessary measures urgently to deal with climate change
14 Use the marine resources, seas and oceans sustainably
15 Restore and protect forests, terrestrial ecosystems; avoid land degradation and desertification, stop loss of biological diversity
16 Develop peaceful and inclusive societies, ensure everyone access to justice, build institutions which are effective, inclusive and accountable
17 Reinforce the tools for revitalizing and implementing the Global Partnership for Sustainable Development (WHO, 2015)

SDGs adopted by UN Member States are a plan of action for humans, the world and wealth. They stress the importance of human rights, effective institutions, adequate financing and partnerships. At the base of 17 SDGs, there is a pledge by the governments to work in partnership for peace, prosperity, dignity and equality for all people in the world. Gender equality is a priority to achieve all of the SDGs (UN, 2018).

Women Empowerment Principles

Women Empowerment Principles (WEPs) are principles signed by more than 1,000 business leaders representing some of the largest companies to develop gender equality (ICRW, 2016: 4). The following seven principles provide guidance to businesses on the ways to empower women at work, marketplace and community:

1 Promoting gender equality through establishment of high-level corporate leadership
2 Supporting non-discrimination, respecting human rights, treating men and women employees fairly at work
3 Ensuring the safety, well-being and health of all employees, regardless of gender
4 Supporting the professional development, training and education of women
5 Instituting marketing and supply chain practices as well as enterprise development to empower women
6 Developing equality through advocacy and community initiatives
7 Evaluating the progress to achieve gender equality and reporting the results publicly(CARE, 2011: 7)

Present Situation

SDRs and WEPs that governments and businesses have committed to can potentially provide a strong base for the empowerment of women and contribute to their families' well-being and the nation's economic development. However, mainstreaming gender equality in both society and business environment is a prerequisite for achieving gender equality in business (ICRW, 2016: 4). Hence, Goal 5 of SDRs is a priority in attempting to achieve the empowerment of women.

The UN 2017 Report evaluating the progress of Goal 5 shows the following:

- The time women spend in unpaid and domestic carework is three times more than that of men according to the data from 83 countries. A large portion of the gender gap in unpaid work results from time spent in domestic chores.
- In most of the 67 countries, women held less than one third of middle and higher management positions between 2009–2015.
- There is a slow progress of women's participation in parliaments; 23.4 % in 2017. Progress was slow between 2000 and 2017, only 10%, emphasizing the need for a stronger political commitment, and more ambitious measures and quotas.

All these indicate that there is still much to be done in the empowerment journey of women. SDGs 15, 16 and 17 of are other important goals since they lead the way towards a society based on justice, accountable to all citizens and having institutions open to the service of all, without any gender discrimination, and preserving the ecosystem and sustainability of natural resources.

A Conceptual Model of Women Empowerment

Women's choices are quite limited because of the gender inequality dictated by the patriarchal system in society. In addition to their lack of assets, women do not have the power to secure more advantageous conditions for themselves in many institutions both within the public and private domains. In building a framework for women empowerment, major elements of the model are the reform in state institutions (both at local and national levels), and women and their organizations. As a result of the interactions between these two, developmental outcomes in women empowerment are expected to emerge.

Elements of Empowerment (Empowerment Support)

There are four elements of empowerment to be used in women's empowerment, singly or in combination:

- having access to information,
- participation and inclusion,
- liability (accountability),
- organizational capacity at the local level.

(World Bank Group, 2018: 12–14)

Positive changes in these items are expected to create synergy in women's empowerment.

Having access to information

Women can be empowered through access to information. Women, who know the rules and their rights as stated by international agreements, national laws and local arrangements, can better exercise their legal rights, such as protection from violence, taking advantage of opportunities offered by state/local authorities, such as getting financial aid in starting their own businesses to develop their capabilities. State authorities (both national and local) and non-governmental organizations (NGOs) are the main actors in providing women with timely, relevant and understandable information.

Participation and inclusion

This involves the share women have of the limited public resources in a community and it may necessitate changes in the rules to enable women to take part as a priority in financial allocation at the national and local levels. For example, a gender sensitive budget can be vital in the economic empowerment of women, and women can contribute to decisions in the budget preparation process. Funds should be reserved and/or once reserved, should be managed wisely to provide the necessary support services for women. The private sector can also be effective in the economic empowerment of women through adopting an equality culture where women enjoy an equal status as men in getting hired, compensated, promoted and being appointed to managerial boards.

Liability (accountability)

Liability (accountability) concerns the public officials' and private employers' answerability to women for their actions, use of funds and policies in empowering them. In other words, it involves the questioning of commitment to gender equality at all levels of government and businesses. Some examples may be the inability of state officials and/or the relevant ministry in fulfilling their commitment for the increased participation of women in formal jobs, in politics or protection from violence and non-lenient laws that may stop the violence at source.

Organizational capacity at the local level

In order to have an effect on government decisions and gain collective power with the financing bodies and private businesses, women should build up associations and cooperative forms of businesses that give them regional or national recognition. Through these organizations, women may have a real voice in society and influence state policies.

Reform in Institutions

Within the context of institutions, empowerment is concerned with changing unequal institutional relationships. Since gender inequality is firmly established in the nature of the institutional relations, it is quite convenient in the context of women empowerment to start reforms in both formal and informal institutions that are nourished by patriarchal norms.

Among the formal institutions that affect the lives of women are norms and rules. Some examples are laws and rules in public and private sectors as well as civil organizations. On the other hand, informal restrictions on women's property inheritance, rituals concerning the treatment of widows and child brides are some examples of gender inequality in informal institutions.

Women and their Organizations

Women and their organizations involve women's capabilities and assets, both individually and collectively. Assets can be financial and physical, such as land, building, investments and savings. A considerable number of women have to stay home to tackle care and domestic works or to endure low paying, low status, informal jobs that are way below their capacity. Despite the fact that women enjoy less of these compared to men, assets can offer women more alternatives in broadening their horizons.

Women also have to possess human, social and political capabilities in the form of education, good health and skills to better their lives, a sense of identity, the potential to represent themselves or others, access information and take part actively in politics, etc. (World Bank Group, 2018: 11). In most parts of the world, women's formal education lags behind that of men, and women's abilities, coping mechanisms and knowledge usually go unnoticed. At many levels of society, relations of power prevent women's achieving healthy and fulfilling lives (UNFPA, 1994).

The Model

A conceptual model is developed based on the institutional reforms necessary in all of the aforementioned elements to come up with improved development outcomes in women's economic empowerment and the nation's economy. When state offices are occupied by individuals that adopt a culture of discrimination against women, women empowerment becomes hard to achieve despite the existence of well-planned policies and programs. Since formal rules can be ignored, it is of utmost importance to take into account the ethics, values and culture of institutions (World Bank Group, 2018: 13).

The empowerment model below shows the relationship between empowerment, institutions and favorable development outcomes for women. Institutional reforms to support empowerment of women involve investing in organizing capabilities of women, both individually and collectively. It is important for the reforms at all levels to concentrate on rules, laws, institutional practices, behavior and values which reinforce all elements of empowerment. A connection should be established between the changes in regulations and rules and the efforts to empower women to interact effectively with both the formal and informal institutions in an environment of equality (World Bank Group, 2018: 19). As a result of these reforms, women should be able to access all types of information about their legal rights, and the state and local authorities' support systems that they can benefit from.

Differences in Empowerment Models

Since the reforms necessary to build up an equality culture in the formal and informal institutions will be affected by various elements like the development of civil society, the state of political freedom, the pattern of exclusion and conflict, there will be differences in the resulting women's empowerment models. As far as the last of these factors is concerned, gender equality and economic empowerment of women will be determined by a culture of inequality and social establishments which embody discriminatory practices towards women, instead of individual characteristics. In other words, women's involvement in social, political and economic life at all levels is controlled by

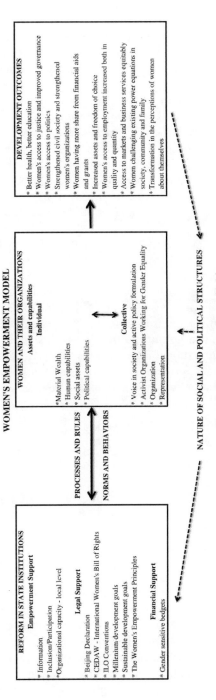

WOMEN'S EMPOWERMENT MODEL

REFORM IN STATE INSTITUTIONS

Empowerment Support

* Information
* Inclusion/Participation
*Organizational capacity - local level

Legal Support

* Beijing Declaration
* CEDAW - International Women's Bill of Rights
* ILO Conventions
* Millenium development goals
* Sustainable development goals
* The Women's Empowerment Principles

Financial Support

* Gender sensitive bedgets

PROCESSES AND RULES

NORMS AND BEHAVIORS

WOMEN AND THEIR ORGANIZATIONS

Assets and capabilities

Individual

*Material Wealth
* Human capabilities
* Social assets
* Political capabilities

Collective

* Voice in society and active policy formulation
* Activist Organizations Working for Gender Equality
* Organization
* Representation

DEVELOPMENT OUTCOMES

* Better health, better education
* Women's access to justice and improved governance
* Women's access to politics
* Strengthened civil society and strengthened women's organizations
* Women having more share from financial aids and grants
* Increased assets and freedom of choice
* Women's access to employment increased both in quality and quantity
* Access to markets and business services equitably
* Women challenging existing power equations in society, community and family
* Transformation in the perceptions of women about themselves

NATURE OF SOCIAL AND POLITICAL STRUCTURES

Figure 1 : Women's Empowerment Model

Figure 2.1 Women Empowerment Model

the other powerful half of the society that is men. Understanding the culture supporting the exclusion of women is vital in determining policies and designing interventions directed at increasing their educational level and upgrading their skills. In dealing with exclusion, changes in rules, regulations and laws may be necessary to eliminate the discriminatory practices against women.

Major responsibility rests with the government in undertaking the required changes in women's lives through empowering them, and the model given demonstrates this. However, businesses can also be effective in reducing the discrimination against women in both private and public domains through empowering them economically. Although businesses invest heavily in the economic empowerment of women, it should be noted that there are other areas of empowerment such as legal rights, norms and practices that are not women friendly and contribute to decision making at the policy level.

Businesses with strong financial standing are capable and very influential in politics. They can influence who (or which party) will govern a nation and for how long. These giant corporations and several others are also very well aware of their responsibilities for the community. Gender equality is an important one in this respect and businesses can do a lot to advance gender equality and in the meantime contribute to the Sustainable Development Goals. At times, businesses can go into partnership with state and local government authorities and international organizations to increase the areas they adapt women empowerment principles. Non-governmental organizations working for women rights can also participate in this process.

Macroeconomic Policies and Social Protection

In achieving women's empowerment and gender equality, macroeconomic and social policies are significant investments. However, these policies should be carefully designed to consider the major inequalities between genders in accessing economic assets and job opportunities; otherwise, failure will be inevitable (UN Women, 2017).

In the process of establishing gender equality, it is vital to eliminate the inequalities in social protection systems. Social security is a basic instrument for developing equal opportunities; so it is highly important to inject a gender point of view to the conception, execution and evaluation of social protection systems, which consider the female labor market characteristics.

Gender budgeting is a key mechanism in eliminating gender gaps and encouraging development and empowerment of women. In gender budgeting, the various effects of changes in budget allocations and fiscal policies on different groups – especially those which influence women disproportionately – are viewed, monitored, and a commitment is made to address the different necessities and circumstances of them through taxes and public spending (ILO, 2017, 37).

As far as employment is concerned, women fall behind men in participating in the labor force. They work in poorly paid, insecure and low status jobs. Although women's education level is rising, they are still directed to jobs traditionally considered appropriate for women in the labor markets. Of these women, only very few can reach higher-level positions in leadership and management. Therefore, collaboration among governments and international nonprofit organizations working for women (such as the United Nations and associated establishments, businesses working for empowerment of women and gender equality) has a good chance of getting results.

Social protection policies help women reach labour markets and help poor households meet basic needs. Governments can also benefit from the works of international nonprofit organizations working for gender equality. For example, UN Women collaborates with governments to design and execute macroeconomic policies through which women get results, handling issues such as the relationship between inclusive growth and paid work for women, the repercussions of economical crises and the effect of gender in trade and agricultural policies. Thus, policies, which are more gender sensitive, are formulated and gender equality advocates and public officials are supported in gaining skills to formulate and execute them. UN Women also encourages the sharing of knowledge and new ideas by bringing together progressive and feminist economists with policymakers (UN Women, 2018)|.

One example is the state family subsidies in Albania. Initially the majority of the subsidies were given to men, because men were typically assumed to be the heads of households. With the help of UN Women, the Albanian government changed the Economic Assistance and Social Services Law for the benefit of economically weak women. The candidates eligible for grants include women who have subjected to domestic violence, women who applied for divorce, and trafficked women (UN Women, 2018).

Another example from India involves the training of elderly illiterate women living in rural settlements in different geographic areas in engineering skills. These women were taught to put together and install solar lamp components in or near their villages. They earned some money and at the same time contributed to a cleaner environment.

The UN and the Central American Bank collaborated to develop a gender strategy for economic integration. The strategy involved assisting over one hundred micro finance institutions tailoring financial services to rural and indigenous women. By 2011 more than 12,000 women had access to training, financing, new technology and encouragement in Guatemala through an organization of service centers focused on women entrepreneurship.

"Women's Empowerment Principles: Equality Means Business", mentioned earlier, was launched by the UN in partnership with the UN Global Compact. Along with other commitments, several hundred chief executives endorsed a support statement of CEOs, for providing corporate leadership to achieve gender equality, encourage professional development of women, and treat men and women equally.

Sustainable development necessitates the transformational economic, environmental and social changes, and rural women are key actors in this process. The food shortage and economic crises and changes in the climate make the problems more complex. Empowering women in rural areas is necessary for the well-being of everyone, including families and communities. Considering the large presence of women in the agricultural workforce worldwide, it is a key factor to improve economic performance globally.

The Works of Women's Rights Organizations

Women's associations and civil society groups can raise the voice and visibility of women (as indicated in the empowerment model) and help their members reach many services and advantages. These associations can reach out to both government and private sector in seeking institutional support for women's activities that provide them income and can also negotiate collective loans and micro-leasing for their members (OECD, 2011: 29).

Women's organizations are crucial in the continuous struggle for human rights and gender equality. They are also the key forces for social change and in pointing out the various directions along which the rights of women have to be promoted (Sen and Mukherjee, 2013: 18). The sustainability of and financial support for women's organizations is crucial to achieve the transformation in MDGs in the form of a development agenda that can advance gender equality in the real sense (Sen and Mukherjee, 2013: 8).

The work of women's rights organizations in women empowerment is directed at making changes in the patriarchal and other oppressive cultures, social structures, beliefs and practices besides the formal realm of law, policy and other resources. Rao and Kelleher's model is a good reflection of this work, and shows the four dimensions for revealing the different domains in which gender power structures operate (Batliwala and Pittman, 2010).

The model is especially useful in presenting the complexity of the changes that women's rights organizations deal with in different domains of women's lives. It also points out the complimentary contribution of these organizations together with the governments and businesses in women empowerment.

One example of the crucial role of women's organizations in empowerment is Saptagram in Bangladesh. This is an organization for women who do not own any land. Saptagram was based on three major objectives:

- To achieve economic independence for women by cooperative loans and savings;
- To structure a critical consciousness level and agency by cultural activities, training sessions and group discussions;
- To institute solidarity among women who possess no land.

The program stimulated positive developments in the living standards such as setting up small businesses and improvements at homes, and more significantly,

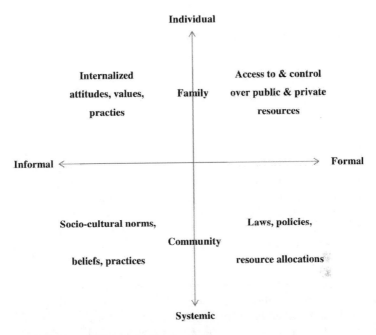

Figure 2.2 Domains of Change in Gender Power

notable changes in confidence, self-esteem and attitude. Thus a transformation took place in the perceptions of women about themselves and they became more confident about interacting with others. In Saptagram case collective action and solidarity became major change instruments and gains took place in access to public services, employment rights and domestic relationships (Cornwall, 2016).

Implementing Women Empowerment and Measuring Progress in Businesses

The most effective evaluation tools stem from the culture of an organization and its goals accompanied by a concise measurement framework. However, under the guidance of WEPs and review of the developments in gender equality, it becomes possible to assess the degree of women empowerment achieved by each company. Although the goals are common, the routes chosen to get there will be diverse. Following are some examples in the assessment of women empowerment achievement of companies in parallel to Women's Empowerment Principles (UN Women, 2018).

Principle 1

In order to be a leader in instituting equality between genders, it can be checked whether the company clearly defined its commitment to developing gender equality within the company and in its area of work. It can be questioned if the stated commitment to developing equality and enhancing nondiscrimination and fairness is publicized on the company web page. The organization's employee selection procedures and sustainability records can be reviewed and analyzed.

Principle 2

As far as equal treatment is concerned, it can be checked whether a clear cut organizational announcement that is against discrimination in hiring, promoting, retention, salary levels and benefits is publicized. Alternatively, compensation of all employees according to gender, job title and employment category can be reviewed and analyzed. It can be questioned if there is discrimination on the basis of gender in the company's senior management and if equitable pay evaluations are made regularly.

Principle 3

It can be checked whether a gender sensitive record of safety and health conditions is undertaken to ensure the safety and well-being of all employees. It can be questioned, for example, if there are washrooms and changing areas separately for women and men.

Principle 4

In promoting the training, education and development of women professionally, it can be checked whether the company promotes training programs tailored for women. The distribution of training and professional development opportunities between women and men can be reviewed.

Principle 5

In organizing company development, marketing and supply chain practices that are related to empowering women, it can be checked whether there exists a policy record at the executive level which indicates the management's positive approach for gender equality among the vendors. It can be questioned if the company analyzes its present list of suppliers to determine the baseline number of vendors that are owned by women.

Principle 6

It can be checked whether there are community-company initiatives of engagement for empowerment. It can be questioned if the company encourages initiatives to develop equality in the community and the number of boys and men, women and girls it employs.

Principle 7

It can be checked whether there are annual reports prepared on the basis of department, company gender equality policies and plans, according to established criteria in measuring and reporting the progress to develop equality. It can be questioned if the benchmarks for promoting women indicate that the company is showing a positive performance.

Women's Economic Empowerment and its Effect on the National Economy

Women's economic empowerment should be provided in order to secure sustainable development and achieve Millennium Development Goals. This is also about rights and equitable societies (OECD, 2011). Economic empowerment seems to offer potential in discovering and developing the productive potential of women and reducing gender bias. The *Global Gender Gap Report* published annually shows the relative gaps in 144 countries measured by the Global Gender Gap Index in four major fields: economy, education, health and politics. The top ten countries in the 2017 index are the same as in 2016: smaller western countries, particularly Iceland, Norway and Finland have the top three positions. Starting from 2006, the World Economic Forum measured the global gender parity. Although slow, the gap was closing until 2017. However, according to the 2017 Report, the gender gap has widened compared with the previous year. The striking point in the Report is that women's gains in earning opportunity, economic independence and leadership are not commensurate with their progress in education (World Economic Forum, 2018).

A woman must have two capabilities for her economic empowerment: to be able to show good economic performance and to have the authority to make decisions on economic matters. To achieve these, an integrated approach based on a human rights framework is necessary. Such an approach will necessitate collaboration between the women's rights sector and businesses supporting women's economic empowerment programs and it may be effective in tackling the structural barriers to women's economic empowerment. The eight building blocks consisting of business assets that companies can activate in this integrated approach are:

1 Availability of equitable and safe employment
2 Education, training
3 Having power over economic opportunities and resources
4 Having a voice in society and policy influence
5 Removing the threat of violence
6 Ensuring freedom of movement
7 Reach and care regarding health and family issues
8 Ensuring social protection and child care.

In such an approach across the corporate value chain, women can play various roles such as suppliers, contractors, distributors, employees, customers and community members. At the same time this can improve business outcomes (ICRW, 2014).

According to a recent report about women in the workplace and the progress over the past 20 years, a woman's decision to take part in the labor market is affected extensively by gender based and socio-economic constraints. However, important economic gains in terms of Gross Domestic Product growth and improved multi-dimensional personal welfare are expected to occur through closing the gaps in the labor market (ILO, 2017).

Research indicates that economic growth through reducing poverty and increasing opportunities for women in the labor market can affect gender equality positively. Thus, improved economic welfare of the households can result in a movement toward gender equality. Women have a critical role in development; in order to achieve efficiency – a prerequisite for achieving MDGs – it is essential to close the gender gap in education, political participation, and employment opportunities. One good example is the micro-credit schemes directed exclusively to women because they use the money for goods and services that provide for the welfare of the families and development (Duflo, 2012: 1054–1064).

Following are some concrete data indicating the favorable effects of economic empowerment of women on a nation's economic development. Data also show the cases of women disempowerment (UN Women, 2017).

- According to the 2012 Report by OECD, economies grow as more women work. An increase of women in the workforce results in faster economic growth. The same OECD Report shows that as the education level of women is raised, economic performance is improved. In OECD countries, better education is the cause of 50 percent of the economic development in the last 50 years; resulting from girls having the opportunity of higher education, and enjoying greater equality in their period of education.
- Women's participation in labor markets is considerably lower than men. The proportion of men employed to population is 72.2% whereas the figure for female employment is 47.0%.
- The 2012 World Bank Report indicates that gender equality in the laws affect both developed and developing economies. Most of the 143 economies (90% of them) have one or more legal differences limiting economic opportunities for women. In 79 of these economies, there are laws that limit the types of jobs in which women can work. In 15 economies, permission and consent of the husbands are necessary before their wives can accept jobs.
- Gender equality is good for business. Giving women better chances for leadership is to the benefit of companies, resulting in higher organizational performance. Firms which have at least three women in higher

management positions perform better in every dimension of the organization's effectiveness.
- Women's reach to formal financial institutions and saving mechanisms is
less than men. The gap is widest in lower middle-income economies, in
Middle East, South Africa and South Asia.

Christine Lagarde, the head of the International Monetary Fund, stated in her
speech at W-20 Summit that women's empowerment is more than a fundamental
moral cause; it is a definite economic necessity. She stressed that gender equality
carries the global capacity to improve economic development, reduce poverty
and income inequality, and increase income per capita (Lagarde, 2015).

There are obvious benefits of women's economic empowerment. When
female labor force participation increases, a faster economic growth can result
(OECD, 2012; Klasen and Lamanna, 2009).

According to the experiences of various countries, as the share of household
income controlled by women increases (through their earnings or cash transfers),
the spending that benefits children also increases (World Bank, 2012: 5).

Higher economic growth can be achieved through increasing women's and
girls' education. Approximately half of the economic growth in OECD
countries during the last 50 years was achieved in this way (OECD, 2012).

In achieving sustainable development, women are key to progress in social,
economic and environmental areas. The 2012 Rio+20 Agreement, which is
committed to ensuring equal rights and opportunities for women, confirms
this statement. To achieve this requires empowering women, and removing
discriminatory barriers in various areas including health, education, employment, energy, agriculture and reduction of disaster risk.

When women do not use their full economic capacity, the world economy
suffers. A report by McKinsey Global Institute points to the economic impacts
of pay inequality between women and men. According to this study, through
enhancing women's equality, global GDP could increase by 12 trillion dollars by
2025. In order to achieve this, it is essential that the private, public and social
sectors act to eliminate gender gaps in the society and at work. A striking finding
in the report is the virtual non-existence of countries with high gender equality in
society, but low gender equality at work. This indicates that although countries
can eliminate gender gaps through economic development, the progress can be
accelerated by improvement in the following areas:

Level of education
Inclusion in financial and digital matters
Protection on legal basis
Care work compensation (McKinsey & Co., 2016)

However, it should be noted that an empowerment strategy on the basis of
access to economic resources only, does not guarantee making changes in all
other areas of women's life because of the limiting potential of the prevailing

social norms in the society. Thus, it becomes vital to use other empowerment strategies along with economic empowerment in dealing with the power relations and norms that are at the roots of inequality. In short, empowered women should be aware of their rights as citizens, should be active partners in the social, economic and political system through participating in decision making mechanisms; they should have decent and secure jobs and separate bank accounts and be respected in the family and society.

Conclusion

In this chapter, the close relationship between a nation's economic development and women's empowerment is investigated. The concept of empowerment, the legal framework, a conceptual model of women empowerment, the role of macroeconomic policies and social protection, works of the businesses and women's rights organizations, implementing women empowerment and measuring success are the major topics presented. It is emphasized that establishing gender equality is a prerequisite of achieving women's empowerment, the latter involving a transformation of women in terms of having legal rights, a voice in financial policy making, and status in all domains of society besides the economic one. It is also underlined that the ways to empower women and achieve gender equality will differ from one nation to other (and also from one woman to another) although the norms, standards and guiding principles are universal.

References

Batliwala, S. & Pittman, A. (2010). *Capturing Change in Women's Realities*, Association for Women's Rights in Development (AWID), 1st Ed. Dec.

CARE (2011). Women's Empowerment Principles: Why Business Should Care. Retrieved from: weprinciples.org/files/attachments_Primer

Cornwall, A. (2016). Women's Empowerment: What Works? *Journal of International Development*, 28(3), April, (342–359).

Duflo, E. (2012). Women Empowerment and Economic Development, *Journal of Economic Literature*, 50(4), (1051–1079).

ICRW (2014). The Business Case for Women's Economic Empowerment. Retrieved from www.icrw.org/publications/the-business-case-for-womens-economic-empowerment-an-integrated-approach/

ICRW (2016, January 01). Building Effective Women's Economic Empowerment Strategies, ICRW. Retrieved from: www.bsr.org/reports/BSR

ILO (2017). World Employment Social Outlook – Trends for Women, Geneva, (1–63).

Klasen, S. & Lamanna, F. (2009). The Impact of Gender Inequality in Education and Employment on Economic Growth: New Evidence for a Panel of Countries, *Feminist Economics*, 15(3), July (91–132).

Lagarde, C. (2015). Delivering on the Promise of 2025, Keynote Address by Christine Lagarde, W-20 Summit, Sep. 15, Ankara, Turkey.

McKinsey & Company (2016). How Advancing Women's Equality can add $12 Trillion to Global Growth. Retrieved from: www.mckinsey.com/featured-insights/emp loyment-and-growth/how-advancing-womens-can-add

OECD (2011). Women's Economic Empowerment, DAC Network on Gender Equality (GENDERNET), (1–31). Retrieved from: www.oecd.org/dac/gender-developm ent/47561694.pdf

OECD (2012). *Gender Equality in Education, Employment and Entrepreneurship: Final Report to the MCM*. Retrieved from www.oecd.org/employment/50423364.pdf. P.17.

Sen, G. & Mukherjee, A. (2013). No Empowerment Without Rights, No Rights Without Politics: Gender-Equality, MDGs and the Port 2015 Development Agenda, Harvard University FXB Center for Health and Human Rights May, (1–50).UN (2017). Sustainable Development Goals. Retrieved from https://sustainabledevelopm ent.un.org/?menu=1300sustainabledevelopmentgoal5

UN (2018, March 15). Deputy Secretary-General's Remarks to the 2018 Women's Empowerment Principles Forum, New York. Retrieved from: www.un.org/sg/en/ content/dsg/statement/2018-03-15/deputy-secretary-generals-remarks-2018-wom en's-empowerment

UN Women (2017). Facts and Figures: Economic Empowerment. Retrieved from: www.unwomen.org/en/what-we-do/economic-empowerment/facts-and-figures

UN Women (2018). *Global Norms and Standards: Economic Empowerment*. Retrieved from: www. unwomen.org/en/what-we-do/economic-empowerment/global-norms-a nd-standards

UNDP (1995). Gender and Human Development. New York: Human Development Report.

UNFPA (1994). Programme of Action, Cairo, September 5–13. Retrieved from: www. unfpa.org/sites/default/files/event-pdf/PoA_en.pdf

UNICEF (2000). Combating Poverty and Inequality: Structural Change, Social Policy and Politics. Retrieved from: https://www.unicef.org/socialpolicy/files/Combating_Po verty_and_Inequality.pdf

World Bank (2002), Chapter 2 What Is Empowerment? p. 10. Retrieved from: http:// siteresources.worldbank.org/INTEMPOWERMENT/Resources/ 486312-1095094954594/draft2.pdf

World Bank (2012). *World Development Report: Gender Equality and Development*. Retrieved from: https://siteresources.worldbank.org/INTWDR2012/Resources/7778105-1299699968583/7786210-1315936222006/Complete-Report.pdf

World Bank Group (2018). Retrieved from: www.steresources.worldbank.org/INTEM POWERMENT/resources/486312–1095094954594/draft2.pdf (10–23)

World Economic Forum (2018). *Global Gender Gap Report 2017*. Retrieved from: www.weforum.org/reports/the-global-gender-gap-report-2017

WHO (2015, September 25). Sustainable Development Goals, UN Sustainable Development Summit. www.who.int/topics/millenium_development_goals/about/en/www. who.in/mediacentre/events/meetings/2015/un-sustainable-development-summit/en/

WHO (2018). Millennium Development Goals (MDGs). Retrieved from: www.who. int/topics/millenium_development_goals/about/en/

3 How Does Women's Empowerment Affect a Country's Economy?

Sonja ĐURIČIN

Introduction

The fact that a country possesses factors of production such as labour force, arable land, natural resources, capital and infrastructure, is an important but not sufficient condition for achieving competitiveness in the global market. The competitive advantage depends on how effectively and efficiently these factors are used. Efficient and effective management of human capital increases productivity. Productive work, with the efficient and effective use of natural and economic resources, affects the growth of economic activity. In order for growth to be sustainable, human capital and knowledge need to be used independently of gender.

Although gender equality represents the imperative of contemporary society, which largely determines national morality within its political and cultural dimension, women still often face discrimination and marginalization. Today, a total of 136 countries by their constitution explicitly guarantee the equality of all citizens and the absence of gender-based discrimination (World Bank, 2012). Nonetheless, more than 50% of these countries limit through their legislation the types of jobs women can get (World Bank, 2014, p.8). Therefore, feminization of poverty and unemployment occur as a consequence of limiting the equal participation of women in political, economic and cultural life.

According to the official World Bank data, the population of the Earth is 7.444 billion people. In the total population, women account for 49.56%. Therefore, approximately the same number of men and women live in the world. According to Eurostat data, the situation is similar in the EU. In the EU population, over the last ten years, women account for 50.66%. In 2017, in Turkey, men make up 50.2% of the total population, and this percentage changes in favour of women in the age group of 65 and over. In the age group of 65 and over, women in the total population, participate with 56%. An almost equal share of women in the total population imposes the need to study their contribution to the development of total economic activity. In order to examine the contribution of women to the development of overall economic activity, it is necessary to conduct an analysis of their position in terms of education, employment, at work, and consequently in economic terms.

This research starts from the hypothesis that empowerment of women contributes to sustainable economic development, improvement of the quality of life and living standards of all citizens, as well as the development of new business activities that stimulate economic growth. The subject of this research is the empowerment of women in terms of education, employment, at work and in economic terms. The subject of the research was defined after analysing the Global Gender Gap (GG) in Turkey. Women's empowerment in terms of education is important because Educational Attainment (EA) is one of the four indexes that determine the Global Gender Gap. On the other hand, women's empowerment in terms of employment, position in the work-place and in economic terms is important because it helps the calculation of the second index that determines GG and refers to economic participation and opportunity (EPO). The aim of the research is to determine how different types of empowerment of women influence the development of the Turkish economy. The aim of the research was realized using the desk research, the results of which were supplemented by examples of good practice.

Theoretical Framework of Research

In recent decades, women have accounted for more than 50% of enrolled students at various universities in the world (World Bank, 2012). One of the basic indicators underlying the implementation of the Europe 2020 Strategy is the number of people who have completed tertiary education and obtained university education. There is a gender gap at the level of the EU in terms of university education. The latest Eurostat data show that, at the age of 30–34, there is a gender gap in the domain of acquiring university education in favour of women of 9.5 percentage points. In all Member States, except in Germany, in the case of tertiary education, at the age of 30–34, a gender gap has been recorded for women.

The results of the Gender Parity Index (GPI) of the Gross Enrolment Ratio show that in Turkey, since 2010, a greater number of girls than boys enrol in primary schools. On the other hand, in the last ten years, i.e. 2007–2016, a consistently large number of men enrolled in secondary and tertiary schools. Although the number of enrolled men in the secondary and tertiary schools dominated in the observed period, the growth of enrolled women was notable. The number of women enrolling in secondary schools grew in the period 2009–2015, while the number of women enrolling in tertiary schools grew in the period 2008–2016. Despite the fact that in the case of a low household budget, girls are the first to leave school, Turkey among OECD countries has the lowest segregation in tertiary education (World Bank, 2012).

In addition to equal opportunities for education, all kinds of discriminatory norms in society must be eliminated, such as job opportunities, job position, and consequently economic independence. According to the United Nations

Table 3.1 Gender parity index of the gross enrolment ratio in primary, secondary and tertiary education, 2007–2016

Year	Primary education	Secondary education	Tertiary education
2007	0.964	0.858	0.880
2008	0.979	0.890	0.801
2009	0.989	0.886	0.834
2010	1.004	0.897	0.862
2011	1.004	0.933	0.874
2012	1.018	0.942	0.881
2013	1.023	0.946	0.892
2014	1.018	0.954	0.902
2015	1019	0.956	0.905
2016	1.009	0.943	0.964

Source: TurkStat, 2017

data, the participation of women in the labour force has stagnated over the last 25 years. In relation to men, women daily spend an average of 1 to 3 hours more than men on household chores, 2 to 10 times more time to take care of children, the old and the sick and daily 1 to 4 hours less in the labour market (World Bank, 2012, p.8). Women spend 26 hours a week in performing unpaid jobs, while men spend only 9 hours (European Women's Lobby, 2015). In the European Union, 25% of women and only 3% of men state provision of care and other family responsibilities as a reason for unemployment (UN Women, 2016, p.84). According to data from the family structure survey for 2016, in Turkey, cooking, as one of the most important household chores, is done by 91.2% of women and 8.8% of men, while wall painting is done by 80.4% of men and 19.6% of women.

Research conducted by the International Labour Organization (ILO) shows that in 2017, in the total population of the world, employees aged 15 and over account for 58.5%. Out of the total male population, 71.3% were employed, while out of the total female population, 45.8% were employed. According to the same source, in the total population in EU-28, aged 15 and over, 52.9% were employed. Out of the total male and female population, 59.1% and 47% were employed respectively. In Turkey, in the same age group, 45.8% of the total population were employed in 2017. Out of the total male population, aged 15 and over, 64.9% were employed, while 27.7% were employed out of the total female population. Compared to the overall population in Turkey, a fewer number of men and women were employed than in the world, by 6.4 and 18.1 percentage points. On the other hand, compared to the overall population, a larger number of men, but fewer women were employed in Turkey than in the EU-28, by 5.8 and 19.3 percentage points respectively.

Table 3.2 Employment-to-population ratio, 2017 (percentage)

Reference area	Age	Total	Male	Female
World	15+	58.5	71.3	45.8
EU-28	15+	52.9	59.1	47.0
Turkey	15+	45.8	64.9	27.7

Source: International Labour Organization (ILO)

The participation of women in the labour force varies in relation to their educational status. According to the Turkish Statistical Institute, illiterate women and women without a high school diploma account for 16.1% and 26.6% in the labour force respectively. Women with a secondary school diploma participate with 32.7% in the total labour force, while women with vocational high school and higher education diplomas account for 40.8% and 71.6% respectively.

The difference in employment in relation to gender varies depending on the age that is being observed. For example, in the EU Member States, according to the latest Eurostat data, differences in employment relative to gender, in the age group 20–64, vary among countries. The lowest gap was recorded in Lithuania, Latvia, Finland and Switzerland, where the percentage of employed men in the 20–64 age group is higher than in women by 1.9, 2.9, 3.3 and 3.8 percentage points respectively. On the other hand, the biggest gap between employed men and women aged 20–64 was recorded in Malta where it was 27.7 percentage points. In addition to Malta, a big gap of 20.1, 19.0, 17.6 and 16 percentage points respectively was recorded in Italy, Greece, Romania and the Czech Republic.

Gender inequality in employment also reflects on the position of women in the workplace. The position of women in the workplace can be viewed through salary received. Gender inequality in employment and wages negotiated varies between countries but is observed in all of them. For example, women in Sweden and France can expect a salary that is by 31% lower than that of men, while in Germany it is lower by 49% (UN Women, 2016, p.69).

In Turkey, according to the latest available data from Turkstat (2016, 2017), the gender pay gap at the level of annual average gross wage amounts to only 1.1% in favour of women. However, from the aspect of the level of education and the type of occupation, the results are different. The highest gender pay gap of 19.5% in favour of men was recorded in the case of those who finished vocational high school, while the lowest one, also in favour of men, of 10.1% was recorded in the case of those who completed high school. From the aspect of occupations, the gender pay gap shows that men in all professions, unless they hold managerial positions, earn more than women. Where women work in managerial positions, they earn more, with the recorded gender pay gap of 7.3%. The highest gender pay gap of 24.1% was recorded in favour of men for the position of plant and machine operators and assemblers, while the lowest one of 6.1% was observed for the position of clerical support workers.

According to the research on the family structure in 2016, 78.1% of men and 91.5% of women approved of women working in Turkey. Observed by statistical regions, the highest percentage of people who approved of women working of 90.6% was registered in İzmir, Aydın, Denizli, Muğla, Manisa, Afyonkarahisar, Kütahya, Uşak, and the lowest of 71.5% in Gaziantep, Adıyaman, Kilis, Şanlıurfa, Diyarbakır, Mardin, Batman, Şırnak, Siirt.

The above data show that Turkey is not unique in terms of gender inequality. Gender inequality is more or less pronounced in most countries. Largely, inequality is expressed in employment, then in wages, and to the least extent in education. According to numerous studies at the international level, gender inequality has been found to have economic effects.

Table 3.3 Annual average gross wage and gender pay gap

Position	Annual average gross wage (TL)			Gender pay gap[1] (%)
	Total	Male	Female	
Total	**17 884**	**17 837**	**18 029**	**-1.1**
Educational attainment				
Primary school and below	12 237	12 597	10 519	16.5
Primary education and secondary school	12 192	12 571	10 470	16.7
High school	15 117	15 531	13 969	10.1
Vocational high school	18 759	19 442	15 647	19.5
Higher education	31 486	33 574	28 184	16.1
Major occupational group				
Managers	43 825	43 073	46 201	-7.3
Professionals	31 520	34 549	27 861	19.4
Technicians and associate professionals	22 082	22 536	20 865	7.4
Clerical support workers	18 875	19 383	18 203	6.1
Service and sales workers	12 922	13 167	12 188	7.4
Skilled agricultural, forestry and fishery workers	14 091	(*)	(0)	(*)
Craft and related trades workers	15 278	15 586	13 004	16.6
Plant and machine operators and assemblers	13 336	13 851	10 518	24.1
Elementary occupations	12 075	12 449	10 713	13.9

Source: TURKSTAT, Structure of Earnings Survey

[1] Calculated based on total wages in 2010, [(male wages-female wages)/male wages*100]

In the OECD countries, in the last 50 years, the increase in the educated population, primarily through the provision of equal opportunities for men and women, accounts for about half of the economic growth (OECD, 2012, p.4). However, the existence of equal opportunities for the education of men and women does not necessarily mean economic growth. According to the World Bank data, in 45 developing countries, there are more girls enrolled than boys in high school, while in more than 60 developing countries, there is a higher number of female students. In these same countries, the increased number of educated women did not directly affect economic growth. It is necessary to change and improve the position of women in the labour market.

Providing equal opportunities in employment, i.e. increasing the participation of women in the total labour force, contributes to the growth of economic activity. Reducing the gap between the participation of women and men in the total labour force contributes to faster economic growth (OECD, 2012, p.17). Reducing the gap between men and women in the labour market does not mean only the percentage growth of women's participation in the total labour force, i.e. their business engagement on any basis and at any price. First of all, it is necessary to create conditions for solving business segregation. Eliminating barriers that discriminate against women in employment in certain sectors and occupations could increase productivity by as much as 25% (World Bank, 2012). Research shows that companies where women hold senior managerial positions have greater chances of efficient business. It is estimated that companies with three or more women holding senior managerial positions are characterized by organizational efficiency and more successful businesses (McKinsey & Company, 2014, p.6). Eliminating the gap in the number of employed men and women and their salaries would contribute to a global increase in women's income by 76%, which in an absolute amount has a value of 17 trillion US dollars (Actionaid, 2015, p.9).

The existence of equal opportunities for men and women in their contribution to the development of family and careers positively reflects on the general social well-being. The change in the structure of household income, through the empowerment of women, has a positive impact on the economic growth and development of children (World Bank, 2012). In a family where a woman has a job, the expenditures in terms of kindergarten and childcare costs are lower than the savings that would have been made if a woman did not work and took over the full care of children and the household. On the other hand, the socialization of children and their social awareness in the early years of life act as a feedback and contribute to the acceptance of gender equality at an early age. Research also shows that the growth in the number of women educated in reproductive age has led to a reduction in child mortality by 9.5% (Gakidou et al., 2010, p.969).

Gender inequality in employment is linked to the economic independence of women. Less than 20% of landowners are women (FAO, 2011). Gender gaps regarding the access to land and funding sources limit women's ability to invest, develop business and use profitable business opportunities in the most efficient way (World Bank, 2012, p.3). It is estimated that the absence of adequate programs and measures can lead to a time period of 30 years that would be needed to overcome the gap in the employment of women and men, 70 years for equal pay, and 40 years for equal share in housekeeping activities (European Women's Lobby, 2015).

The efficiency and effectiveness of the use of production factors depends to a large extent on government policy. Government policy, at all levels, can improve or reduce the competitive advantage. According to the World Bank data, the right of boys and girls to inherit is the same in practice as under the law in Turkey. Furthermore, the attitude about the need for women's education in Turkey is changing. In the last ten years, the number of people who believe that higher education is more important for men than for women has decreased from 34% to 20%. In addition, the gap in control over earned money has significantly decreased. In Turkey, only 2% of married women from the richest population have no control over earned money (World Bank, 2012).

Data and Methodology

The subject and aim of the research were derived from such a defined theoretical framework. The aim of the research is to determine how different types of women's empowerment influence the development of the Turkish economy. For achieving this goal, the subject of the research is to analyse the possibility of empowering women in terms of education, employment, at work and in economic terms.

The aim and subject of the research were realized by applying desk research, where the results were supplemented by examples of good practice. An example of good practice is presented through results obtained by analysing the performance of Sabancı Holding's business owned by women. Analytical and synthetic methods were mostly used during the desk research. Analysis and deduction were used as analytical methods, and induction as a synthetic method of research.

In the analysis method, descriptive and explicit analyses were used, then content analysis, comparative spatial, temporal, and financial analysis (Đuričin, 2012; Đuričin et al., 2013; Đuričin and Beraha, 2013; Đuričin and Pantić, 2014). Descriptive analysis is used for description, while explicit analysis was used in explaining the subject of the research. Content analysis helped collection and classification of data from the expert literature, from the web pages and relevant documents. The subject of the research determines the relevance of the documents. The subject of the research conditioned the analysis of professional literature, primarily in the area of equality of women in education, employment, at the workplace and in economic terms (Đuričin and Pantić, 2015; Đuričin and Beraha, 2016). Comparative analysis has led to knowledge of certain similarities and differences that exist in the subject of research in different geographical areas. This is a spatial comparative analysis that includes a global case study of the subject of research at the level of the EU, the OECD countries and the territory of Turkey. In addition to the spatial analysis, a temporal analysis was carried out to determine the characteristics of the subject of the research, depending on the observation period. By observing the movement of changes in the quantitative and qualitative characteristics of the subject of research in time and space, we have learned about the factors of occurrence and future expectations regarding the gender gap. Thus, attempts were made to identify, through determining the factors causing a gender gap in Turkey, the measures that would have the effect of reducing the gap between the sexes. The financial analysis was used to obtain data on the performance of Sabanci Holding, which was used as an example of good practice. Starting from general to special aspects, using the deduction method from the general data, specific and individual views and conclusions are derived. In addition to analytical methods, a synthetic method of research was used. Using the induction method, the general view and conclusion are defined from several pieces of specially acquired information about the subject of research and its constituent elements.

Gender Gap in Turkey and Recommendations for Women's Empowerment

The gender gap in Turkey was analysed through educational attainment level and through economic participation and opportunity. These two factors have been highlighted as important because they substantially define Turkey's position on the global level in the domain of gender gap. In other words, educational attainment and economic participation and opportunity represent two out of four sub-indexes participating in the assessment and ranking of countries in terms of gender gap on a global level. In addition to these two sub-indexes, Health and Survival and Political Empowerment are also taken into account, but they are not the subjects of this research.

The sub-index of educational attainment is calculated by measuring the rate of female literacy and access to primary, secondary and tertiary education. The analysis of these factors will contribute to the realization of a part of the research objective concerning the identification of the way in which women's empowerment in terms of education improves the development of the Turkish economy. On the other hand, the realization of the second part of the aim of the research, which deals with determining the way in which women's empowerment in terms of employment, at the workplace and in economic terms influences the development of the Turkish economy, will be carried out by analysing the sub-index of economic participation and opportunity. The sub-index of economic participation and opportunity is calculated through three segments. The first segment refers to the gap that exists in the domain of participation in labour. The second segment takes into account the gap that exists in the domain of salaries, i.e. compensation for similar work and in the domain of total revenues realized. The third segment takes into account the prospects for the advancement of women and men observed through the relationship between women and men among legislators, senior officials and managers, on the one hand, and among professional and technical workers, on the other hand.

In 2017, according to Global Gender Gap Index, out of a total of 144 countries, Turkey held 131st position (World Economic Forum, 2017, p.11) with a score of 0.625 (0 means irregularity, while 1 means parity). Observed individually, according to the sub-index of educational attainment, Turkey holds 101st position with a score of 0.965, while according to sub-index of Economic participation and opportunity, Turkey holds 128th position with a score of 0.471.

At a regional level, in the Middle East and North Africa with a total of 17 countries, according to the Global Gender Gap Index, Turkey occupies the 8th position. Israel, Tunisia, United Arab Emirates, Bahrain, Algeria, Kuwait and Qatar have a better position than Turkey, while Mauritania, Egypt, Jordan, Morocco, Lebanon, Saudi Arabia, Iran Islamic Rep., Syria and Yemen have a lower position than Turkey. The Middle East and North Africa region records by eight percentage points lower Global Gender Gap Index than its average weighted value and as such, compared to other regions, occupies the lowest position.

Compared to 2006, when the Global Gender Gap Index was measured for the first time, Turkey recorded a better score and parity in 2017, while its worse position was the result of an increase in the number of countries used for ranking references. The Global Gender Gap Index was measured for 115 countries in 2006, while in 2017 it was measured for 144 countries.

Although Turkey's position deteriorated in 2017 compared to 2006, the Global Gender Gap was improved from 0.585 to 0.625. The score of Economic participation and opportunity and Educational attainment is also improved from 0.434 to 0.471 and from 0.885 to 0.965 respectively. For the purposes of the research, the sub-index of Educational attainment and Economic participation and opportunity in Turkey were analysed in more detail below.

Table 3.4 Global Gender Gap score, 2006/2007

Index/sub-index	2006		2007	
	Rank	Score	Rank	Score
Global Gender Gap	105	0.585	131	0.625
Economic participation and opportunity	106	0.434	128	0.471
Educational attainment	92	0.885	101	0.965
Rank out of	115		144	

Source: World Economic Forum, 2017

Educational attainment

Turkey's position on educational attainment has improved significantly. Compared to 2006, the score of educational attainment in 2017 not only improved from 0.885 to 0.965, but Turkey also recorded above-average values on the global level. Unlike in 2006, when Turkey achieved a score for educational attainment by 0.054 lower than its average global value, the average global educational attainment score in 2017 was exceeded by 0.012.

In 2006, only in the case of the literacy rate, a full parity was recorded and the score was higher than the average global value by 0.09. This year, the score for primary, secondary and tertiary education was below their average global value. However, in 2017, although literacy rate parity was not achieved, the score was higher than their average global value in the case of primary and secondary education by 0.011 and 0.01. In the case of tertiary education, Turkey recorded a lower score than its average global value by 0.064, which is again more favourable than in 2006.

In 2006, only in the case of literacy rate, a full parity was recorded and the score was higher than the average global value by 0.09. This year, the score for primary, secondary and tertiary education was below their average global value. However, in 2017, although literacy rate parity was not achieved, the score was higher than its average global value in the case of primary and secondary education by 0.011 and 0.01. In the case of tertiary education, Turkey recorded a lower score than its average global value by 0.064, which is again more favourable than in 2006.

An improved score in 2017 means that Turkey has made progress in overcoming the gender gap in educational attainment, especially when it comes to sub-indexes relating to primary and secondary education. However, the lack of parity on the educational attainment and all of its sub-indices points to the fact that there are opportunities to improve the position of women. Empowerment of women in the field of education would directly affect the gender gap reduction and also the improvement of Turkey's global position. Women's empowerment in terms of education could be achieved by implementing measures that enhance their literacy, primary, secondary and tertiary education.

The empowerment of women in terms of education contributes to the improvement of Turkey's Global Gender Gap position. A better position in Global Gender Gap is also the strengthening of the competitive advantage in the global market and greater potential for economic growth.

Economic participation and opportunity

Turkey's position on economic participation and opportunity improved in 2017 compared to 2006. Compared to 2006, the score of economic participation and opportunity in 2017 improved from 0.434 to 0.471. Unlike in 2006, when for economic participation and opportunity Turkey received the

Table 3.5 Educational attainment (EA) score card, 2006/2017

Year	2006						2017					
GG subindexes	Rank	Score	Sample average	F	M	F/M ratio	Rank	Score	Sample average	F	M	F/M ratio
EA	92	0.885	0.939	-	-	-	101	0.965	0.953	-	-	-
Literacy rate	1	1.00	0.91	98	98	1.00	94	0.940	0.883	92.6	98.6	0.94
EA in primary education	99	0.95	0.97	87	92	0.95	97	0.990	0.979	93.7	94.6	0.99
EA in secondary education	105	0.75	0.94	-	-	0.75	110	0.981	0.971	85.5	87.2	0.98
EA in tertiary education	84	0.73	0.86	24	34	0.73	105	0.874	0.938	88.3	101.0	0.87

Source: World Economic Forum, 2017

Table 3.6 Recommendations for women's empowerment in terms of education in order to improve the Global Gender Gap position

---

Women's empowerment in terms of education

Literacy

- overcoming social inequalities
- overcoming illiteracy at its earliest stage
- identifying households at the local level that are at high risk of illiteracy
- promoting social entrepreneurship at local, regional and national level
- improving approaches, programs and methods of formal and non-formal education
- committing all businesses and institutions that use budget funds to promote literacy
- offering the possibility of becoming literate in the workplace

---

Primary, secondary and tertiary education

- developing a mechanism for equal opportunities for the education of boys and girls in socially vulnerable families
- developing mechanisms to increase the number of adults aged 25–64 to gain primary, secondary and/or tertiary education in the workplace in cooperation with educational institutions
- developing mechanisms to increase the number of adults aged 65+ to acquire primary, secondary and/or tertiary education through pension schemes or special programs in cooperation with educational institutions
- developing a mechanism for equal chances for completing PhD studies
- developing a mechanism for equal opportunities for using the Internet

---

Source: Author's research

score by 0.162 lower than its average global value, in 2017, the score was by 0.114 lower than its average value.

In 2017, similar to 2006, there was no full parity in the case of each of the observed sub-indexes. In 2006, the value of 0.64 for wage equality for similar work was equal to its average value at the global level. In this year, the value of the score in terms of labour force participation, estimated earned income, legislators, senior officials and managers and professional and technical workers were below their average global value. Furthermore, in 2017, in the case of each of the observed sub-indices, the score was lower than its average global value. Observed individually by sub-indices, in 2017, in comparison with 2006, the value of labour force participation, legislators, senior officials and managers and professional and technical workers increased by 0.079, 0.118 and 0.208 respectively. In the case of the sub-index wage equality for similar work and estimated earned income in 2017, compared to 2006, the global position deteriorated and the value fell by 0.05 and 0.02 respectively.

The absence of parity in the case of economic participation and opportunity and all of its sub-indices points to the fact that there are opportunities to improve the position and empower women in employment and in the workplace. Empowering women in employment and at the workplace would lead to the improvement of their economic position and Turkey's position at the

Table 3.7 Economic participation and opportunity score card, 2006/2017

Year	2006						2017					
GG subindexes	Rank	Score	GG sub-indexes	Rank	Score	GG sub-indexes	Rank	Score	GG sub-indexes	Rank	Score	GG subindexes
EPP	106	0.434	0.596				128	0.471	0.585			
Labour force participation	110	0.36	0.69	28	77	0.36	131	0.439	0.667	33.6	76.6	0.44
Wage equality for similar work	54	0.64	0.64	-	-	0.64	94	0.590	0.634	-	-	0.59
Estimated earned income (PPP, US$)	72	0.46	0.52	4.276	9.286	0.46	122	0.440	0.509	14,917	33,867	0.44
Legislators, senior officials and managers	98	0.06	0.37	6	94	0.06	107	0.178	0.320	15.1	84.9	0.18
Professional and technical workers	82	0.43	0.79	30	710	0.43	104	0.638	0.758	39.0	61.0	0.64

Source: World Economic Forum, 2017

Table 3.8 Recommendations for women's empowerment regarding employment and positions in the workplace in order to improve the Global Gender Gap position

Empowering women in terms of employment and the workplace

Employment

- improvement of regulations in case of prevention of discrimination of women in employment
- development of support measures for subsidizing women when starting their own business
- development of support measures for the employment of women in higher positions
- development of a mechanism for assisting women in household chores

Position at the workplace

- development of regulations that encourage equal compensation for men and women according to their education, experience and position in which they perform their duties
- development of regulations in the case of preventing discrimination against women in selection of top management, members of the board of directors, etc.

Source: Author's research

global level. Empowerment could be achieved by implementing measures that improve the position of women in the labour market.

One way to overcome the gender gap is to impose an obligation on businesses to define in their strategic documents goals related to gender equality in terms of employment, promotion, earnings, assumption of responsibility, etc. According to the McKinsey research, in 2016, only 14% of companies in Turkey cite gender equality among the first three strategic priorities. Gender equality is mentioned in the top five strategic priorities in 19% of companies, and in the top ten priorities in 30% of companies. Gender equality, which is not in the top ten priority strategic goals, was recorded in 24% of companies, while the complete absence of dealing with gender equality issues was recorded in 12% of companies.

If gender equality was one of the basic strategic priorities, women would be given the same chances in relation to men when entering into employment, and later, through providing opportunities for improvement and promotion. Equal chances when entering a working relationship can be created by a transparent assessment of all candidates who have applied without hidden prejudices and subjective assessments. An equal opportunity for promotion is possible if men and women could equally meet the conditions for the job vacancy. Furthermore, it is necessary to introduce a higher degree of flexibility in the workplace for women who are expected to be equally good mothers and housewives.

Encouraging gender equality is possible through the change of organizational culture. Organizational culture should promote the basic postulates of gender equality with equal respect for the competencies, efforts, devotion and abilities of women and men. Persistence is very important because it takes time to achieve the first results. Therefore, gender equality should be one of the long-term strategic priorities.

Example of good practice – Sabancı Holding

Güler Sabancı is an example of good practice in Turkey and according to the latest data she is among the 100 most powerful women in the world on the list of Forbes magazine. Compared to 2016, the position has improved by 12 places.

Sabancı Holding operates in accordance with the Declaration of UN Women's Empowerment Principles and Equality at Work Platform Policies. Gender equality is one of the basic business postulates, as indicated by the fact that Sabancı Holding was the first Turkish company to sign the UN Women's Empowerment Principles in 2011. Compliance with the principle of gender equality resulted in the fact that in 2016, 34% of all employees and 24% of the administration were women. The participation of women in the labour force if Sabanci Holding (2016) is twice higher than the average participation of women in the labour force of Turkish companies.

According to the Sabanci Holding's sustainability report for 2016, the Women's Empowerment Principles that they adhere to are the following:

- To create senior level corporate leadership for the gender equality,
- To treat women and men fairly at work – respecting and supporting the human rights and non-discrimination principle,
- To ensure the health, safety, and well-being of all female and male employees,
- To encourage the training, professional training and career development of women,
- To adopt such practices as initiative development, supply chain and marketing that empower women,
- To enhance equality through social initiatives and defence,
- To measure and to publicly report the developments to ensure gender equality.

In addition, Sabanci Holding operates in accordance with the Equality Platform at Work, under the supervision of the Ministry of Family and Social Policies. The World Economic Forum (2017) created Equality Platform at Work in order to reduce gender inequality through a higher involvement of women in the workforce, a decision-making mechanism, providing equal opportunities, etc. By adopting these business principles, Sabancı Holding has committed itself to eliminating discrimination by gender, transparent reporting on the progress of achieving this goal, and spreading good practice in this area at the national level.

Sabancı Holding successfully implemented volunteer projects, and some of them related to bilingual trainings attended by 10,000 employees. By conducting trainings such as Social Gender Equality for Group Employees: "Concept and definitions," "Education and Social Gender," "Business World and Social Gender," "Violence against Women," and "Forced Marriage at an

Early Age", Sabancı Holding represents an example of socially responsible business.

Implementation of gender equality in the strategic objectives of Sabancı Holding and the business operation in accordance with the Declaration of the UN Women's Empowerment Principles and Equality at Work Platform Policies has positively influenced the growth of financial performance (Sabancı Holding, 2017). This does not mean that financial performance grows solely because of respect for gender equality, but it shows that compliance with the basic postulates of equality between women and men does not damage the business. Sabancı Holding is an example of good practice that, with respect for gender equality, has enormous financial results and significantly contributes to the overall economic growth and development of Turkey.

Conclusion

Desk research has confirmed the hypothesis that empowerment of women contributes to sustainable economic development, improved quality of life and living standards of all citizens, and the development of new business activities that stimulate economic growth. The hypothesis is confirmed by the good practice example. Providing an example of compliance with the basic postulates of gender equality and consequently a very successful business, Sabanci Holding confirms that empowerment of women contributes to sustainable economic development, improvement of the quality of life and living standards of all citizens, and the development of new business activities that stimulate economic growth.

The above-mentioned data show that Turkey is not unique in terms of gender inequality. Gender inequality is more or less pronounced in most countries. Largely, inequality is expressed in employment, then in wages, and to the least extent in the case of education. In addition, among the OECD countries Turkey has the least segregation in tertiary fields of study. The data obtained from the research are the basis for the possible construction of an economic model that could directly measure the contribution of women's empowerment in terms of education, employment and at the workplace in national economic growth.

The basic research results are recommendations for improving the literacy and empowerment of women in terms of education, employment, and at the workplace. Accepting these recommendations would lead to Turkey's improved position in the Global Gender Gap and the promotion of national competitiveness.

References

Actionaid (2015). Close the Gap! The Cost of Inequality in Women's Work, Retrieved from: https://www.actionaid.org.uk/sites/default/files/publications/womens_rights_on-line_version_2.1.pdf

Đuričin, S. (2012). Book: *Analiza Poslovanjai Mimogućnosti Izlaska Preduzeća Iz Zone Gubitka* (Business analysis and opportunities for companies to leave the zone of loss), Institute of Economic Sciences, Belgrade, Republic of Serbia

Đuričin, S. & Beraha, I. (2016). *SME Clustering in Serbia: Finding the Right Business Partners and Improving the Business Environment for SMEs*, Final Workshop Report on "SME clustering: finding the right business partners and improving the business environment for SMEs", Konrad-Adenauer-Stiftung, Ankara, ISBN 978-605-4679-15-7, pp. 213–236

Đuričin, S. & Pantić, O. (2014). Harmonization of National Strategic Documents with The Documents of EU: Licenses and Permits for SMEs, *Contemporary Trends and Prospects of Economic Recovery*, CEMAFI International Association, Nice, ISBN 978-2-9544508-5-8, pp. 616–631

Đuričin, S. & Pantić, O. (2015). The Development of Micro-crediting as a Factor of Promoting Women's Entrepreneurship in Serbia, *Journal of Women's Entrepreneurship and Education*, Institute of economic sciences, Belgrade, Republic of Serbia, ISSN 1821–1283, 1/2, pp. 50–66

Đuričin, S. & Beraha, I. (2013). Alternative Forms of Financing of Small and Medium Sized Enterprises for The Purpose of Strengthening Competitiveness at The International Level, Economic Sciences on the Crossroad/International Scientific Conference on the Occasion of the 55th Anniversary of the IES [4th December], Institute of Economic Sciences, Belgrade, Republic of Serbia, ISBN 978-86-89465-10-5, pp. 382–392

Đuričin, S., Stevanović, S. & Baranenko, E. (2013). Monograph: *Analiza i Ocena Konkurentnosti Privrede Srbije* (Analysis and assessment of the competitiveness of the Serbian economy), Institute of Economic Sciences, Belgrade, Republic of Serbia

European Women's Lobby (2015). From Words to Action 1995–2015, Retrieved from: https://www.publicpolicy.rs/arhiva/796/ekonomska-nezavisnost-zena-kao-osnova-svih-prava#.WwlAGu6FOUl

FAO (Food and Agriculture Organization) (2011). *The State of Food and Agriculture 2010–11: Women and Agriculture, Closing the Gender Gap for Development*. Retrieved from: http://www.fao.org/docrep/013/i2050e/i2050e.pdf

Gakidou, E., Cowling, K., Lozano, R. & Murray, C.J. (2010). Increased Educational Attainment and its Effect on Child Mortality in 175 Countries between 1970 and 2009: A Systematic Analysis, *The Lancet*, 376(9745)

International Labour Organization (ILO). Retrieved from: http://www.ilo.org/ilostat/faces/oracle/webcenter/portalapp/pagehierarchy/Page3.jspx?MBI_ID=7&_adf.ctrl-state=ik3w9nms9_66&_afrLoop=1138827621655884&_afrWindowMode=0&_afrWindowId=ik3w9nms9_63#!%40%40%3F_afrWindowId%3Dik3w9nms9_63%26_afrLoop%3D1138827621655884%26MBI_ID%3D7%26_afrWindowMode%3D0%26_adf.ctrl-state%3D16698iof8s_4

McKinsey & Company (2014). *Women Matter*. Retrieved from: https://www.mckinsey.com/business-functions/organization/our-insights/promoting-gender-diversity-in-the-gulf

McKinsey & Company (2016). *Women Matter: Turkey 2016*. Retrieved from: http://www.mckinsey.com.tr/arastirma-ve-yayinlarimiz/WomenMatterTurkey2016Report.pdf

OECD (Organization for Economic Cooperation and Development). (2012). *Gender Equality in Education, Employment and Entrepreneurship: Final Report to the MCM 2012*. Retrieved from: http://www.oecd.org/employment/50423364.pdf

Sabanci Holding (2016). *Sabanci Holding Sustainability Report*. Retrieved from: https://www.sabanci.com/documents/raporlar/surdurulebilirlik/sabanci_SR_2016_en_v2.pdf

Sabanci Holding (2017). *Financial Reports*. Retrieved from: https://yatirimciiliskileri.sabanci.com/en/financial-reports/-/2017/-

TurkStat (Turkish Statistical Institute) (2016). Women in Statistics, 2016. Retrieved from: http://www.turkstat.gov.tr/PreHaberBultenleri.do?id=24643

TurkStat (Turkish Statistical Institute) (2017). Women in Statistics, 2017. Retrieved from: http://www.turkstat.gov.tr/PreHaberBultenleri.do?id=27594

UN (2018). Facts and Figures: Economic Empowerment, Benefits of Economic Empowerment, UN WOMEN. Retrieved from: http://www.unwomen.org/en/what-we-do/economic-empowerment/facts-and-figures

UN Women (2016). *Progress of the World's Women 2015–2016*. Retrieved from: http://progress.unwomen.org/en/2015/chapter2/

World Bank (2012). *World Development Report: Gender Equality and Development*. Retrieved from: http://siteresources.worldbank.org/INTWDR2012/Resources/7778105-1299699968583/7786210-1315936222006/Complete-Report.pdf

World Bank (2014). *Women, Business and Law 2014: Removing Restrictions to Enhance Gender Equality*. Retrieved from: http://documents.worldbank.org/curated/en/893551468147874555/pdf/922710PUB0v20W00Box385355B00PUBLIC0.pdf

World Economic Forum (2017). *The Global Gender Gap Report*. Retrieved from: http://www3.weforum.org/docs/WEF_GGGR_2017.pdf

4 Women Empowerment and Income Inequality during the Great Recession in the United States

Mehmet Erdem YAYA

Introduction

Researchers have defined women's empowerment as the ability to access health, education, earning opportunities, and legal rights. Women's empowerment has been a topic of extensive research due to the fact that in many parts of the world women are disempowered. Women are not only unable to access basic healthcare and education but also have difficulty attaining equal opportunities for employment in the labor markets. Consequently, women across the nations are suffering from worse health outcomes, lower educational attainments, and unequal pay. The literature is filled with research on the lack of women's access to resources and institutions that results in non-uniform outcomes for women and men (Mackenbach et. al, 1999; Burnette, 2017). Duflo (2012) in her overview of women's empowerment argued that the fundamental goal of empowerment policies should be the equality of women and men.

The earning differential between women and men is starker in under-developed economies compared to the developed ones. Although, some of the earlier researches have focused on underdeveloped economies, the empowerment of women still remains an important issue in developed economies such as the United States. Recent studies have shown that women earn only 78 cents for every dollar men earn in United States (Blau and Kahn, 2017). Furthermore, the literature has not examined the impact of recessions on women's empowerment. The United States fell into a deep recession in 2008, also known as the Great Recession. Although the recession started in the financial sector with the bankruptcy of Lehman Brothers, the recession quickly spilled into the entire economy. The Great Recession has been examined in the literature, especially issues related to income inequality (Yaya, 2018; Danzinger et al., 2013; Hellebrandt et al., 2015; Picketty and Saez, 2013; Salgado et al., 2014). Most of these papers, nevertheless, did not delve into the possible non-uniform impact of the Great Recession on inequality between women and men. This chapter fills this gap in the literature by offering descriptive results related to the impact of the recession on income inequality for women and men.

Overall, this study aims to inform the public and policymakers about the possible changes in inequality for women and men during the Great Recession in the United States. After all, not only the absolute level of income inequality but also inequality between women and men is a social problem in the United States. The literature on women's empowerment suggests that the roots of women's empowerment problems can be traced back to the economic dependence of women on men; hence income inequality between these groups.

The findings of this research are both relevant and timely given the fact that policymakers frequently underscore the importance of inequality between women and men. As Senators Sanders and Clinton made this issue part of their platforms during 2016 Presidential Election, the findings can be used to advocate for public policies such as the Women, Infants, and Children (WIC) program to increase women's empowerment particularly during recessions.

The Great Recession and Inequality

The American Community Survey (ACS) is a nationally representative survey that allows the public to obtain information on personal income as well as demographic information of respondents. For this research, data from 2005 to 2016 cohorts is employed, which provides information five years prior and five years after the Great Recession. The recession years are 2010 or 2011. The respondents of ACS were asked about their income in the previous year, making 2010 and 2011 the ideal years for the recession variable in the dataset. Meyer and Sullivan (2013) and Yaya (2018) used the same years as the years of the Great Recession in their studies. Only working age adults aged 18 to 65 are used for the study. The income variable is the sum of all personal incomes from various sources, including wages, salaries, and self-employment income. The nominal income values are adjusted for inflation.

Table 4.1 shows the inflation-adjusted income for the entire sample as well as women and men. The table clearly shows that the average income in the United States was $45,224 in 2005 and after a recession-inflicted period, the economy did not recover fully for 12 years. The average income reached only $43,032 in 2016, five years after the Great Recession. The second column shows the average income of women, which is much lower than men, starting out at $32,090 in 2005. The income of women has also declined during the Great Recession but bounced back to $32,884 in 2016. Finally, the third column exhibits the inflation-adjusted income for men, which was $59,352 in 2005, almost double that of women's income. Men's income took a harder hit during the recession, and did not recover in the post-recession period. In 2016, the income of men was only $53,521, approximately a 10% decline compared to 2005.

Table 4.1 Inflation-adjusted average income by gender

Year	Income (All)	Income (Women)	Income (Men)
2005	$45,224.31	$32,090.78	$59,352.04
2006	$44,198.47	$31,807.77	$57,128.93
2007	$45,101.17	$32,543.13	$58,235.10
2008	$45,144.18	$32,931.52	$57,927.18
2009	$42,354.14	$31,450.29	$53,750.72
2010	$41,194.80	$31,227.40	$51,572.79
2011	$39,079.57	$29,935.83	$48,457.07
2012	$39,372.12	$29,921.74	$49,110.45
2013	$40,304.59	$30,578.29	$50,319.42
2014	$40,511.25	$30,914.93	$50,387.86
2015	$41,606.27	$31,681.04	$51,795.08
2016	$43,032.42	$32,884.62	$53,421.64

Using personal income, the Gini coefficient has been computed for women and men over 12 years from 2005 to 2016. The Gini coefficient is a commonly used measure of inequality that takes a value between zero and one. The higher the coefficient, the more unequal the income distribution is. The Gini coefficient is popular in the literature, since it is sensitive to the changes in income at the bottom and the top of the distribution. More specifically, the changes in Gini coefficient are higher than other inequality metrics such as Relative Mean Deviation when the share of income earned by the poor (or rich) changes (Yaya, 2018). Gini coefficient can be calculated as:

$$Gini = \frac{\sum_{i=1}^{n} \sum_{j=1}^{n} |x_i - x_j|}{2_n \sum_{i=1}^{n} x_i}$$

Figure 4.1 depicts the Gini coefficient for the entire sample and gender groups between 2005 and 2016. The gray shaded area is the period of the Great Recession for the years 2010 and 2011. The figure exhibits an increasing trend in overall inequality in the United States. This overall increase in income inequality can be attributed to the structure of the US economy that rewards the skills generously, combined with low income taxes. Furthermore, structural changes such as immigration, skill-biased technological change, and declines in union power contributed to the upward swing in inequality in the United States since the 1980s. During the Great Recession in 2010 and 2011, the Gini coefficient increased at a much faster rate mostly due to decreases in income as well as non-uniform labor market outcomes for workers during the recession. Income inequalities for women and men also exhibit increasing trends, but there are few points to note: First, income inequalities for women

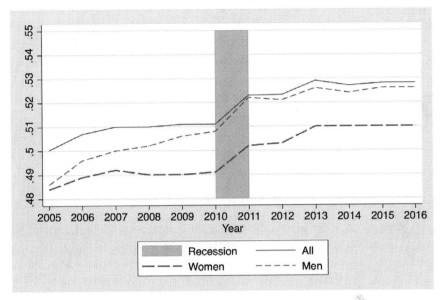

Figure 4.1 Gini Coefficient by Gender: 2005–2016

and men started out very close in the period prior to the recession. Second, inequalities for both women and men rapidly grew during the recession years, slightly more for men. Finally, in the post-recession period, these income inequalities are fairly flat with one difference; income inequality for men is now much higher than women. Consequently, it is possible to argue that the Great Recession has increased the overall income inequality which has not reverted back to pre-recession levels. Moreover, the recession had a non-uniform impact on women and men, such that the income inequality for men is now much higher than the income inequality for women.

Pyatt (1976) suggested that it is possible to break down the Gini coefficient into three components; namely within-group, between-group, and overlap. The within-group inequality component shows the share of inequality that arises from the dispersion of income among the poor and rich within each group that make up the population. On the other hand, the between-group inequality can be obtained if every income in every subgroup were replaced by each relevant subgroup mean (Lambert and Aronson, 1993). The remaining portion of the Gini coefficient can be named residual or overlap. Mookherjee and Shorrocks (1982) discussed the residual and the interaction effect, and they argued that it is impossible to interpret the overlap component precisely, except it is needed to maintain identity.

Figure 4.2 shows the within-group inequality based on Pyatt's (1976) break down of the Gini coefficient. The within-group inequality in the United States explains approximately half of the overall income inequality. It exhibits a consistent increase over the time period analyzed. However, it is also true

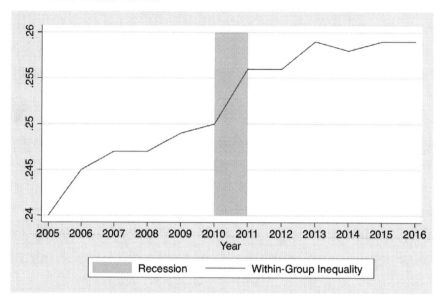

Figure 4.2 Pyatt's Within-Group Inequality by Gender: 2005–2016

that the rate of inequality change is very high during the recession years of 2010 and 2011. The descriptive results on this figure suggest that over time the within-group inequality accounted a larger share of the overall income inequality in the United States. It is possible that a larger share of women finds themselves in professions that are mainly located at the bottom of the income distribution as suggested by their lower average income. These professions, such as those in the hospitality or healthcare industry, might be heavily hit by the recession, which leads to more dispersion of income within gender groups. The same argument can be made for men, but this time, it should be noted that men have higher income on average, and recession again might hit the earnings of men but this time at the top of the distribution, leading to more unequally distributed income for men.

Between-group inequality based on Pyatt's (1976) break down of the Gini coefficient measures how much of the overall inequality can be attributed to the inequality between these gender groups. For example, the between-group inequality for women measures the inequality between women and men. It should be noted here again that the between-group income inequality based on Pyatt's decomposition can be obtained if every income in every subgroup is replaced by each relevant subgroup mean. In other words, the between-group inequality of women and men can be calculated by replacing the incomes of men with the average income of women. Once the replacement is completed, the Gini coefficient is calculated as usual.

Figure 4.3 exhibits the between-group inequality, showing visible decline in inequality between women and men. Interestingly, although the within-group inequality in the United States has been increasing during the time period ana-lyzed, between-group inequality has been declining even before the Great Reces-sion. The between-group inequality has reached the bottom in 2011, following a flat path in the post-recession period. The decline in between-group inequality for women and men during recession is expected. The dispersion of income between women and men decreased during the Great Recession, possibly due to men's disproportional exposure to the adverse effects of the recession, such as declines in income due to the fact that men who suffered more from declines in income work in industries heavily dominated by men such as manufacturing, banking, and construction. During the recession, these industries posted double digit declines in employment and earnings that led to a decrease in between-group inequality for women and men.

To summarize, the women's empowerment in the United States during the last 12 years has been analyzed in this descriptive study. The external shock that is incorporated into the analysis of women's empowerment is the Great Recession. The indirect measure of women's empowerment in this study is the income inequality. When the economic freedom, and opportunities available to women decline, the income inequality reflects these with increasing levels. As the results suggest that overall income inequality for women as well as within-group inequality has increased in the United States during the Great Recession. These findings indicate that women are less empowered in the post-recession period since these inequalities did not revert back to pre-

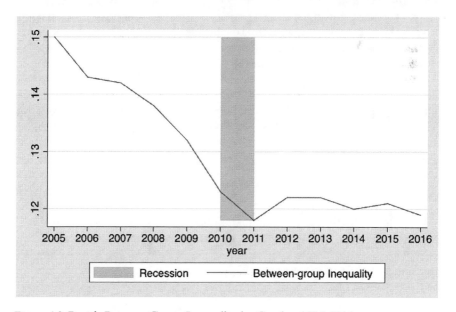

Figure 4.3 Pyatt's Between-Group Inequality by Gender: 2005–2016

recession levels five years after the Great Recession as shown in Figure 4.1 and Figure 4.2. Furthermore, the income inequality between women and men has significantly declined prior and during the recession; however, this general trend has halted in the post-recession period. This is a signal that economic gains and opportunities that lead to convergence of income between women and men have stopped due to the Great Recession. If the decline in between-group inequality is assumed to be another indirect measure of empowerment, the Great Recession slowed down the convergence of earnings, and hence the inequality between women and men.

Conclusion

Women facing discrimination, dependence on men, lack of educational and employment opportunities are disempowered around the world. Disempowerment of women reveals itself with lower earnings and educational attainments, and lack of entrepreneurial activities for women in both developed and developing countries. Although economic progress alleviates some of the disempowerment problems in developed economies, women in these countries still suffer from economic dependence on men and lower labor market participation. For instance, women still earn only 78 cents for every dollar men earn in the United States (Blau and Kahn, 2017).

Given the importance of women's empowerment, there has been an increasing level of interest and research on this issue. From the measurement of empowerment to the policies that empower women, researchers have analyzed this phenomenon extensively. Unfortunately, to my knowledge, the status of women and their empowerment during the economic crises has not been analyzed in the literature. To this end, this paper provides initial descriptive analysis of women empowerment in the United States over the last 12 years with special emphasis on the Great Recession.

The results from the initial estimates of income and inequality based on American Community Survey (ACS) over the last 12 years suggest that inflation adjusted income has gone through a big drop and recovery but average income has not reached the 2004 level even by 2016. The trend is similar for earnings of men. In contrast, women were able to reach the pre-recession earnings level after the recession. However, it should be noted that women earn significantly lower than men. Using the personal income provided by the ACS, I then calculated the overall income inequality as well as the within- and between-group inequalities for women and men. As expected, overall and within-group income inequalities have increased during the recession. Furthermore, between-group inequality has dropped for women and men. These results coupled with the average income suggest that women are less empowered in the post-recession period in the United States. The findings of the research call for more quantitative research such as regression-based analysis to shed light on the channels that recession affects the inequality for women and men. Furthermore, given the fact that women are less empowered during and after the recessions, the government may initiate public policies targeting women to alleviate not only the effects of recessions but also the inequality related disempowerment of women.

References

Blau, F. D., & Kahn, L. M. (2017). The Gender Wage Gap: Extent, Trends, and Explanations. *Journal of Economic Literature*, 55(3), 789–865. https://doi.org/10.1257/jel.20160995

Burnette, J. D. (2017). Inequality in the Labor Market for Native American Women and the Great Recession. *American Economic Review*, 107(5), 425–429.

Danzinger, S., Pfeffer, F. T., & Schoeni, R. F. (2013). Wealth Disparities Before and After the Great Recession. *The ANNALS of the American Academy of Political and Social Science*, 650(1), 98–123. https://doi.org/10.1177/0002716213497452

Duflo, E. (2012). Women Empowerment and Economic Development. *Journal of Economic Literature*, 50(4), 1051–1079. https://doi.org/10.1257/jel.50.4.1051

Hellebrandt, T., Jarand, M., Kirkegaard, J. F., Moran, T., Posen, A. S., Wolfers, J., & Zilinsky, J. (2015). *Raising Lower-Level Wages: When and Why It Makes Economic Sense*. Peterson Institute for International Economics.

Lambert, P. J., & Aronson, J. R. (1993). Inequality Decomposition Analysis and the Gini Coefficient Revisited. *The Economic Journal*, 103(420), 1221–1227.

Mackenbach, J. P., Kunst, A. E., Groenhof, F., Borgan, J. K., Costa, G., Faggiano, F., & Valkonen, T. (1999). Socioeconomic Inequalities in Mortality Among Women and Among Men: An International Study. *American Journal of Public Health*, 89 (12), 1800–1806.

Meyer, B. D., & Sullivan, J. X. (2013). Consumption and Income Inequality and the Great Recession. *American Economic Review*, 103(3), 178–183.

Mookherjee, D., & Shorrocks, A. (1982). A Decomposition Analysis of the Trend in UK Income Inequality. *The Economic Journal*, 92(368), 886–902.

Piketty, T., & Saez, E. (2013). Top Incomes and the Great Recession: Recent Evolutions and Policy Implications. *IMF Economic Review*, 61(3), 456–478.

Pyatt, G. (1976). On the Interpretation and Disaggregation of Gini Coefficients. *The Economic Journal*, 86(342), 243–255. https://doi.org/10.2307/2230745

Salgado, M. F., Figari, F., Sutherland, H., & Tumino, A. (2014). Welfare Compensation for Unemployment in the Great Recession. *Review of Income and Wealth*, 60 (S1), S177–S204.

Yaya, M. E. (2018). Great Recession and Income Inequality: A State-level Analysis. *Journal of Economics, Race, and Policy*, 1(2), 112–125. https://doi.org/10.1007/s41996-018-0016-6

5 National Economic Policies and Women's Economic Inclusion

The Case of Turkey and South Africa

Humaira HANSROD and Hatice Ahsen UTKU

Introduction

Women's economic empowerment (WEE) as a socioeconomic imperative is seldom contested these days, resting on the notion that empowering women economically is good both socially and economically. Research has long been indicating the links between WEE and the effectiveness of development approaches in reducing poverty (Dwyer et al., 1988; Kabeer, 2003; Quisumbing, 2003; World Bank, 2011). Empowerment-focused approaches promote economic growth that includes poor and marginalized people through investments, such as education, that build and improve people's capabilities and access to opportunities (Narayan, 2005). There also seem to be more positive economic growth outcomes where there are concurrent expansions in women's employment, suggesting that public policies may be crucial to removing barriers to women's labor force participation (Kabeer & Natali, 2013). There are sometimes disadvantages to macro-level policy actions however, and simply relaxing one constraint toward women's employment may neglect other constraints women face, suggesting the need for more holistic approaches to labor force participation.

Women's labor force participation, more simply known as "work", is widely accepted as key to women's economic empowerment. What exactly does "women's economic empowerment" mean? If one looked only at the labor force participation rates globally, standing at 49 percent of working-age women (World Bank, 2017a) as compared to 76 percent of working-age men (World Bank, 2017b), women's participation lends a negative picture to their empowerment. It is however not straightforward, nor recommended, to translate female labor participation into claims about women's welfare and empowerment. For example, women still dominate the unpaid labor domains such as housework and childrearing, and working conditions can affect whether work is "more" or "less" empowering for women. It is hard to predict what employment indicates about women's empowerment until both quantitative and qualitative factors are considered on a case-by-case basis, which is beyond the scope of this chapter. Nonetheless, if considering work as a stepping-stone or element of a broader set of factors that influence or represent empowerment, then understanding women's position in the labor force serves to enhance our understanding of empowerment. It is along this line of thinking that we approach this chapter's focus on women's economic inclusion.

We define "women's economic inclusion" as women's uninhibited participation in the workforce as wageworkers, entrepreneurs, and business owners. Empowerment is a key factor for women's wellbeing and in ensuring sustainable economic development. Facilitating empowerment rests on "improving the ability of women to access the constituents of development—in particular health, education, earning opportunities, rights, and political participation" (Duflo, 2012, p.1053). Policy action is key to facilitating this improvement. Women's economic inclusion thus emphasizes a dimension of empowerment focusing on the access to labor markets and opportunities for women who choose to participate in the labor force. Understanding the local and gender-specific priorities for enabling women's economic inclusion therefore contributes to our understanding of one factor of women's economic empowerment and plays an important part in maintaining a healthy economy and democracy. This chapter will specifically review particular national policies of two countries—Turkey and South Africa, which underwent significant economic transformation in their post-independence transitions—and examine how women especially were targeted and affected.

Between Family and Work: Century-old Contradictions on the Ideal Image of Turkish Women

Located between Europe and Asia, the Turkish Republic is a secular nation state founded in 1923 after the collapse of the Ottoman Empire in the First World War. Despite being invaded by the European states during the First World War on multiple fronts, Turkey was never colonized as a result of a lengthy Independence War led by Mustafa Kemal Atatürk, the founding father of Turkey. Atatürk removed the European armies from the Turkish lands, yet his visions of Turkey were inspired by European ideals. The Turkish state was founded on six principles: republicanism, nationalism, populism, statism, *secularism* and reformism—some of which were contested and disputed, creating the enduring political contradictions of the modern Turkish history. In addition to the ongoing candidacy of membership to the European Union, multiple coups d'état, and unrelenting political instability and coalition governments before the AK Party took power defined the political environment in Turkey for decades. The gender question just adds another layer of complexity to these contradictions. It is also essential to note that this section will examine the policies and laws up to the failed coup on July 15, 2016 since in the aftermath of the failed coup and in the process of transition to the presidential system, many laws and policies are subject to change.

Gender analysis of Turkish politics and particularly Turkish nationalism merits greater attention given the role of gender in the nation-building process and development. This section explores the gender implications of modernization in Turkey, and how they translate into the economic inclusion of women into the workforce. The case of Turkey manifests some intriguing questions and contradictions in terms of national ideals and expectations, and social norms and traditions. The creation of the new Turkish citizenship defined by nationality rather than religion resulted in the establishment of strict boundaries among entangled identities that survived for centuries in the Ottoman Empire. The new "perfect" Turkish citizen was assumed to be Sunni Muslim, secular, ethnically Turkish—and if not, smoothly assimilated into Turkish society—and westernized. Women became the face of modern Turkey: "unveiled, dressed in Western clothes, yet still the chaste mother" (Willis et al., 2015, p.20). However, the contradictions that made up these ideals of modernization are yet to be resolved. Turkish women had to "catch up" with their Western peers, yet they were still assigned to the traditional gender roles, which created divergent profiles of women throughout generations and eventually left many women in a limbo of identities.

The significant introduction of female workforce participation, as a relevant notion and major leap in the practice of female employment, took place during the urbanization, industrialization, and migration processes of the 1950s. This process also marked the transition of women working in unpaid jobs within their family homes or farms to female employment in paid jobs in industrial sectors (Kılınç, 2015). Some of the first important legal and policy changes regarding women and gender equality were endorsed in the late Ottoman period, particularly during the Tanzimat period. The foundation of the Turkish Republic in 1923 entailed the re-definition of the notion of Turkishness, which certainly had gender aspects. In a series of pro-Western reforms initiated by Mustafa Kemal Ataturk, the founder of modern Turkey, changes in the political, economic and social status of women took place. However, these reforms and changes did not materialize in the smoothest way. Change came with resistance, enforcement, and segregation. This section will further analyze the policies, and their implications for the economic inclusion of women into the workforce in Turkey.

As a part of the Kemalist reforms, *Tevhid-i Tedrisat* law was adopted in 1924, which entailed equal opportunities for male and female students. In 1926, the new Civil Code, adapted from the Swiss Civil Code, abolished polygamy and provided the right to divorce and parental right to women. Women were also granted the right to vote and be elected in local elections in 1930, and in national elections in 1934. Although the first signs of transformation in the clothing of Ottoman women can be traced back to early 1900s, this transformation principally took place in the urban settings and elite circles. Smaller cities and rural populations perceived the top-down policies with either resistance or indifference, and the empowerment of women in Turkey turned out to be a process of "forced inclusion" (Willis et al., 2015). Government officials cooperated with the laws and policies of forced inclusion, mainly because "they viewed Atatürk as a national hero" (Willis et al., 2015, p.24). These laws and policies of forced inclusion did not defy patriarchy radically, and there seemed to be only limited threat to the hegemonic masculinity both in the state and the society (Willis et al. 2015). This is essential to keep in mind in order to comprehend and to interpret the motivations underlying subsequent policies, such as those within the context of the National Action Plan, and their results.

Economic Inclusion within the Policy Framework

The membership process of the European Union also entailed some legal and policy changes regarding the status of women, and their contribution to the workforce. These changes are framed within a series of National Action Plans Regarding Social Gender Equality and Development Plans. Major changes include but are not limited to the amendments to the Civil Code (2002), amendment to Article 10 of the Constitution (2004), Labor Law No. 4857, and Social Security Law No. 5510. The Labor Law addresses and outlaws discrimination and pay gap based on language, race, gender, political affiliation, ideology, religion, or sect in the workplace. The law also ensures that gender is not a valid reason for the termination of labor contracts (Korkmaz & Korkut, 2012). The Labor Law has also prohibited women working underground or under water, and regulated working conditions in a favorable way for women including night shifts, maternity leave, working hours for pregnant women, conditions for breastfeeding rooms, and nurseries in workplaces. According to the Labor Law Article 74, maternity leave is 16 weeks, extended by two weeks in cases of multiple pregnancy. If necessary, female employees can take up to six months of unpaid leave in addition to 1.5 hours (per day) of breastfeeding leave until the child is weaned. An additional clause to the Labor Law suggests that fathers can take five days of paternity leave. The Civil Servants Law Article 104, on the other hand, authorizes ten days of paternity leave and up to 24 months of unpaid leave in necessary cases. Article 108 allows female civil servants to ask for the same extension at the end of their maternity leave. Recent regulations allow similar maternity leave conditions for parents who adopt children who are under the age of three.

While these laws and policies aim at promoting the inclusion of women into the workforce, and ameliorating the social and economic status of women against the traditional gender norms rooted in Turkish society, the underlying assumption still remains that the primary responsibility of child care belongs to women. As a result, many employers tend to hire men rather than women in order to avoid responsibilities and obligations of positive discrimination (e.g. to provide a breastfeeding room or nursery), or avoid these responsibilities and obligations with fines in cases where there is no sufficient number of female employees (Korkmaz and Korkut, 2012, p.61). Regardless, the Employment Law (2008) has revoked the requirement of providing the above-stated rooms and nurseries, resulting in the separation of the workplace and nurseries, and creating more pressure on female employees with children (Korkmaz and Korkut, 2012, p.61).

The aforementioned policies and laws are part of the broader strategic plan, including the National Action Plan on Women's Employment, which addresses various issues of development including gender equality and empowerment. The National Action Plan on Women's Employment was created in 2014 as a collaboration between the International Labor Organization (ILO) and the Turkish Employment Agency (IŞKUR) in order to promote gender-sensitive employment policies while supporting government efforts such as the national strategic plans. Successive governments have envisioned these strategic plans that often cover a span of five years since 1963, and the latest one, the Tenth Strategic Plan, has framed the policy changes addressing inclusion and empowerment from 2014 to 2018 (TUIK, 2014). The Tenth Strategic Plan envisages gender equality as one of the broader objectives; however, it is intriguing that women empowerment stands as a sub-issue to family-relation issues. "Women" are relegated to a sub-section entitled "Family and Woman", and with only three clauses that briefly mention targets and aims of increasing women's labor force participation as a strategy within the development plan (The Tenth Development Plan: 2014–2018, clauses #246, 247, 251). This kind of hasty attention to women's labor force participation is frustrating as it does not provide explicit aims for *how* women will be empowered through labor force participation, nor clear targets for achieving those aims. The plan promises the enhancement of opportunities for women, and improvement of gender equality in employment and participation in the workforce. In the following clauses, it also ensures to achieve gender equality without harming the Turkish family structure, which raises the assumption that women's economic inclusion is still perceived as a threat to existing family dynamics and traditional gender roles. The plan's section on the amelioration of the labor market also mainly focuses on the inclusion of women into the workforce, envisioning an increase in the participation rate, and easier access to child and elderly care.

It is essential to investigate to what extent these policies are implemented and with what results. The National Action Plan for Women's Employment for instance aims to increase the opportunities available to women for *decent work* mainly through policy action and enhancing the capacity of relevant local and national institutions to create and provide employment for women (ILO, 2016). One should be aware that an in-depth examination would include survey data, interviews, and on-site observations which are beyond the scope of this chapter. Hence, this section will only scan statistical data provided by the Turkish Statistical Institute (TurkStat) and conduct a basic review of the literature and laws to try to explain some of the trends in the economic inclusion of women. Another limitation that should be kept in mind is that the most recent statistical data by the TurkStat is up to 2013 at the time of writing this section, which can be analyzed in the context of earlier policies and laws, but that unfortunately has not allowed us to place the data in the context of the Tenth Strategic Plan and the National Action Plan on Women's Employment, both of which started in 2014.

Economic Inclusion in Statistical Figures

Participation of women in the workforce manifests significant fluctuations from the early days of the Turkish Republic to date. According to statistics from TurkStat, female participation in the workforce was 70 percent in 1955 while it declined to 30 percent in the 1990s. Migration from the rural areas to the urban regions is considered to be the primary reason for the decline (Ağlı & Tor, 2016). TurkStat statistics reveal that in 1988, the participation rate of illiterate women in the workforce was 32.3 percent which dropped to 26.8 percent in 1999. The participation of women with high school diplomas dropped from 45.7 percent in 1988 to 32.2 percent in 1999. Most surprisingly, the participation of women with a bachelor's degree dropped from 82.5 percent in 1988 to 71.4 percent in 1999. The participation rate of women with bachelor's degree had been in decline since 2000, but with slight fluctuations it has been on the rise again in the last few years. In 2000, 70 percent of women with a bachelor's degree participated in the workforce, dropping to a low of 68.8 percent in 2006, and reaching 72.2 percent in 2013. One potential factor that could have partly affected the decline and recent rise in women's labor participation, and that is worth further investigation as it is beyond the scope of this chapter, is the headscarf ban that began in the 1980s and was strictly implemented in the public sector as well as selectively adhered to in the private sector in the 1990s. Under the ban, women employed in public sectors were not allowed to wear a headscarf, and many were not hired in private sector companies often as a result of discrimination against the headscarf. The ban continued officially until the mid-2010s, although many would argue it is still a cause of discrimination in some employment practices.

Unlike illiterate women, women with no degree, or women with a two-year college degree, some other groups of women have increasingly participated in the workforce over the last decade. The most significant increase can be observed among women with only primary school education. While in 2000 only 7.9 percent of women with primary education participated in the workforce, 21.5 percent of women in this group were in the workforce by 2013. Further inquiry should verify if this rise in this group's workforce participation might be a result of relatively recent government support and subsidies to female-owned small enterprises.

Barriers and Constraints on Economic Inclusion

Three groups of factors can hinder economic inclusion of women: socio-cultural factors, socio-economic factors, and political factors. These groups of factors are not exclusive to one and other, but instead, they intertwine in

many cases. Patriarchal culture in society also prevails in the mainstream literature on economic development and the policy-making world. Anti-feminist
approaches in the economic and policy-making world often ignore the invisible
and unpaid labor by women, leaving women out of economic participation by
definition on the first hand. Patriarchy defines the traditional gender roles and
expectations in Turkish society, and defines the limits and boundaries within and
between genders. Despite policies encouraging women to get educated and to
work, society can prioritize roles within the family as daughters, wives, and
mothers, and disdain higher education or career goals for women (Korkmaz and
Korkut, 2012, p.45). Having said that, Turkish culture is not monolithically
patriarchal, and the degrees of patriarchy also hinge on the disparities between
rural and urban settings. On the other hand, extending education processes is
another factor delaying the active participation of women in the workforce.
Finally, civil status—being single, married, or divorced/widowed, as well as
having children—is another factor that has an impact on the economic inclusion
of women (Korkmaz and Korkut, 2012, p.42).

According to data from TurkStat in 2013, the highest share of women who
participated in the workforce were divorced. Namely, 50.9 percent of divorced
women were employed, a rise from 41.0 percent in 2000. In 2013, only 30.5
percent of married women were in the workforce while 37.9 percent of single
women were in the workforce. These two categories show a slight increase compared to 25.2 percent and 35.0 percent respectively in 2000. However, for the
latter category this increase is not even close to what the rate was in 1988 when
47.8 percent of single women participated in the workforce. The only category in
steady decline is widowed women. While 16.0 percent in 1988 and 11.5 percent
in 2000 were in the workforce, only 9.0 percent of widowed women were active in
the workforce in 2013. Extended education, like seeking higher education and
pursuing graduate studies, might be a cause of the fluctuation in the participation rate of single women. Migration from rural to urban settings is one of the
most significant socioeconomic barriers against economic inclusion for unskilled
or low-skilled women looking for decent jobs. Women who work in farms or
similar settings are likely to not get jobs in the cities, or switch to informal and
less secure jobs like cleaning, cooking, or babysitting (Korkmaz and Korkut
2012, p.42). On the other hand, in the last few years, participation of women in
the workforce has been on the decline in rural settings while it has been on the
rise in the urban settings (Korkmaz and Korkut 2012, p.44). While urbanization
may be bringing more work opportunities for both men and women, these gains
will need to be combined with efforts to directly address women's economic
inclusion for women with different skill levels and abilities.

South Africa – Economic Inclusion at the Intersection of Race and Gender

South African history cannot be read in any one-dimensional way. James
Michener was on the right track in his exhaustive account of the country's

history in his 1980 book *The Covenant*. In this historically phenomenal publication, Michener reviews the history of the land from 15,000 years ago till
the 1970s, describing the connecting histories of South Africa's five major
population groups of the 20th century—the Bantu (indigenous Black African
tribes), the British, Colored (those of racially mixed descent), Indian (and
other Asians), and Afrikaner (those of Dutch, French Huguenot, and
German descent who migrated to South Africa seeking religious freedom).
Although at the time of writing South Africa was still under its apartheid
regime, the book's conclusion, imbued with disappointment at the terrible
political ideology, is part of the current narrative that is most often associated
with South African history.

Apartheid

Apartheid is the term for a policy or institutional system of racial segregation
and discrimination. The term has most notoriously been associated with
South African history, although it also existed in the country that is presently
known as Namibia. While racial laws have existed since the 19th century in
South Africa, apartheid as a legitimate policy became official in 1948 promoted by Afrikaners who ruled through the National Party. This system
established a government ruled by the White minority in order to extend
White, in particular Afrikaner, privilege and systematically discriminate
against Blacks. Under apartheid, Black South Africans (which include Bantu,
Colored, and Indian people) were restricted from meaningful participation in
the economy through constraints on property ownership, lack of or limited
access to quality education, and systematic discrimination in hiring laws and
processes. Under such conditions, many saw limited economic opportunities
for employment, skill-development, and asset ownership.

Society

South African society is often referred to as the *rainbow nation* due to the
many cultures that have throughout the centuries created a diverse nation.
Despite the legacy of apartheid, which not only sought to establish the
superiority of the White race but also restrict the intermingling between non-
Whites, the country is a collage of different cultures living together. This is
not to say that it is a paradigm for social cohesion. Racism, nowadays more
internalized, and distrust of "other" groups is a persisting feature (Hofmeyr &
Govender, 2015). What is obvious however is the rampant poverty and massive inequality that plague the country. The widening gap between the poor
and the rich, the latter of whom in the post-apartheid era have included a
small group of Blacks that comprise the elite, has serious implications not
only for social peace but also economic and political stability. Women in
particular seem more inclined than men to view the rich–poor divide as the
primary division in South Africa (Meiring et al., 2018).

South Africa remains one of the most unequal countries in the world with limited progress on reducing poverty. For an upper middle-income country with GDP per capita of about US$6,000, the country has a few high-income earners and a small limited middle-class. There is low intergenerational mobility and the labor market is "polarized", creating a wide wage gap (World Bank, 2018, p. xi). Meanwhile there is massive poverty with half the population living on less than US$3 a day and about 18 percent living on less than US$2 per day (World Bank, 2018). The bearers of this poverty display the persistent legacy of apartheid, comprising of mainly Blacks, female-headed households, large families, the unemployed, and less educated. Gender inequalities are evident in South African society considering its patriarchal roots, and many women still find themselves accorded lower social status to men (UNICEF SA, 2006). In a country with over 7 million people living with HIV, women have among the highest rates of HIV infection—about double the rate for men—and face high levels of gender-based violence. Many girls feel socially pressured to relinquish higher educational pursuits in favor of domesticity. Considering the high physical insecurity widespread throughout the country, girls face greater dangers when travelling to and from schools that are far from their homes. Sexual abuse is not uncommon within many schools and perpetrated by students as well as some teachers. There are high rates of teenage pregnancies and this places greater burdens on single under-age mothers who often have to quit school amid social and financial pressure (UNICEF SA, 2006).

Economy

South Africa's economy boasts a nominally free market system with limited government intervention in economic planning measures like price setting. Mining is the historical driver of the economy, and still accounts for the majority of the country's exports particularly in the form of precious metals and stones, coal, and processed petroleum oils. Other main sectors of the economy involve manufacturing, including automobiles and agro-processing, and financial services.

The *Quarterly Labour Force Survey* of August 2018 indicates that women's status in the labor force during the past decade has deteriorated (Stats SA, 2018a). Unemployment is high, ranging from a narrow rate of 27 percent and expanded rate (which considers those who are not actively searching for work) of 37 percent. In both categories, unemployment among women is higher than men. There are, however, more women employed in the informal sector, which comprises about 17 percent of total employment. Widespread unemployment represents loss of income to individuals and their families, and decline in production and consumer spending nationally. While the informal sector is a source of employment to many, its potential to promote economic growth and reduce poverty is often dismissed by its shadowy nature bordering on illegality in many instances, offering workers much less protection, benefits, and income security, and an even greater gender gap in earnings, with women dominating the "bottom segment" jobs (Chen, 2007). In the formal sector, women again dominate occupations in the "bottom segments" such as domestic and clerical work. Some jobs like machinery operators, tradesmen, and skilled agricultural workers continue to display a strong male preference, with a quarter or less female presence.

Severe inequality is highlighted in the country's wealth and income distribution. As Figure 5.1 shows, South Africans who comprise the top 10 percent of the class level own and control about 90 percent of the country's wealth and assets while earning about 55 percent of total income (Orthofer, 2016). The middle 40 percent, which can arguably be called the *middle class*, earn about 35 percent of total income while owning only about 10 percent of its wealth. The other half of the population earns a meager 10 percent of the total income while their wealth ownership remains numerically insignificant.

Politics

South Africa's transition to democracy occurred through regime *transformation* that centered on procedural continuity and economic development

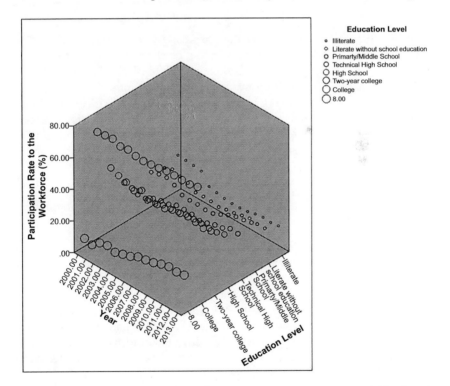

Figure 5.1 Distribution and Control of Wealth and Income in South Africa by Class (percentage)

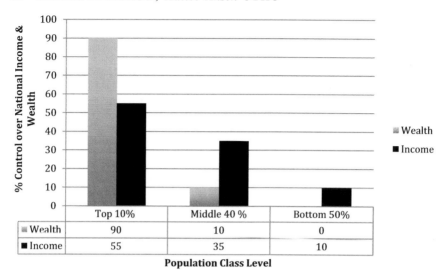

	Top 10%	Middle 40 %	Bottom 50%
▦ Wealth	90	10	0
■ Income	55	35	10

Population Class Level

Figure 5.2 Percent Distribution & Control of Wealth and Income in South Africa by Class

(Giliomee, 1995; Sisk, 1995). Rather than regime *breakdown* that would create a complete cut from the past for instance, as occurred in neighboring Zimbabwe's transition through nationalization of White-owned lands and businesses, South Africa's White-led government provided limits to the process of democratization. The leading Black political party, the African National Congress (ANC, 1994), led by Nelson Mandela restrained plans for nationalization "in return for pledges to promote Black advancement through affirmative action and the restitution of some of the losses sustained under apartheid" (Giliomee, 1995, p.97).

Broad-Based Black Economic Empowerment Policy – Background and Aims

The policy termed Broad-Based Black Economic Empowerment (BBBEE) was first developed in 2001, reformed in 2007, and amended in 2013. One of the world's broadest and most complicated set of affirmative action policies, BBBEE (or BEE in its short form) rules cover affirmative action mainly in companies' ownership, procurement, and employment activities by prioritizing those from previously disadvantaged backgrounds. Inherently a racial law, the rationale for BEE was to remove "all the obstacles to the development of black entrepreneurial capacity" in a country where Blacks did not have capital or land for investment (ANC, 1994, pp.4–5).

The Broad Based Black Economic Empowerment strategy is a necessary government intervention to address the systematic exclusion of the majority of South Africans from full participation in the economy. The defining feature of Apartheid was the use of race to restrict and severely control access to the economy by Black persons. The accumulation process was one of restricted wealth creation and imposed underdevelopment on Black communities to ensure that they were, in the main, suppliers of cheap labor (Act 53, 2003).

As amended by Act 46 of 2013, Section 1(c) of the BBBEE Act stipulates:

> Broad-based black economic empowerment means the viable economic empowerment of all black people including, in particular women, workers, youth, people with disabilities and people living in rural areas, through diverse but integrated socio-economic strategies that include, but are not limited to:
>
> a   increasing the number of black people that manage, own and control enterprises and productive assets;
> b   facilitating ownership and management of enterprises and productive assets by communities, workers, co-operatives and other collective enterprises;
> c   human resource and skills development;
> d   achieving equitable representation in all occupational categories and levels in the workforce;
> e   preferential procurement from enterprises that are owned or managed by black people; and
> f   investment in enterprises that are owned or managed by black people.

The Department of Trade and Industry (DTI) subsequently laid out numerous strategies against which the successful implementation and assessment of BEE would be conducted by establishing key objectives that emphasized BEE's focus on Blacks in positions of ownership, control, and management. To guide the implementation of the BEE objectives and initiatives, and provide clear criteria for measurement of BEE compliance, the DTI also released the Codes of Good Practice in 2007 (revised in 2013) in accordance with elements of a BEE Scorecard. The scorecard is a measurement system that assigns points to various elements of empowerment that aligns with BEE's main objectives in order to determine the level of an organization's compliance. It is also the primary way for the government to evaluate the extent of *Black empowerment* from individual organizations to the broader economy. The Codes of Good Practice further aim to reduce the practice of *fronting*— whereby a Black person or entity is placed in a high-level position, without substantial contributions and/or gains, in order for a company to gain BEE points—and broaden the spectrum of empowered individuals from a relatively smaller Black "elite" group to a wider category of people including women, youth, workers, the disabled, and rural people (Brand South Africa, 2017). The Codes are binding on all state entities with respect to employment guidelines and public transactions such as procurement and public–private partnerships while remaining technically a discretionary measure for private companies.

BEE's Critics

There are understandably many critics and criticisms of the policy. BEE has undoubtedly become a normalized feature of the new South Africa. It has shaped the political character of the new nation in many ways, particularly through the state's manipulation of labor markets. These labor market interferences were first seen in the precursor to BEE, the 1998 Employment Equity Act that demanded employers to classify their employees by race and reduce racial under-representation at various levels of the workforce by meeting targets for Black representation. For instance, the expected Black share (including Indians and Coloreds) of the national labor force (those working or actively looking for work) is about 87 percent, which is also the target for Black representation that employers are expected to meet. Aside from a number of strains that this put on employers, the "target" system did not consider the human capital—or stock of knowledge and skills—of the Black labor force, of which in 2001 only 276,000 held a post-grade 12 qualification (Jeffery, 2014). BEE not only widened the inequality gap between the rich and the poor, by ensuring that those who pursued business-oriented objectives benefited the most financially, but it created a Black elite that was disconnected from the masses.

BBBEE has been the democratic state's, particularly the ANC government's, main instrument to use state power in order to transfer the majority-White-controlled economy into Black hands. Southall (2007) aptly made this proposition:

> The essence of the negotiated settlement was that the ANC would secure political power while simultaneously accepting the principles of market economy. If this, in shorthand, translated into "black" control of politics and "white" control of the economy, large-scale capital was nonetheless aware of the need to reduce its political exposure by developing alliances and class interest with aspirant black capitalists.
>
> (p. 70)

The "negotiated settlement" therefore highlights three key features. First, the distribution of political power was affirmed to Blacks while economic power was left to Whites. Second, democratic South Africa chose to follow a pro-market path to development rather than a people's revolution approach to state socialism, which would shape the character of the neoliberal policies adopted. The ANC's establishment of neoliberal macroeconomics' authority in the new democracy benefited the existing White bourgeoisie and upcoming Black elite—mostly ANC-connected—while excluding the poorest half of the population (Terreblanche, 2002). Third, the new settlement birthed a new but small Black elite that was largely indifferent to ensuring the distribution of economic wealth to the majority of Blacks in the country (Du Toit et al., 2008). While BBBEE is technically an optional measure for private companies, being a non-BEE-compliant entity in South Africa is akin to organizational suicide. Applying the codes is mandatory for any company that intends to engage in business with the government. These business engagements can be small or large, and include tenders for public projects, purchasing state-owned assets, applying for licenses and concessions, and entering into public–private partnerships.

BBBEE & Women

The development of the BBBEE policy emerged from the government's need to have a focused and key strategic framework that would set the pathway to post-apartheid Black economic empowerment. Through the policy, Black economic empowerment was now positioned within a broader development strategy whose target would be the historically disadvantaged groups. These groups included not just the racial classifications of Blacks, coloreds, and Indians, but also other categories such as gender, disability, age, and community status (i.e. rural). To legally support this Black-empowerment-based economic growth, the policy calls on the Bill of Rights' principle of equality and the Constitution's allowance for affirmative action. Using affirmative action as an approach to empowerment, BBBEE focused on: 1) increasing the number of Blacks in middle to senior-level positions; and 2) increasing the number of Blacks to own, control, and/or manage existing and new companies.

Women's Economic Inclusion – 1995–2018

The state has opened many doors, such as its redistributive policies and skill-building programs, to facilitate women's economic involvement across all sectors, especially those that have been White-dominated in the apartheid era. While historically disadvantaged women during apartheid participated in the labor force, they were largely unskilled and low-skilled labor, driven into more insecure livelihoods of the post-apartheid "casualization" and "proletariatization" of labor (Hall et al., 2013). The democratic state through its policy mechanisms however is deliberately aiming to pull more women into skilled positions.

BBBEE tackled many barriers that women from previously disadvantaged groups faced in entering the formal labor force. In fact, the policy placed women (i.e. Blacks, Indians, Coloreds) at the forefront of hiring practices by making it both an imperative for some—as certain employers like state entities were legally mandated to abide by the policy—and an incentive for all—as women employees increased a company's BBBEE "score" used to provide tax incentives and access to government contracts—to hire women. The following four sub-sections give a glimpse into four key spaces for women's economic inclusion.

Employment

Women comprised about 44 percent of the skilled employed population in 2017 (Stats SA, 2017a, Table 3.5); it was 44 percent in 2002 (Stats SA, 2009, Table 4.3). Regardless of race, men are more likely to have paid employment than women. This indicates that the labor market is still more favorable to men than to women. Some qualitative studies indicate that part of the increase, in absolute numbers, in women's general labor force participation in the post-apartheid years "may be a response to long-term processes of impoverishment," and in the African context emerged from women's declining incomes in traditional occupations (Whitehead, 2009). While general poverty in South Africa has declined since 2000, women are not only poorer than men (by 30 percent) but they are also worse off in well-being dimensions such as water, health, and sanitation (Rogan, 2014). While there has been "feminization'—an increase in female workers—in the labor force since democratization, women are still in the most disadvantaged positions in the labor force as they largely occupy insecure and low-income jobs (Casale, 2004; Barker, 1999). Even when including women in relatively better off positions, women still earned less than men in wages (Finn, 2015). Some note that this feminization of the labor force was due to a "push" factor, notably that women who lacked adequate education and skills entered the labor force out of financial need and not because the labor market increased its demand for female labor in particular (Casale & Posel, 2002; Bhorat & Kanbur, 2006).

Business

In business, the scorecard system ensures that having Black women within any aspect of firm activity—from procurement and management to skills development—counts more than having Black men. Through a specific allocation in the scorecard called the Adjusted Recognition for Gender principle, Black women can earn a company up to double the BEE points it could score if hiring Black men. The principle essentially aims for firms to uphold both the Equality Clause of the Bill of Rights and the Constitution's affirmative action clause by encouraging women to account for at least 50 percent of some of the scorecard's targets. In addition to the principle, the scorecard further allows a company to gain higher compliance status through the exclusive inclusion of Black women. For instance, companies earn extra points by having at least 10 percent of voting rights in Black women's hands and having at least 6 percent of procurements from Black female-owned companies. Note that a Black female-owned company is defined by the BEE scorecard as being at least 30 percent owned by a Black woman or group of women. The need for applying and monitoring BBBEE underlies a complicated set of regulations that has also created a BBBEE compliance sector. This sector comprises of state-approved and often industry-specific firms and consultants that assist other organizations in understanding and achieving their respective BBBEE compliance targets.

At the board level, if having enough women in decision-making positions will lead to actual impact on profitability and gender diversity, the current policy context does not particularly target one aspect—CEOs. Female representation at the CEO-board level is not legislated. If rewarding Black ownership and management alone was sufficient, the data does not look so favorable to women. According to a Bain & Co report (Fajardo & Erasmus, 2017), the percentage of female CEOs was 10 percent (the global average is 12 percent). The report, which surveyed over 1,000 women and men in both private and listed companies, also found that as Black women climbed up the management ladder, they had to navigate certain corporate dynamics that their male counterparts did not necessarily face as the latter had the support and guidance of mentors and sponsors. The Businesswomen's Association of South Africa (BWASA, 2017) reported in its latest census that only 22 percent of women were board directors and out of these only 7 percent were executive directors. BWASA (2017) further found that only 4.8 percent of companies listed on the Johannesburg Stock Exchange (JSE) had three or more female CEOs, while 2 percent of listed companies had a gender-balanced board with at least 50 percent of female CEOs.

Between 2004, around the time BBBEE came into force, and 2017, the percentage of women holding senior leadership positions only rose by 2 percent, rising from 26 percent to 28 percent. Fajardo & Erasmus (2017) indicated hampered progress on broader gender equity because "for minorities to have their voices heard as an influential body and not as a token, this figure needs to be 30% or higher". Women in middle- and senior-management in particular have diminished access to mentors and sponsors who share their race and gender, lowering their aspirations and confidence in reaching higher-level positions. Considering that women made up 46 percent of people who entered the workforce, and having a highly scrutinized policy context like BBBEE aiming to increase underrepresented women's economic representation, the findings indicate persisting constraints to Black women's professional upward mobility in corporate settings.

Education

Part of the "bottom-up" approach to development and change, education has been a renowned path through which normative and behavioral transformations have been channeled. Furthermore, beyond basic literacy and numeracy, ensuring that this instruction facilitates higher education that equips both male and female learners with adequate knowledge and skills commensurate with the needs of the market (anticipating participation in the labor force) aligns with broader development goals for economic growth. South Africa's male literacy rate is 84.9 percent, almost the same as the female literacy rate of 84.3 percent (Stats SA, 2017b, pp.xi and 40). Although only about 23 percent of women are acquiring a tertiary education, enrolment statistics show more women are entering universities than men (around 18 percent) and acquiring 62 percent of tertiary degrees (BWASA, 2017). Girls' school attendance was over 90 percent at both primary and secondary level. Completion rates however are lower at the secondary level, especially for Blacks and Coloreds, reducing many of these women's employability and prospects for higher studies. Furthermore, the data show that completion of secondary schooling is not sufficient to ensure women's economic inclusion. Unemployment among those with only a secondary education attainment was 26.3 percent in 2015, which is almost double the unemployment rate of those with a post-secondary education (Stats SA, 2017b, p.44).

Female leadership in the education sector is also a cause for concern, if one understands such leadership to promote greater inclusion of women in pursuing higher education. In higher-education institutions, women held only 15 percent of vice-chancellor positions (BWASA, 2017, p.77). While women filled the majority of chancellor positions, this role was mostly ceremonial and the actual decision-making roles were the vice-chancellors. There were only nine women who were deans of science, technology, engineering and mathematics (STEM) departments (BWASA, 2017, p.78). Data on the composition of executive managerial and director positions shows less than a third being held by women, casting further doubt on women's potential to climb up the leadership ladder (BWASA 2017, p.79).

Entrepreneurship

One of the pertinent gender-relevant BBBEE "sister" strategies is the DTI's 2007 *Strategic Framework on Gender and Women's Economic Empowerment* (DTI, 2007). Aiming to support "women's equal access to, and control over, economic resources," its driving motive was to facilitate and increase women's access to and participation in the DTI's programs and policies (DTI, 2007, p.5). Through this document, the DTI proposed several interventions aimed at addressing underdevelopment and unemployment in order to support women's full participation in the economy and "accelerate the empowerment of women" (DTI, 2007, p.ii). As outlined by the framework, the proposed interventions sought to improve the quality of manufactured goods and increase employment opportunities for women by increasing support for women's entrepreneurship through accessible and affordable financial and technological services. Given DTI's mandate to support business development, it is clear from this document and its initiatives that the focus is on *women's entrepreneurship* specifically through helping women build and/or sustain their businesses. The approach has been to "target women and to empower them to take control of their lives, to set their own agenda, to gain skills and knowledge, to increase self-confidence, and solve problems" (DTI, 2007, p.8).

There is little however in the document to indicate how the supported female entrepreneurs will be able to distribute the economic benefits of entrepreneurship such as, for example, by employing other women. After all, one of the main aims of entrepreneurial development is the supposed creation of supporting jobs—those within the business sector—and secondary jobs— those within the wider economy. A critical view of this framework, for instance, shows the limited grasp and impact of such programs to benefit rural women's economic inclusion, those who are hard to reach and often with low educational attainment.

Implications for South Africa's National Development

BBBEE has been the main instrument to use state power in order to transfer the majority-White-controlled economy into Black hands. However, the post-apartheid settlement birthed a new but small Black elite that was, and remains to some extent, largely indifferent to ensuring the distribution of economic wealth to the majority of Blacks in the country (Du Toit et al., 2008). A study by scholars at the University of Cape Town on perceptions of personal financial situation and broader inequality found that South Africans who identified their financial status as "better off" or "the same" were "less likely to recognize the pervasiveness of inequality as a source of division," further casting doubt on social cohesiveness at the national level (Meiring et al., 2018). Inequality and poverty are perpetuating realities in post-apartheid South Africa, both of which reinforce experiences of disempowerment. One of the main features of South Africa's democratic consolidation, the BBBEE affirmative action policy, has altered and created certain channels and pro-cesses through which the South African state aimed to create, allocate, and "democratize" employment—thereby reducing poverty—that largely, though not exclusively, targeted women. Women however seem particularly more inclined than men to view the rich–poor divide as the primary division in South Africa (Meiring et al., 2018). BEE and development are viewed as complementary and linked processes in the broader growth strategy. National unemployment however, ranging from 26 percent to 37 percent, is still as high as it was during apartheid.

A cursory view of the public sector could suggest that women working in state institutions experienced greater economic inclusion. At the parliamen-tary level, South Africa ranks tenth in the world with women holding four out of every ten seats in parliament. At the municipal level, women held about 42 percent of mayoral seats in 2017 (Stats SA, 2018b, Table 1.4). However, even the public sector raises questions on the effectiveness of BBBEE in increasing female representation at the top levels. The BWASA (2017) report researched 297 companies, of which 277 were JSE-listed and 20 were the largest state-owned enterprises (SOEs). Only two of these SOEs had female chairpersons

(BWASA, 2017). Despite the public sector being the upholder of equity targets and employing more female workers than males, the BWASA (2017) report also indicated a declining trend in female executives among SOEs, with about 41 percent of senior management being women and a decrease of female executive managers to 28.5 percent.

There is also evidence of workplace culture needing an overhaul. The Bain and Company report found nearly 80 percent of men and women in senior management positions supportive of gender equality in the workplace. When pressed for *why* they believed in gender equality however, less than 30 percent cited "business performance" as their main reason for supporting gender equality. This finding casts doubts on actual potential for women's progress in the workplace where some companies may meet legislated gender targets but a lack of recognition of the serious implications of gender equality on business performance limits women's actual potential to flourish. Many women describe feeling "stuck" in mid-management roles as they are excluded from corporate social networking events, the out-of-office interactions between senior and middle management that most often lead to promotions (Fajardo & Erasmus, 2017, p.9).

There are additionally societal factors to consider. When it comes to women earning more than men who are close to them, only 63 percent of surveyed women reported that it was not an issue to those men, while Black women were 1.6 times less likely to report their higher earnings not being an issue to the men close to them (Fajardo & Erasmus, 2017, p.6). Social norms thus reinforce the "double burden" on women to balance work and family life within a society that still demands that women be the primary caregivers. A broader approach that targets gender biases within the workplace and outside—in households, communities, and schools—is likely needed to change mindsets and support a gender equity culture.

In analyzing how the state is addressing its development objectives through an emphasis on women's economic inclusion, this section aims for future research and programs to position female employment and the BEE policies within a more holistic empowerment structure. One step of this structure will consider the actual and perceived realities that women face on the path to economic inclusion, considering their individual capabilities as well as the societal and organizational factors influencing them, and what may be excluding them from reaping the benefits of development that the democratization discourse and rhetoric had promised them. Another step will further assess South Africa's democratic consolidation process, prospects and objectives, and the implications for the social contract between women workers-citizens and the post-apartheid democratic state. From one political extreme—apartheid—to potentially another—the BBBEE policy within democratic consolidation—the jury is still out on whether the path on which South Africa is treading is the most effective for broader development, economic inclusion, and women's economic empowerment.

Current Context—Considering Turkey and South Africa

In juxtaposing Turkey and South Africa, this chapter does not aim to compare and contrast these two countries. Both countries have unique histories, cultures, economies, and politics that cannot be placed in the same comparative basket. Rather, by drawing on our personal research concentrations and disciplinary focus, we present an overview of the status on women's economic inclusion from particular policy perspectives. Based on the objective of this presentation, the benefit of such a chapter therefore hopefully rests in the reader's choice of what to glean from the descriptions we have laid out. This chapter also does not intend to favor a policy or set of policies over another, but instead chooses to present the broad circumstances surrounding recent and relevant policies in each country with particular respect to women's economic inclusion. Evaluating economic policies with gender equality objectives can be a sensitive subject and we would argue that ideals of "fairness" and "access" cannot be merely viewed as statistics, but their value in terms of empowering women is better perceived and more inherent to the individuals and societies that grow from and through such policies.

One such inherent value of the empowerment of women is decision-making power. While the field for measuring women's decision-making power is vast, this chapter has mostly considered decision-making and leadership potential in the workplace. There is growing evidence supporting the *economic* case for empowering women in the workforce, especially through positions of greater decision-making power. A 2016 report by the Peterson Institute for International Economics showed a 15 percent increase in profitability when companies shifted from having no female representation to a 30 percent representation on boards (Noland et al,. 2016). On the equity front, gender diverse boards can increase returns by as much as 36 percent (MSCI, 2015). Currently, only five countries worldwide have managed to achieve at least 30 percent representation on company boards, with Iceland and Norway being the best performing through a legislated quota of 40 percent female representation (MSCI, 2016). The case for having gender diverse boards is premised on the added value that different perspectives bring to the table. Sufficient female representation in the seats of power, in public and private entities, should enable governments and companies to be better positioned to understand and tackle a wider set of challenges that women face in particular within their growing economies.

Given Turkey's historically politicized experience in modernization and secularization, the role of women in the workforce can be a particularly touchy subject in some regards. For example, the headscarf ban that prevented many adherent women from seeking and finding work in the public sector also allowed the private sector to follow a similar hiring policy that only served to deter such women's economic inclusion. By not allowing for adequate economic inclusion, the ban disempowered those women who were prematurely rejected for work they qualified for and discouraged from seeking certain jobs simply due to their religious adherence. If the First Action Plan for Women's Employment is contextualized within the removal of the head-scarf ban, it is possible to view the policy initiative not only as a testament to espoused ideals of gender equality but also cautiously as a step to redress past employment discrimination toward certain women. The statistics however show that several categories of women may still be facing barriers to economic inclusion, among whom are rural women. Also notable are married women, who tend to be less active in the labor force than single and divorced women. More research needs to ascertain the reasons and motivations behind these numbers in order to understand how the current policy context can address or be modified to relieve present challenges women face toward economic inclusion.

In light of gender-inclusive development, one may question the effectiveness of an affirmative action (labor) policy, like South Africa's BBBEE, that pulls historically disadvantaged groups to the forefront of hiring practices—expecting that employment would empower them—but elusively addresses the underlying causes of disempowerment such as persistent inequality and unemployment within those groups. There is limited empirical research examining whether and how those from previously disadvantaged groups, the supposed intended beneficiaries of BBBEE, are benefiting directly and indirectly from the social transformation agenda promoted by the policy. BBBEE deals still favor and benefit empowerment partners, the investors and companies, more perceptibly amidst widespread social marginalization and economic inequality (Patel & Graham, 2012). While a simpler labor market regulation, such as a female quota, is often necessary to increase women's participation in the labor force, the latter may not automatically empower women (Elson, 1999). In light of South Africa's particular policy considerations, a look at deeper institutional transformations is needed to understand if women have the opportunities, abilities, and decision-making power to empower themselves in the context of BBBEE.

Conclusion

By distinguishing between economic inclusion and economic empowerment, we aim to encourage readers to consider and inquire about other factors that have contributed to less than ideal development results for women in these two countries, despite the noble intentions of the particular policies in Turkey and South Africa. The economic empowerment of women cannot be diluted in the broader empowerment agenda as it currently stands, nor should "empowerment" be viewed as a panacea for development. Economic inclusion is a valid and necessary component for national economic development and the advancement of women, but it is not the equivalent of women's economic empowerment.

Women's economic empowerment is a multidimensional effort requiring simultaneous and integrated interventions from multiple fronts. These fronts include, but should not be limited to: governments, through policies and programs, the rule of law, and the application of gender equity laws within the state institutions themselves; private companies, especially through organizational culture, practices, and rules; and civil society, from advocacy for changes through direct representation of voices and needs from the bottom to ensuring transparent corporate behavior and implementation of appropriate rules, and holding organizations accountable for breaches, and governments responsible for supporting inclusive policies. While it is still too early to make definitive claims about the national strategic and action plans and their impact on women's economic inclusion in Turkey, further research and action will need to take into account the less noticeable factors, some of which this chapter raises, that relate to women's economic empowerment in the context of their economic inclusion. The status of women's work in South Africa convinces us that the polarized nature of the workforce within a society that is still highly unequal within and between racial lines is not catering for the spread of skills necessary for women's adequate economic inclusion and building an inclusive economy. In both countries, ensuring the diversity of economic sectors and women workers with necessary skills and opportunities to participate as equal members of society will be key to sustainable economies.

References

Act 53 of 2003, South Africa. Now known as the B-BBEE Act, which came into force in 2004.

Act 46 of 2013, South Africa.

African National Congress (ANC). (1994, April 15). *Affirmative Action and the New Constitution*. Retrieved from: http://www.anc.org.za/content/affirmative-action-and-new-constitution.

Ağlı, E. & Tor, H. (2016). An Analysis of Turkish Women's Status in Educational, Social and Political Life since the Proclamation of the Republic of Turkey until Today. *International Journal of Social Sciences and Education Research* 2(1), p.77.

Barker, F.S. (1999). *The South African Labour Market*. Pretoria: J.L. van Schaik.

Bhorat, H. & Kanbur, S.M.R. (2006). *Poverty and Policy in Post-Apartheid South Africa*. Cape Town: HSRC Press.

Brand South Africa. (2017, August 12). *Black Economic Empowerment Codes of Good Practice*. Retrieved from: https://www.brandsouthafrica.com.

Business Women of South Africa (BWASA). (2017). *BWASA South African Women in Leadership Census*. Retrieved from: https://bwasa.co.za/wp-content/uploads/2018/04/2017-BWASA-CENSUS-report.pdf.

Casale, D. (2004). What has the Feminization of the Labor Market 'Bought' Women in South Africa? Trends in Labor Force Participation, Employment and Earnings, 1995–2001. *Journal of Interdisciplinary Economics*, 15(3–4), 251–275.

Casale, D. & Posel, D. (2002). The Continued Feminization of the Labor Force in South Africa. *South African Journal of Economics, 70* (1), 156–184.

Chen, M.A. (2007). Rethinking the Informal Economy: Linkages with the Formal Economy and the Formal Regulatory Environment. UN/DESA Working Paper No. 46, Retrieved from: http://www.un.org/esa/desa/papers/2007/wp46_2007.pdf.

Department of Trade and Industry (DTI). (2007). Draft Strategic Framework on Gender and Women's Economic Empowerment. Retrieved from: http://www.dti.gov. za/economic_empowerment/docs/women_empowerment/Draft_Framework.pdf.

Duflo, E. (2012). Women Empowerment and Economic Development. *Journal of Economic Literature*, 50(4), 1051–1079.

Du Toit, A., Kruger, S. & Ponte, S. (2008). Deracializing Exploitation? "Black Economic Empowerment" in the South African Wine Industry. *Journal of Agrarian Change*, 8(1), 6–32.

Dwyer, D. H., Bruce, J. & Cain, M. (1988). *A Home Divided*. Stanford: Stanford University Press.

Elson, D. (1999). Labor Markets as Gendered Institutions: Equality, Efficiency and Empowerment Issues. *World Development*, 27(3), 611–627.

Fajardo, C. & Erasmus, M. (2017). *Gender (Dis)parity in South Africa. The Bain & Company*. Retrieved from: https://www.bain.com/insights/gender-disparity-in-south-africa/.

Finn, A. (2015). A National Minimum Wage in the Context of the South African Labour Market. SALDRU Working Paper Number 153. Retrieved from: http://op ensaldru.uct.ac.za/handle/11090/786.

Giliomee, H. (1995). Democratization in South Africa. *Political Science Quarterly*, 110(1), 83–104.

Hall, R., WisborgP., Shirinda, S. & Zamchiya, P. (2013). Farm Workers and Farm Dwellers in Limpopo Province, South Africa. *Journal of Agrarian Change*, 13(1), 47–70.

Hofmeyr, J. & Govender, R. (2015). *National Reconciliation, Race Relations and Social Inclusion*. South African Barometer Briefing Paper 1. Cape Town: Institute for Justice and Reconciliation. Retrieved from: http://www.dac.gov.za/sites/default/files/ reconciliation-barometer.pdf.

International Labor Organization (ILO). (2016, May 23). Turkey's First Action Plan Focusing on Women's Employment was Introduced to the Public on May 17th. Retrieved from: http://www.ilo.org/ankara/news/WCMS_484712/lang–en/index.htm.

Jeffery, A. (2014). *BEE: Helping or Hurting?*Cape Town: Tafelberg Publishers Limited.

Kabeer, N. & Natali, L. (2013). Gender Equality and Economic Growth: Is There a Win–Win? IDS Working Papers, 2013(417), 1–58.

Kılınç, N. Ş. (2015). Küresel Eğilimler Çerçevesinde Kadın İstihdamı. *HAK-İŞ Uluslararası Emek ve Toplum Dergisi*, 4(9), 121–135.

Korkmaz, A. & Korkut, G. (2012). Türkiye'de Kadının İşgücüne Katılımının Belirleyicileri. *The Journal of Faculty of Economics and Administrative Sciences (Suleyman Demirel University*, 17(2), pp.41–65

Meiring, T., Kannemeyer, C. & Potgieter, E. (2018). The Gap between Rich and Poor: South African Society's Biggest Divide Depends on Where You Think You Fit In. SALDRU Working Paper Number 220, Cape Town. Retrieved from: www.opensa ldru.uct.ac.za.

MSCI. (2015). Women on Boards: Global Trends in Gender Diversity on Corporate Boards. Retrieved from: https://www.msci.com/www/research-paper/research-in sight-women-%20on/0263428390.

MSCI. (2016). *The Tipping Point: Women on Boards and Financial Performance: Women on Boards Report 2016*. Retrieved from: https://www.msci.com/documents/ 10199/fd1f8228-cc07-4789-acee-3f9ed97ee8bb.

Narayan, D. (2005). Conceptual Framework and Methodological Challenges. In *Measuring Empowerment: Cross-Disciplinary Perspectives*, 1st ed. The World Bank. Retrieved from: https://openknowledge.worldbank.org/handle/10986/7441.

Noland, M., Moran, T. & Kotschwar, B. (2016). Is Gender Diversity Profitable? Evidence from a Global Survey. Peterson Institute for International Economics Working Paper 16-13. Retrieved from https://piie.com/publications/wp/wp16-3.pdf.

Orthofer, A. (2016). Wealth Inequality in South Africa: Evidence from Survey and Tax Data. REDI3x3 Working Paper 15 June 2016. Retrieved from: http://www.redi3x3.org/.

Patel, L. & Graham, L. (2012). How Broad-Based is Broad-Based Black Economic Empowerment? *Development Southern Africa*, 2 (29), 193–207.

Quisumbing, A.R. (2003). *Household Decisions, Gender, and Development*. Washington: Johns Hopkins Press & IFPRI.

Rogan, M. (2014). Poverty May Have Declined, but Women and Female-Headed Households Still Suffer Most. Retrieved from: http://www.econ3x3.org/.

Sisk, T. (1995). *Democratization in South Africa: The Elusive Social Contract*. Princeton: Princeton University Press.

Southall, R. (2007). Ten Propositions about Black Economic Empowerment in South Africa. *Review of African Political Economy*, 34(111), 67–84.

Stats SA. (2009). *Labor Force Survey, Historical Revision, September Series 2000 to 2007*. Retrieved from: http://www.statssa.gov.za/.

Stats SA. (2017a, October 2). *Quarterly Labor Force Survey*, Retrieved from: http://www.statssa.gov.za/.

Stats SA. (2017b). *Education Series Volume III: Educational Enrolment and Achievement, 2016*. Retrieved from: http://www.statssa.gov.za/.

Stats SA. (2018a). *Quarterly Labor Force Survey*. Statistical Release P0211. Retrieved from http://www.statssa.gov.za/.

Stats SA. (2018b, June 4). *Non-financial Census of Municipalities for The Year Ended 20 June 2017*. Statistical Release P9115. Retrieved from: http://www.statssa.gov.za/.

Terreblanche, S. (2002). *A History of Inequality in South Africa 1652–2002*. Pietermaritzburg: University of Natal Press.

TUIK. (2014). *The Tenth Development Plan: 2014–2018*. Retrieved from: http://www.mod.gov.tr/Lists/RecentPublications/Attachments/75/The%20Tenth%20Developm ent%20Plan%20(2014-2018).pdf.

UNICEF South Africa (SA). (2006). *Girls Education Movement—South Africa*. Retrieved from: https://www.unicef.org/southafrica/SAF_resources_gembrief.pdf.

Whitehead, A. (2009). The Gendered Impacts of Liberalization Policies on African Agricultural Economies and Rural Livelihoods. In S. Razavi (Ed.), *The Gendered Impacts of Liberalization: Towards 'Embedded' Liberalism?* London: Routledge.

World Bank. (2011). *World Development Report (WDR)*. Washington DC: The World Bank.

World Bank. (2017a). Labor Force Participation Rate, Female. ILOSTAT Database. Retrieved from: https://data.worldbank.org/indicator/SL.TLF.CACT.FE.ZS.

World Bank. (2017b). Labor Force Participation Rate, Male. ILOSTAT Database. Retrieved from: https://data.worldbank.org/indicator/SL.TLF.CACT.MA.ZS.

World Bank. (2018). *Overcoming Poverty and Inequality in South Africa: An Assessment of Drivers, Constraints and Opportunities*. Retrieved from: http://documents.worldbank.org/.

Willis, J., Hansrod, H. & Utku, H.A. (2015). Policies, Propaganda, and Purdah: Forced Inclusion of Women in the Early 1900s in Turkey and Soviet Central Asia. Paper presented at the Annual International Conference Interdisciplinary Legal Studies (AICILS), Oxford. ISBN: 978-0-9930368-3-5.

6 Provoking Gender-Related Institutional Changes

A Case of a Returnee Female Entrepreneur in India

Quynh Duong PHUONG, Sharon MAYER, Viktoria THEOHAVORA, Aki HARIMA and Jörg FREILING

Introduction

Over thousands of years, migration has been inextricably tied to human history. The recent technological advancement driven by globalization, however, has strengthened the growing trend in migration. The overall size and frequency of global migration waves have increased, and directions, as well as motivations for migration, have diversified. One notable trend is the emergence of the phenomenon called 'circular migration' (Saxcnian, 2005; Cassarino, 2008). People migrate not only from one country to another to seek for their next lifetime settlement, but also return to their homeland after some time or travel back and forth between two countries. This wave creates the people called diaspora and returnee who have been considered to be unique developmental agents for their country of origin.

Scholars have investigated various types of contributions to the development of home countries that returnee entrepreneurs make (Pruthi, 2014; Dai and Liu, 2009; Wright et al., 2008). By exploring and exploiting transnational opportunities and utilizing their unique human and social capital, returnee entrepreneurs have contributed to the emergence and development of entrepreneurial ecosystems in their homelands (Dai and Liu, 2009; Saxenian, 2001), to the internationalization of homeland industry (Alon et al., 2011; Filatotchev et al., 2009), to facilitate knowledge (Saxenian, 2005; Bao et al., 2016), and to drive innovation (Kenney et al., 2013; Liu et al., 2015).

While the roles of returnee entrepreneurs in the context of homeland development have attracted growing interest from policy-makers and scholars, their potentials have not fully been understood for two reasons. First, most of the previous research contributions highlight their economic contributions. Returnees' experience and resources applied to their business have more potential than small economic contributions. The entrepreneurship literature shows that entrepreneurial activities can change and develop institutions of the country (Koene, 2006; Kalantaridis and Fletcher, 2012; Smallbone and

Welter, 2012). There are numerous reasons to believe that returnee entrepreneurs can make distinctive institutional changes in their homeland. Roles of returnees as institutional entrepreneurs are not yet well understood. Second, previous discussions on returnee entrepreneurs have not paid enough attention to gender issues. Especially in countries with a significant gender gap, female returnees can make distinctive contributions to gender equality. Against these backgrounds, combining institutional entrepreneurship and gender aspects with the phenomenon of returnee entrepreneurship seems to give a basis for advancing our understanding of returnee entrepreneurship.

Based on the arguments above, the purpose of this book chapter is to explore the roles of female returnee entrepreneurs as institutional change makers. What we want to achieve with our research endeavor is to gain new insights into under-investigated relations between gender-related institutions and female returnee entrepreneurs – and to stimulate the debate on their potentials. The research question of this chapter is, therefore: *How do female returnee entrepreneurs initiate and drive homeland institutions?* To respond to this research question, we conducted a single case study with a critical case of a well-known woman-driven enterprise in India. The enterprise is called *KAARYAH* and was founded by Nidhi Agarwal, who is a returnee from the United States and has a strong media presence in the country.

Structurally, this study will begin by outlining the various literature from the fields of returnee entrepreneurship, institutional entrepreneurship, and female entrepreneurship. After the literature review, we briefly portray our methodological approach and present a case. Subsequently, we demonstrate how the enterprise influenced three different institutions – (1) the Indian women's community, (2) media, (3) education – in different ways. Finally, we discuss theoretical contributions, practical implications, limitations, and future perspectives.

Conceptual Backgrounds

Returnee Entrepreneurs as Institutional Change Agents

Recent trends of globalization have fostered technological advancements in transportation and communication which have created immense and complex migration streams (Tung and Lazarova, 2006). Nowadays, migration takes place not only from less developing countries to developed countries, but also from developed to developing countries, or from developing to developed countries (Harima et al., 2016; Harima, 2016). Furthermore, some migrants also move between countries and have a transnational lifestyle, while others return to their home countries after spending some years in another country. These phenomena are described as circular migration (Venturini, 2008).

Scholars have investigated how this changing environment and nature of migration has influenced entrepreneurial activities of migrants (Freiling and Harima, 2018; Harima, 2014). Migrants start their business for different reasons: some of them start their business out of necessity (Chrysostome, 2010), while others are driven by opportunities (Dai and Liu, 2009; Bao et al., 2016). Regardless of their motivation, migrants transfer unique human, social and financial capital from one country to another through their entrepreneurial activities. The dominant migration waves used to be mostly unidirectional in the past. Therefore, this phenomenon used to be called a 'brain drain' for their homelands and 'brain gain' for receiving countries (Bhagwati and Hamada, 1973; Venturini, 2008; Straubhaar, 2000; Lien and Wang, 2005). The nature of migration waves has changed over time, and it has become rather common for migrants to return home or to re-build their homeland relations after a while. Having witnessed migrant entrepreneurs in Silicon Valley who transfer their knowledge to their homelands, Saxenian retitled this phenomenon as a 'brain circulation' (Saxenian, 2000; Saxenian, 2005).

The discussion over brain circulation raised awareness of the existence of migrant entrepreneurs who conduct their business back in their home countries, leveraging from their experience outside. Scholars named them returnee entrepreneurs (Qin et al., 2017; Farquharson and Pruthi, 2015; Dai and Liu, 2009; Wright et al., 2008). A returnee entrepreneur is defined as a person 'who gathered vocational or educational experiences as diasporans in developed countries before returning to their country of origin to establish their businesses' (Mayer et al., 2015: 99).

The literature has predominantly investigated highly skilled returnee entrepreneurs in high-tech industries, particularly in China, India and Taiwan, with the question how they contribute to the emergence and development of entrepreneurial ecosystems in their home countries (Wright et al., 2008; Filatotchev et al., 2009; Lin et al., 2015; Kenney et al., 2013). These studies reveal significant contributions of returnee entrepreneurs as economic agents to the economic growth of homelands. However, returnee entrepreneurs' contributions are not limited to their economic activities. Due to their diasporic nature, returnee entrepreneurs have distinctive personal characteristics – risk-taking, optimism, persistence, resilience, creativity, and adaptation (Dutia, 2012). Furthermore, migrants are embedded in two different institutional environments, which fosters their cognitive and behavioral flexibility (Rouse, 1986; Kloosterman et al., 1999; Kloosterman, 2010). Through experience in host countries, returnees gain different types of knowledge such as entrepreneurial, cultural and institutional knowledge.

With their distinctive nature, returnee entrepreneurs have potentials to develop their homelands as so-called institutional entrepreneurs. Scholars have discussed complex relations between entrepreneurial actors and institutions (Khavul et al., 2013; Kalantaridis and Fletcher, 2012; Garud et al., 2007). The major challenge that scholars face, when researching entrepreneurship and institutions, is to consider entrepreneurial actions' influence and the institutional structure in which entrepreneurs are embedded simultaneously (Leca and Naccache, 2006). While scholars have not found a consensus to resolve this paradox, the concept of institutional entrepreneurs has become one of the primary focuses in the entrepreneurship research field (Bruton et al., 2010). This concept highlights entrepreneurs' roles as active agents to initiate and drive institutional changes (Garud et al., 2007; Levy and Scully, 2007; Misangyi et al., 2008; Maguire et al., 2004). Institutional entrepreneurs possess unique skills to remove and reform existing institutions from their grassroots perspective (Li et al., 2006). The underlying premise of this concept is that entrepreneurs are not only influenced by the existing institutions, but they also influence institutions, both intentionally and unintentionally (Kalantaridis and Fletcher, 2012; Smallbone and Welter, 2012). According to Svejenova et al. (2007), there are four approaches how institutional entrepreneurs initiate change: (1) creativity to create new ideas continuously; (2) theorizations that evaluate these ideas and recognize patterns; (3) reputation from inside and outside of the community which recognizes the value of ideas; and (4) dissemination that bridges ideas to the public domains.

The concept of institutional entrepreneurship provides a robust theoretical underpinning for investigating homeland contributions of returnees. While this concept has seldom been applied to the phenomenon of returnee entrepreneurship, there are a few previous studies which applied institutional logics to economic activities in transnational settings. For instance, Kwok and Tadesse (2006) investigate direct foreign investment of multinational corporations which can influence host-country institutions and result in corruption. Riddle and Brinkerhoff (2011) conducted a case study with a diaspora venture in Nepal to show how diaspora entrepreneurs can transform institutional arrangements in their country of origin through 'institutional acculturation.' Similarly, Wijers (2013) also investigates Cambodian returnees who act as institutional entrepreneurs. While these studies made first steps to examine relations between returnee entrepreneurship and institutions, we still know little about how returnees can change institutions and what enablers and hindrances exist in the change process.

Female Returnee Entrepreneurship in India

Gender equality and female entrepreneurship are considered to be critical drivers for economic development (Sarfaraz et al., 2014). Henry (2008) argues that strong customer orientation, application of 'soft' management style, emphasis on human capital and cultural aspects of their business, and passion towards the quality of products and services characterize female entrepreneurship. Generally, women are believed to face gender-specific challenges when entering the fields of entrepreneurship. For instance, there is a limited number of female entrepreneurial role models and mentors compared to male counterparts so that they tend to be left alone with their career challenges. Another challenge is related to the exclusiveness of male-dominated networks and the lack of managerial experience, which makes it difficult for them to integrate into the business world (McGowan et al., 2012).

In recent years, the number of studies on female entrepreneurs increased, and their research focus has been widened (Estrin and Mickiewicz, 2011; Brush and Cooper, 2012; Warnecke, 2013; Baughn et al., 2006). Not only 'hard' topics like financing and capitalization of female-owned ventures, but also 'soft' ones like motivation and work–family balance have become research objectives (Brush and Cooper, 2012; Orhan and Scott, 2001). The previous studies, however, predominantly focused on female entrepreneurs in developed countries, which calls for more research on female entrepreneurship in emerging countries (Brush and Cooper, 2012; Wong-MingJi et al., 1999).

Addressing the research gaps, this paper investigates highly skilled female returnee entrepreneurs in India. The context of India is of particular interest, as the traditional moral concept still determines the behaviors of Indian women (Field et al., 2010). Various societal factors such as access to education to strict cultural norms hinder Indian females in becoming independent entrepreneurs (Sinha, 2003; Shastri and Sinha, 2010). Indian female returnees have spent considerable time outside of such a traditional society and became familiar with foreign institutions, which led them to greater emancipation. When Indian female returnees develop business back in India, they cannot avoid facing the traditional society expecting them to play a particular role, which is taken for granted as a female in India. The underlying assumption of this study is that such returnee female entrepreneurs can trigger some changes in gender-related institutions of their homeland to improve female participation in the economy and society (Isaac et al., 2002).

Methodology

Research Design

This chapter applies an inductive qualitative research approach with the purpose of theory building (Charmaz, 2014; Eisenhardt, 2007). The inductive research process starts with searching for patterns from specific observations and will then develop explanations for these to eventually enable theory building (Hodkinson, 2008). We selected this approach for two reasons: first, while a few studies provide some meaningful evidence as for potential contributions of returnee entrepreneurs as institutional change agents, their findings are, regarding both quality and quantity, insufficient to develop a priori concrete causal assumptions to be validated. Second, since this chapter involves both home and host country institutions, findings are highly context-specific, which makes the application of extant theories almost impossible.

A single case study has been selected as a research method. Following arguments by Yin (2009), a single case study is an active research method, when the selected case is a critical case which meets all the conditions for fulfilling the research aims. The selected case can be considered as a critical case, as it is about an Indian female entrepreneur whose business is related to empowerment of domestic Indian women. Moreover, the entrepreneur has a strong media presence, which makes her a well-known female entrepreneur icon in the country. Also, investigating one case offers this research endeavor the opportunity to gather rich insights into this phenomenon that helps us to explore new causal relations (Eisenhardt and Graebner, 2007). The single case study approach allows understanding of the dynamics within a single research setting (Eisenhardt, 1989).

Case Selection and Data Collection

This study conducts a case study with *KAARYAH*, which is a newly founded startup in the metropolitan city of New Delhi. This startup was founded and led by a female entrepreneur, Nidhi Agarwal, who had been in the United States for the period of her master's program and then returned to India recently. This company is well known as a successful female startup and has a strong media presence.

The primary data consists of qualitative interviews conducted via Skype and telephone by two members of the research team. Besides that, some secondary data accompanied data sourcing for purposes of contextualizing the research setting by selected publications. The interview is semi-structured with the focus on questions with regards to the impact of the female founder and her company on gender-related institutional changes in India. The interview consists mainly of three parts: the first part covers general information about the interviewee and his or her connection to the founder and company. The second part focuses on the entrepreneurial activities of the returnee and their potential impact on environments. The third part addresses explicitly gender-related issues in India to explore whether and how *KAARYAH* has influenced institutional environments. In total, five interviews were conducted. More specifically, one interview took place with the founder, one interview with her employee, one interview with an expert of the Indian startup scene, and two interviews with Indian diaspora members in Germany. The overview of interviewees is given in Table 6.1.

Data Analysis

All the interviews are transcribed from their original language. In the first step, every interview was analyzed by following an open-code principle (Charmaz, 2008). As we apply an inductive qualitative research method, we did not have any a priori category system. The coding's were purely derived from the analysis of interviews inductively. For the sake of triangulation (Denzin, 1973), all the interviews were coded independently by three scholars. Afterward, codings of individual scholars have been compared and discussed to identify similarities and differences between interpretations of researchers. As the second step, the research team analyzed patterns of all the codes and categorized them into thematic groups to build theoretical codes. Figure 6.1 visualizes this process of analysis.

Table 6.1 Overview of interviewees

Name	Experience	Case connection
Nidhi Agarwal	• Previously Director Strategy, Honeywell India • Drafted new B2C market entry strategy at Bain & Co. • Launched India's first m-Commerce product with Airtel in 2006 • Statutory Auditor for B2C clients at KPMG • MBA Kellogg, Recipient of Dean's Service Award • Certified C.A., B.Com (H) Delhi	Founder and CEO of *KAARYAH*
Bushra Ismail	• Previously worked with Value360 Communications, Turkish Airlines, Perfect Relations & CNN-IBN, 8 years of experience in Media & Communications • BA English Honors, St. Xavier's College, Degree in Journalism & Film Study	Employee (head of communication) at *KAARYAH*
Tanvi Dubey and her co-worker	• Employed at YOURSTORY • Previously worked with Delhi University, Dept of History and Indian Economic Social History Review • Master's Degree at St. Stephen's College, India.	Head and Editor of *HerStory*, female startup platform that featured Agarwal
Indian Diaspora Member in Germany1 &2	• Master Student in Germany (Global Management) • Bachelor Degree from India	Information about the Indian context

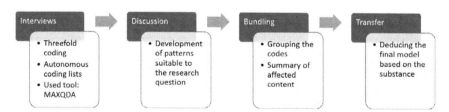

Figure 6.1 Coding Process
Source: own illustration

The qualitative content analysis software program MAXQDA 12 supported the process of data analysis. This software is a useful tool for analyzing a large amount of complex data. It helps to find a useful and fitting category system and allows conducting a deeper level of analysis. It is also suitable for group work, as it makes the individual analysis process traceable and transparent.

Case Descriptions

Research Settings – Female Entrepreneurs in India

India has a booming economy especially in urban cities which has created world-leading entrepreneurial ecosystems (Genome, 2017). For instance, the number of investors in urban Indian cities has more than doubled from 2014 to 2015, and the number of 'unicorn' startups has risen above the Indian average in the last year (Ghoshal, 2016). In such urban ecosystems, regional institutions have been drastically changing. The literature suggests that a large part of economic development in urban areas can be attributed to contributions of returnees who came back to India from Silicon Valley or other dominant startup regions (Lin et al., 2015). Many such returnees find entrepreneurial opportunities in India, which is one of the primary drivers for their homeland investment. Especially, metro cities profit from these trends and have become more and more international. For this reason, this study also selected a case in the urban context.

India offers particularly interesting contexts for gender-related research. India is a country gender inequality is still active. In the last years, however, several changes towards gender equality have taken place. Traditionally, the Indian society perceives it desirable for a woman to be a good mother and to stay at home as a housewife (Patel and Parmentier, 2005). Recent trends show that the middle classes in metropolitan cities in India are starting to accept women not only as a good mother taking care of the family as a housewife but also as an economic participant in the business world. This improvement is also visible in the Global Gender Gap Index developed by the World Economic Forum. In 2011, India was placed as number 113 out of 135 countries with regards to gender equality within the society. In 2016, however, India's position had been moved up to number 86 (Hausmann et al., 2011; World Economic Forum, 2015).

Despite such improvements, the vocational situation of Indian women shows that they are still suffering from gender inequality. Women-owned business contributes only 3.09% of the economic output of Indian industries. Some 90% of female businesses in India are still conducted in informal settings (International Finance Corporation, 2014).

Responding to the still existing societal challenges related to gender inequality, the Indian government launched in 2016 a new campaign to support female entrepreneurship in the country called *Startup India! Startup India!* aims at supporting female businesses in the country. Additionally, numerous online platforms have been established for Indian female entrepreneurs to feature stories about women and their opportunities and challenges. Such platforms also facilitate conversation among female entrepreneurs and offer consultations. One of these platforms is *HerStory*, which is a sub-brand of *YourStory* – a large and well-known platform for Indian entrepreneurs.

KAARYAH – Emergence of the Company

Nidhi Agarwal is a founder of *KAARYAH* Lifestyle Solutions; a successful startup focused on Western wears for Indian women. Agarwal was born in New Delhi, which is one of the four metro cities in India. She grew up in a family with a Western orientation. She was the only girl among thirteen boys and was taught to value her success and independence over marriage. Furthermore, the family frequently traveled a lot. As a consequence, she became familiar with different cultural settings. To date, her family has been strong support for her business.

Agarwal acquired her bachelor's degree in accounting in India. After that, she made a brave decision to move to the United States in order to pursue her master's degree in business administration. After completing her master's in 2008, Agarwal decided to return to India, as the US economy was severely affected by the world economic crisis, making her homeland's condition more appealing to her. After her return to India, she worked in different positions at several companies such as KPMG, Airtel, Bain & Co, until she started her own business. She has more than 15 years of experience in the fields of strategy, innovation, management, and finance.

During the time in which she was working for existing companies, she relaised there was a lack of fitting formal and business wear for Indian women, which led her to come up with the business idea for *KAARYAH*. It was relatively easy for Agarwal to find and buy business clothes for women in the United States. However, she soon started asking herself why it is almost impossible to find perfectly fitting business wear for women in India. Responding to her question, she conducted her own study. The study revealed that 80% of Indian women also face the same problem in finding comfortable business wear. Facing the struggles of Indian female businesswomen, Agarwal decided to develop a business which offers solutions for the problems. That was how *KAARYAH* came into existence. *KAARYAH* was founded in 2013. The brand offered formal Western wear for Indian businesswomen. The innovative part of *KAARYAH*'s business model was that they identified six typical body sizes of Indian women and offer 18 different sizes based on the basic body structure. The brand aimed at bridging the gap between Western formals and the Indian silhouette.

The startup had minimal resources in the beginning. Agarwal did not seek any external support such as public or private women entrepreneurship programs. Still, only after 18 months of its establishment, *KAARYAH* was recognized as one of the top digital companies in India, and Agarwal was ranked within India's top 60 women entrepreneurs. Despite rapid development, Agarwal faced numerous challenges in finding external investors for scaling up her business. Being a female and single entrepreneur, she had considerable difficulties in convincing investors of the potentials of her business, and even more of herself. Investors expressed their concerns about the future prospects of the company, especially whether she would get married or have children. She approached 113 investors over 365 days until she found Ratan Tata from the Tata Group, who was willing to invest in her entrepreneurial endeavor. One notable issue is that *KAARYAH* engaged in incubating two small startups, which are now working exclusively for the brand.

As a CEO of the firm, Agarwal has encountered several incidents where she confirmed the disadvantages of being a female entrepreneur in India. For instance, a male distributor refused to hand over her goods, because he could not believe that a woman could be a CEO of the company. One of her male employees needed to directly communicate with the distributor in order to 'prove' that Agarwal was the CEO of the company. After the explanation from this male employee, the distributor finally believed that a woman could also lead a successful company.

KAARYAH has now 13 employees in its main team, 70% of whom are female. The department heads are all female employees, even though the company does not actively promote the employment of female workers. This high ratio of female employees can only be justified by the fact that *KAAR-YAH* is a rapidly growing brand and well known for a large population of Indian businesswomen. As a consequence, some women in India are inspired by Agarwal's story, which naturally motivated them to work for the company. In this vein, one of the interviewees for this study started working for the company as an employee, since she perceived Agarwal as a role model who can inspire Indian women.

KAARYAH – Influencing Indian Society

The company started to operate in metropolitan cities and has gradually expanded its target market to rural regions, namely to Tier 2 and Tier 3.[1] While the most visible change in mindsets of Indian businesswomen takes place in metropolitan regions, the wave of emancipation has moderately reached women in rural areas, too. There has been an increasing number of the population of businesswomen in rural areas. This has enhanced the demand for female business wear in such regions.

KAARYAH has a strong media visibility, having acquired considerable attention as a successful and influential entrepreneurial initiative. Agarwal also shared her hard time in finding investors due to her gender with everyone else in India, which evoked extensive discussions over gender inequality in the entrepreneurship context of the country. Stories about *KAARYAH* can be found everywhere, in the press, online articles, newspaper reports, as well as some television programs.

It is worth noticing that Agarwal is a part of a network for Indian female entrepreneurs where she receives and gives supports. Since members in this network specialize in different areas, they can help each other by using their expert knowledge. Agarwal feels that this female entrepreneurs' network is one of the most significant support she receives for her business apart from her family. This holds especially true for her father who is her entrepreneurial role model and gives her entrepreneurial advice. Furthermore, Agarwal is an active mentor for women on the platform called *SHEROES*. *SHEROES* is a community for women who share about their different types of problems and seek advice about their business or careers.

Agarwal has been active in different startup events, giving speeches and taking part in panel discussions where she often represented the female startup community in India. Moreover, outside of the startup community, Agarwal was invited to schools and universities to give guest lectures to future leaders in the country. From time to time, Agarwal even became a case study for students to learn about the success story of female entrepreneurship in India.

Interviewees share their perception that there has been a change in India concerning gender equality. There has been much noise regarding women empowerment, not only from the women community itself but also from the government. Women's platforms such as *HerStory* also support the voice of Indian women who are thriving to prove women's potential, which has encouraged Indian women to take a step forward. Agarwal was also active on this platform, writing columns and articles to empower Indian women by sharing her own stories.

The transition has seen slow and steady progress where Indian women have been encouraged to start perceiving their potentials. Gradually, women started taking jobs, which used to be considered as 'jobs for men', such as the army or navy. One factor contributing to this gender-related change in Indian society is the strong and continuous presence of women engaging in various economic activities in the media. Even though *KAARYAH* does not intend to set the focus of their communication strategy on female entrepreneurship, Agarwal has received considerable attention and visibility from Indian society as a successful and influential female entrepreneur. Especially in women entrepreneurship platforms, Agarwal has been continuously and repeatedly featured, since there is a huge demand for female entrepreneurial icons. Such platforms emphasize the challenges she faced as a female entrepreneur and her strong will to achieve her goals. In the media she has always been labeled as a role model for female entrepreneurs to inspire future talents.

Agarwal herself recalls that she did not have any female entrepreneurial role models when she was young. At that time, it was not common for women to pursue entrepreneurial careers. After some years, the societal perceptions towards gender roles have changed, and there has been an increased number of working women and female entrepreneurs. Agarwal is convinced that the next generation will have numerous role models of female entrepreneurs in India.

Triggering Gender-Related Institutional Changes in India through Entrepreneurial Activities

In this section, the case study is analyzed through conceptional lenses to investigate how Agarwal (and her company *KAARYAH*) has directly or indirectly influenced homeland environments. The case shows that Agarwal has utilized her resources as a returnee to explore and exploit this particular business opportunity. In line with the literature on returnee and migrant entrepreneurship (Kloosterman et al., 1999; Kloosterman, 2010), it is evident that Agarwal is embedded in contexts of the United States and India, which enabled her to recognize unmet needs of Indian businesswomen. As Rouse (1986) suggests, Agarwal used her institutional knowledge about two different countries and cognitive flexibility to identify this gap in the market. In contrast, without this kind of embeddedness, this specific kind of opportunity recognition would not have taken place. As a result of a data analysis process, three institutional domains in India are identified where Agarwal and *KAARYAH* had either direct or indirect impact: (1) The Indian women's community; (2) media; (3) further; we expand on her impact in each domain.

Indian Women's Community

The main idea of *KAARYAH* is to offer comfortable and perfectly fitting business clothes for Indian businesswomen. Agarwal's consideration behind this business idea is that Indian businesswomen can raise their self-confidence when they feel comfortable with their appearance as businesspersons, which encourages them to participate in formal business activities more.

The Indian women's community is actively and directly influenced by Agarwal's entrepreneurial activities. Agarwal is actively supporting female entrepreneurs as well as women who are interested in pursuing an entrepreneurial career in the future. As a mentor, Agarwal provides hands-on support for women who seek advice for their entrepreneurial endeavors, while facing numerous gender-related obstacles in their private and business life. Agarwal studied business administration in the United States, which built her technical business know-how. In a way, Agarwal transfers her technical knowledge related to business to local Indian entrepreneurs. This is similar to what previous scholars discuss in the context of knowledge transfer of returnee entrepreneurs (Saxenian, 2005; Filatotchev et al., 2009; Qin et al., 2017). In female entrepreneurship, however, mentors play notable roles (Laukhuf and Malone, 2015; Kyrgidou and Petridou, 2013; Sarri, 2011). Facing similar obstacles related to family–work balance and societal expectation with regards to the gender roles, mentors are those who can share their experience in how they deal with such gender-related challenges and motivate female entrepreneurs (Fowler et al., 2007).

Agarwal also writes columns for several women's platforms, which encourage Indian women through her real-life success stories. Agarwal does not only share her story but also delivers a strong message to Indian women that they should believe in their capability and never lose faith in themselves. Emancipation is not a new phenomenal wave in the world. Indeed, there are considerable numbers of role models of successful and influential female entrepreneurs who empower the future generation in other countries (Mueller and Dato-On, 2008; Muofhe and Du Toit, 2011). What this study could observe, however, was that such international female entrepreneurs' impact on Indian women is limited. One reason for this is that challenges that female entrepreneurs face vary to a large extent depending on their institutional environments (Welter, 2004; Estrin and Mickiewicz, 2011; Warnecke, 2013). Therefore, Agarwal's messages touch the heart of Indian women.

In the literature, there is still a lack of studies about female returnees and their entrepreneurial activities. Agarwal had skills and knowledge about business from her study in the United States and unique attitude towards challenges. Her attitude did not allow her to obey customs based on men's logic in India but decided to develop her own business to empower other Indian women. Although she grew up in a Western-oriented family in India, her socialization in the United States strengthened her attitude, as she witnessed that the US-society perceives women differently than in her homeland and women pursue equal vocational opportunities to men. It is, however, worth mentioning that not everyone can transfer knowledge and resources from outside and inspire domestic women. This has to be someone who is embedded in both institutions and can fully understand the situation of Indian women. Having dual embeddedness (Harima et al., 2016; Kloosterman et al., 1999), returnees are ideal agents to transfer knowledge and to change women's perceptions.

Indian Media influence and play a vital role in forming public opinion (Coyne and Leeson, 2009). Different types of media have approached Agarwal to ask her for interviews. In the media, she is portrayed as an inspirational woman and labeled as a role model, both as an entrepreneur and as a woman. In interviews, Agarwal shares her stories of fighting against and overcoming all the gender-related obstacles in order to realize her dream. These stories are easy to understand for everyone, and deliver a robust and clear message: even as a single woman, nothing is impossible as long as she believes in herself and keeps her will and strength. Agarwal presents a balanced and harmonious picture of a businesswoman who is strong, dedicated, independent, successful, but also caring for others. The media also promotes this picture. Agarwal has been featured in a variety of media shows, which reach a vast number of Indian citizens. Her media presence raises the awareness of the Indian population of the topic of female entrepreneurship. As a result, Indian society has gradually started accepting women as successful entrepreneurs and recognized the economic potential of women.

Interestingly, the media mainly feature the fact that she is a female entrepreneur and the fact that she is a returnee entrepreneur is disregarded. The media occasionally address that Agarwal studied abroad as a side note, mentioning the name of the university, although her business would not have been realized without her experience in the United States and diasporic capabilities.

Being a role model in electronic and print media, Agarwal has a strong influence on Indian society. Her story has sparked a new debate on the role of women in society. In India, women's desirable roles are those of a mother and housewife (Patel and Parmentier, 2005). There are numerous male role models in almost every field, ranging from sports players to successful entrepreneurs. However, women do not have role models in media who enable them to find their orientation. Accordingly, they have to find role models in their surroundings such as family and friends (BarNir et al., 2011). Such role models are often housewives and do not inspire Indian women to start changes in society. Therefore, the media representation of Agarwal is something entirely new to Indian women. This holds especially for the fact that Agarwal shares not only beautiful success stories but also honest experience with gender discrimination in India. Her honesty made her story realistic and credible. Agarwal has received public empathy from Indian women who see that Agarwal is not an unrealistic and superhuman entrepreneurial icon, but a regular Indian woman with a strong will. The literature on role models supports this finding. Bosma et al. (2011), for instance, find that one of the essential attributes for an effective role model is to be the 'next-door-example' that is trustworthy rather than an iconic role model that is beyond reach. Through media presentation, the awareness of women in the business environment can be encouraged, and this helps to gradually change the perception of a society (Coyne and Leeson, 2009).

Education in India

As the media presence of Agarwal has been intensified, various educational institutes in India have become interested in her success story. As a consequence, the story of *KAARYAH* has become a teaching case study used in the classroom at universities. Furthermore, Agarwal has been invited to hold workshops, give guest lectures or talk sessions at several universities in India. Through her engagement, the subject of female entrepreneurship has gained academic attention. Moreover, students who will create the future of the country become aware of this topic and have opportunities to proactively think and discuss gender inequality and entrepreneurial potentials of Indian women. Becoming a successful entrepreneur as a woman in India is by no means easy. The very fact that Agarwal has overcome numerous challenges is the reason for students to take her seriously and respect her story.

The literature on entrepreneurship education shows that it is a common pedagogical method to bring role models into lecture rooms to inspire students (Muofhe and Du Toit, 2011). Bosma et al. (2011) also suggest that 'each year educational institutions (...) employ their scarce resources to provide students and audiences at large with entrepreneurial role models in the classroom (p. 3)'. In the case of Agarwal, she not only offers entrepreneurial inspiration but also stimulates discussions about gender issues in India, which can change the mindset of students. Furthermore, such interactions between Agarwal and students can influence vocational decisions of female students (Mueller and Dato-On, 2008). The more female students who make decisions to pursue entrepreneurial careers like Agarwal, the more considerable institutional change will take place.

In Table 6.2, selected quotes for each institutional domain are listed.

Discussion and Conclusions

Research Contributions and Practical Implications

The research findings of the single case study with *KAARYAH* show that a female returnee entrepreneur influences homeland institutions in different ways. On one side, the female returnee entrepreneur has direct impacts on Indian women by transferring knowledge and mindsets through mentoring. On the other side, she indirectly reaches a large part of the Indian population by being a role model of female entrepreneurship. This finding is similar to what Svejenova, Mazza, and Planellas (2007) suggest, that institutional entrepreneurs need to disseminate their idea by bridging their idea to the public domains. In Agarwal's case, this bridge was made through media presence and active participation in education.

This study highlights the fact that returnee entrepreneurs can change homeland institutions by being a role model. While previous research has investigated how returnee entrepreneurs can influence homeland institutions (Wijers, 2013; Riddle and Brinkerhoff, 2011) and economic development (Wright et al., 2008; Filatotchev et al., 2009), how returnee entrepreneurs can change homeland institutions as a 'role model' indirectly, has not yet been discussed. Being a role model, returnee entrepreneurs can make a stronger institutional change. This chapter shows the new potential of returnee entrepreneurs in the context of homeland development.

This study offers implications for policymakers who wish to promote gender equality in their countries. The findings of this study provide them with arguments how and why returnee female entrepreneurs can make distinctive contributions in this regard. Another practical implication is for returnee female entrepreneurs. Often, female returnees do not know about their potential as institutional change agents. This study shows that they can change gender-related institutions in their homelands by actively becoming a role model of successful female entrepreneurs.

Limitations

In order to clarify the scope of this study, it is essential to discuss its limitations. First, researchers at the German university who are not familiar with Indian institutional contexts conduct research 'remotely.' While this research

Table 6.2 Selected Quotes for Each Institutional Domain

Element	Pattern	Selected Quotes
Indian Women	Women feel heard and taken seriously Workplace for women Encouraging women to work Agarwal contributes to the number of female role models	• 'Once *KAARYAH* started as a brand, women started realizing that these were major problems that were not being addressed…' (Agarwal) • 'Urban India has a growing number of working women like Nidhi with well-paying corporate jobs. Most of them prefer western wear at work, so what are their options?' Tech in Asia (Online article) • 'The brand focuses on **bridging the gap** between **western formals and the Indian silhouette.**' (Agarwal) • 'And I would venture to say that not the majority but **a significant amount of workforce is also women** which then therefore adds to their financial sustainability and growth.' (Agarwal) • 'New age women, us women, I think, have a lot more role models. We don't only have our mothers around. We have a lot of women entrepreneurs, we have a lot of women in business, we have women in art and arts craft industries.' (Dubey) • '…she is also someone who **writes columns** for us and you know, talks about the same thing she is doing about being comfortable with who you are but also about dressing and you know, **your own empowerment and you know, being comfortable in your own skin…**' (Dubey) • 'Yes, Nidhi is actually **really actively involved** in this student and women community…in fact she is also playing **mentor** for a couple of you know, **women only platform**, so in India, if you look it up, there is a platform called Sheroes.' (Ismail)
Media	Media approaching Agarwal and pushing her into spotlight	• '[…] internet is really prevalent in India, like even smaller cities have great amount of connectivity and a smartphone area really active. So I think when people start looking up things on the internet whether it is an actor or an entrepreneur, you also want to, you also tend to want to dress like them.' (Ismail) • 'A lot of perception of women because of what we do is that we follow up a lot with events. So we often announce events on certain topics and we have **meetings of women entrepreneurs when we discuss some of their challenges** and most of these women come to know us because of our stories, because they **read of the challenges of other women entrepreneurs.**' (Dubey) • 'That does happen on its own. We push her as an entrepreneur, she gets pushed as a women entrepreneur by default, I would say.' (Ismail) • 'Then Nidhi is also representing *KARYAAH* and the, you know, **women startup community** in a lot of panel discussion.' (Ismail)

(Continued)

Table 6.2 (Cont.)

Element	Pattern	Selected Quotes
Education	Focus on female entrepreneurship in university education	• 'And then alongside that Nidhi and *KAARYAH* have also **become a case study for a lot of universities and schools in India**.' (Ismail) • 'She has been invited every now and then to be, you know, either a guest to remember or someone to conduct a talk session or a workshop. Sometimes these are in house panel discussions. Yes, Nidhi is actually really actively involved in this student and women community.' (Ismail)

Source: Own illustration

setting gives investigators a chance to observe the phenomenon objectively, it is challenging for them to understand a foreign institution profoundly. This setting makes it unavoidable to rely on the statements of the interviewees. In order to reduce bias of interviewees, we conducted interviews with Indian diaspora members in Germany. It is questionable to what extent our contextual understandings are comparable to native Indian people.

Another limitation is related to the interview language. Interviews were conducted in English, which turned out to be a challenge for this study due to the strong Indian accent. It hindered smooth conversation during the interview, which unavoidably affected the interview quality and led us to struggle to interpret the interviews. The fact that we conducted interviews remotely via telephone or skype also negatively influences the quality of the audio data.

Moreover, the phenomenon we observe in this study is specific to Indian country-context. Moreover, the focus of this study lies on well educated, middle-class women coming from the metropolitan cities in India. We could observe that they got emancipated directly or indirectly through entrepreneurial engagements of Agarwal. We still have no clue about women in other societal classes or other cultural contexts.

Finally, this study focuses on gender-related institutions. On one side, this focus highlights under-researched gender issues in the context of returnee entrepreneurship and its contributions to homeland development. On the other side, however, other types of institutions in India have not been considered in this study. Furthermore, this study has a research setting in India – as a country, which is characterized by a substantial gender gap. This study does not offer any evidence whether and to what extent one can apply its research findings to other country contexts where, for instance, fewer gender gaps exist.

Future Perspectives

In order to overcome the limitations mentioned above, this study recommends future investigators to conduct multiple case studies in different institutional contexts to further explore returnee entrepreneurs' contributions to the development of homeland institutions. For instance, scholars in the future can investigate the role of female returnee entrepreneurs in the country, which has fewer gender gaps to explore, and whether and to what extent their roles are different from the findings of this study.

Future research is recommended to emphasize more the qualitative mechanisms about influence made by returnee entrepreneurs. Returnee entrepreneurs influence the development of their home countries in various ways. The scholars in the past, however, have predominantly focused on 'hard' contributions of returnees such as transfer of knowledge and technology. This study shows that potential contributions of returnees' entrepreneurial activities go far beyond these aspects. Therefore, we suggest that future researchers should focus more on 'soft' sides of returnee entrepreneurs' homeland contributions.

Note

1 The Reserve Bank of India classifies centers into six tiers based on population. Tier-1 is a population classification for 100,000 and above, Tier-2 is for between 50,000 and 99,999, and Tier-3 is 20,000 to 49,999.

References

Alon, I., Misati, E., Warnecke, T. & Zhang, W. (2011). Comparing Domestic and Returnee Female Entrepreneurs in China: Is There an Internationalisation Effect? *International Journal of Business and Globalisation*, 6(3–4): 329–349. doi:10.1504/IJBG.2011.039391.

Bao, Y., Miao, Q., Liu, Y. & Garst, D. (2016). Human Capital, Perceived Domestic Institutional Quality and Entrepreneurship among Highly Skilled Chinese Returnees. *Journal of Developmental Entrepreneurship*, 21(01): 1650002. doi:10.1142/S1084946716500023.

BarNir, A., Watson, W. E. & Hutchins, H. M. (2011). Mediation and Moderated Mediation in the Relationship among Role Models, Self-Efficacy, Entrepreneurial Career Intention, and Gender. *Journal of Applied Social Psychology*, 41(2): 270–297.

Baughn, C. C., Chua, B. & Neupert, K. E. (2006). The Normative Context for Women's Participation in Entrepreneurship: A Multicountry Study. *Entrepreneurship Theory and Practice*, 30(5): 687–708.

Bhagwati, J. & Hamada, K. (1973). The Brain Drain, International Integration of Markets for Professionals and Unemployment: A Theoretical Analysis. 102. *Working Paper Development of Economics*.

Bosma, N., Hessels, J., Schutjens, V., Praag, M. & Verheul, I. (2011). Entrepreneurship and Role Models. 11–061*3. Tinbergen Institute Discussion Paper. Amsterdam and Rotterdam.

Brush, C. G. & Cooper, S. Y. (2012). Female Entrepreneurship and Economic Development: An International Perspective. *Entrepreneurship & Regional Development*, 24(1–2): 1–6. doi:10.1080/08985626.2012.637340.

Bruton, G. D., Ahlstrom, D. & Li, H.L. (2010). Institutional Theory and Entrepreneurship: Where Are We Now and Where Do We Need to Move in the Future? *Entrepreneurship: Theory and Practice*, 34(3): 421–440. doi:10.1111/j.15406520.2010.00390.x.

Cassarino, J. P. (2008). Patterns of Circular Migration in the Euro-Mediterranean Area: Implications for Policy-Making. 2008/29. Circular Migration Series: Political and Social Module. CARIM Analytic and Synthetic Notes.

Charmaz, K. (2008). Grounded Theory as an Emergent Method. In *Handbook of Emergent Methods*, edited by S. N. Hesse-Biber and P. Leavy, 155–170. New York: The Guilford Press.

Charmaz, K. (2014). *Constructing Grounded Theory*. 2nd Edition. London: SAGE Publications.

Chrysostome, E. (2010). The Success Factors of Necessity Immigrant Entrepreneurs: In Search of a Model. *Thunderbird International Business Review*, 52(2): 137–152.

Coyne, C. J. & Leeson, P. T. (2009). Media as a Mechanism of Institutional Change and Reinforcement. *Kyklos*, 62(1): 1–14. doi:10.1111/j.14676435.2009.00421.x.

Dai, O. & Liu, X. (2009). Returnee Entrepreneurs and Firm Performance in Chinese High-Technology Industries. *International Business Review*, 18(4): 373–386.

Denzin, N. K. (1973). *The Research Act: A Theoretical Contribution to Sociological Methods*. Transaction Publishers.

Dutia, S. G. (2012). Diaspora Networks: A New Impetus to Drive Entrepreneurship. *Innovations: Technology, Governance, Globalization*, 7(1): 65–72.

Eisenhardt, K. M. (1989). Building Theories from Case Study Research. *The Academy of Management Review*, 14(4): 532–550.

Eisenhardt, K. M. (2007). Theory Building from Cases: Opportunities and Challenges. *Academy of Management Journal*, 50(1): 25–32.

Eisenhardt, K. M. & Graebner, M. E. (2007). Theory Building from Cases: Opportunities and Challenges. *The Academy of Management Journal*, 50(1): 25–32.

Estrin, S. & Mickiewicz, T. (2011). Institutions and Female Entrepreneurship. *Small Business Economics*, 37(4): 397–415. doi:10.1007/s11187-011-9373-0.

Farquharson, M. & Pruthi, S. (2015). Returnee Entrepreneurs: Bridging Network Gaps in China after Absence. *South Asian Journal of Management*, 22(2): 9–35.

Field, E., Jayachandran, S. & Pande, R. (2010). Do Traditional Institutions Constrain Female Entrepreneurship? A Field Experiment on Business Training in India. *American Economic Association*, 100(2): 125–129.

Filatotchev, I., Liu, X., Buck, T. & Wright, M. (2009). The Export Orientation and Export Performance of High-Technology SMEs in Emerging Markets: The Effects of Knowledge Transfer by Returnee Entrepreneurs. *Journal of International Business Studies*, 40(6): 1005–1021. doi:10.1057/jibs.2008.105.

Fowler, J. L., Gudmundsson, A. J. & O'Gorman, J. G. (2007). The Relationship between Mentee-Mentor Gender Combination and the Provision of Distinct Mentoring Functions. *Women in Management Review*, 22(8): 666–681. doi:10.1108/09649420710836335.

Freiling, J. & Harima, A. (2018). Refugee Entrepreneurship – Learning from Case Evidence. In *Refugee Entrepreneurship: A Case-Based Topography*, edited by S. Heilbrunn, J. Freiling & A. Harima. Basingstoke: Palgrave Macmillan.

Garud, R., Hardy, C. & Maguire, S. (2007). Institutional Entrepreneurship as Embedded Agency: An Introduction to the Special Issue. *Organization Studies*, 28 (7): 957–969.

Genome. (2017). *Global Startup Ecosystem Report 2017*.

Ghoshal, A. (2016). The Indian Startup Ecosystem – Perspectives & Implications. *Global Journal for Research Analysis*, 5(9): 318–320.

Harima, A. (2014). Network Dynamics of Descending Diaspora Entrepreneurship: Multiple Case Studies with Japanese Entrepreneurs in Emerging Economies. *Journal of Entrepreneurship, Management and Innovation*, 10(4): 65–92.

Harima, A. (2016). Classification of Diaspora Entrepreneurship. In *Diaspora Business*, edited by M. Elo & L. Riddle, 1st edition, 59–71. Inter-Disciplinary Press.

Harima, A., Elo, M. & Freiling, J. (2016). Rich-to-Poor Diaspora Ventures : How Do They Survive? *International Journal of Entrepreneurship and Small Business*, 28(4): 391–413.

Hausmann, R., Tyson, L. D. & Zahidi, S. (2011). *The Global Gender Gap Report*. Cologny/Geneva.

Henry, C. (2008). *Women Entrepreneurs. 21st Century Management: A Reference Handbook*, 51–59. Thousand Oaks, CA. Sage.

Hodkinson, P. (2008). Grounded Theory and Inductive Research. In *Life*, edited by N. Gilbert, 3rd edition, London: Sage.

Hugo, G. (2005). *Migrants in Society: Diversity and Cohesion*. Adelaide: Global Commission on Migration.

International Finance Corporation. (2014). *Improving Access to Finance for Women-in India*.

Isaac, T. T. & Franke, R. W. (2002). *Local Democracy and Development: The Kerala People's Campaign for Decentralized Planning*. Rowman & Littlefield.

Kalantaridis, C. & Fletcher, D. (2012). Entrepreneurship and Institutional Change: A Research Agenda. *Entrepreneurship & Regional Development*, 24(3–4): 199–214. doi:10.1080/08985626.2012.670913.

Kenney, M., Breznitz, D. & Murphree, M. (2013). Coming Back Home after the Sun Rises: Returnee Entrepreneurs and Growth of High Tech Industries. *Research Policy*, 42(2): 391–407. doi:10.1016/j.respol.2012.08.001.

Khavul, S., Chavez, H. & Bruton, G. D. (2013). When Institutional Change Outruns the Change Agent: The Contested Terrain of Entrepreneurial Microfinance for Those in Poverty. *Journal of Business Venturing*, 28(1): 30–50. doi:10.1016/j.jbusvent.2012.02.005.

Kloosterman, R. (2010). Matching Opportunities with Resources: A Framework for Analysing (Migrant) Entrepreneurship from a Mixed Embeddedness Perspective. *Entrepreneurship & Regional Development*, 22(1): 25–45. doi:10.1080/08985620903220488.

Kloosterman, R., Leun, J.P. & Rath, J. (1999). Mixed Embeddedness: (In)Formal Economic Activities and Immigrant Businesses in the Netherlands. *International Journal of Urban and Regional Research*, 23(2): 252–266. doi:10.1111/1468-2427.00194.

Koene, B. A. S. (2006). Situated Human Agency, Institutional Entrepreneurship, and Institutional Change. 2*Journal of Organizational Change Management*, 19(3): 365–382. doi:10.1108/IJBM-07-2013-0069.

Kwok, C. C. Y. & Tadesse, S. (2006). The MNC as an Agent of Change for Host Country Institutions: FDI and Corruption. *Journal of International Business Studies*, 37(6): 767–785. doi:10.1057/palgrave.jibs.8400228.

Kyrgidou, L. P. & Petridou, E. (2013). Developing Women Entrepreneurs' Knowledge, Skills and Attitudes through e-Mentoring Support. *Journal of Small Business and Enterprise Development*, 20(3): 548–566. doi:10.1108/JSBED-04-2013-0061.

Laukhuf, R. L. & Malone, T. A. (2015). Women Entrepreneurs Need Mentors. *International Journal of Evidence Based Coaching and Mentoring*, 13(1): 70–86.

Leca, B. & Naccache, P. (2006). A Critical Realist Approach to Institutional Entrepreneurship. *Organization*, 13(5): 627–651. doi:10.1177/1350508406067007.

Levy, D. & Scully, M. (2007). The Institutional Entrepreneur as Modern Prince: The Strategic Face of Power in Contested Fields. *Organization Studies*, 28(7): 971–991.

Li, D. D., Feng, J. & Jiang, H. (2006). Institutional Entrepreneurs. *Economic Association*, 96(2): 358–362.

Lien, D. & Wang, Y. (2005). Brain Drain or Brain Gain: A Revisit. *Journal Economics*, 18(1): 153–163. doi:10.1007/s00148-003-0174-x.

Lin, D., Lu, J., Li, P.P. & Liu, X. (2015). Balancing Formality in Business Exchanges as a Duality: A Comparative Case Study of Returnee and Local Entrepreneurs in China. *Management and Organization Review*, 11(02): 315–342.

Liu, X., Wright, M. & Filatotchev, I. (2015). Learning, Firm Age and Performance: An Investigation of Returnee Entrepreneurs in Chinese High-Tech Industries. *International Small Business Journal*, 33(5): 467–487. doi:10.1177/0266242613508147.

Maguire, S., Hardy, C. & Lawrence, T. B. (2004). Institutional Entrepreneurship in Emerging Fields. *The Academy of Management Journal*, 47(5): 657–679.

Mayer, S. D., Harima, A. & Freiling, J. (2015). Network Benefits for Ghanaian Diaspora and Returnee Entrepreneurs. *Entrepreneurial Business and Economics Review*, 3(3): 95–121.

McGowan, P., Redeker, C. L., Cooper, S. Y. & Greenan, K. (2012). Female Entrepreneurship and the Management of Business and Domestic Roles: Motivations, Expectations and Realities. *Entrepreneurship and Regional Development*, 24(1–2): 53–72.

Misangyi, V. F., Weaver, G. R. & Elms, H. (2008). Ending Corruption: The Interplay among Institutional Logics, Resources, and Institutional Entrepreneurs. *Academy of Management Review*, 33(3): 750–770. doi:10.5465/AMR.2008.32465769.

Mueller, S. L. & Dato-On, M. C. (2008). Gender-Role Orientation as a Determinant of Entrepreneurial Self-Efficacy. *Journal of Developmental Entrepreneurship*, 13(1): 3–20.

Muofhe, N.J. & Du Toit, W. F. (2011). Entrepreneurial Education's and Entrepreneurial Role Models' Influence on Career Choice. *SA Journal of Human Resource Management*, 9(1): 1–15. doi:10.4102/sajhrm.v9i1.345.

Orhan, M. & Scott, D. (2001). Why Women Enter into Entrepreneurship: An Explanatory Model. *Women in Management Review*, 16(5): 232–247.

Patel, R. & Parmentier, M. C. J. (2005). The Persistence of Traditional Gender Roles in the Information Technology Sector: A Study of Female Engineers in India. *Information Technologies and International Development*, 2(3): 29–46. doi:10.1162/1544752054782457.

Pruthi, S. (2014). Social Ties and Venture Creation by Returnee Entrepreneurs. *International Business Review*, 23(6): 1139–1152. doi:10.1016/j.ibusrev.2014.03.012.

Qin, F., Wright, M. & Gao, J. (2017). Are 'Sea Turtles' Slower? Returnee Entrepreneurs, Venture Resources and Speed of Entrepreneurial Entry. *Journal of Business Venturing*, 32(6): 694–706. doi:10.1016/j.jbusvent.2017.08.003.

Riddle, L. & Brinkerhoff, J. (2011). Diaspora Entrepreneurs as Institutional Change Agents: The Case of Thamel.Com. *International Business Review*, 20: 670–680.

Rouse, R. (1986). Making Sense of Settlement: Class Transformation, Cultural Struggle, and Transnationalism among Mexican Migrants in the United States. *Annals New York Academy of Sciences*, 25–52.

Sarfaraz, L., Faghih, N. & Majd, A. (2014). The Relationship between Women Entrepreneurship and Gender Equality. *Journal of Global Entrepreneurship Research*, 2(1): 6. doi:10.1186/2251-7316-2-6.

Sarri, K. K. (2011). Mentoring Female Entrepreneurs: A Mentors' Training Intervention Evaluation. *Journal of European Industrial Training*, 35(7): 721–741. doi:10.1108/EL-012014-0022.

Saxenian, A. (2000). *Silicon Valley's New Immigrant Entrepreneurs.* 15. Working Paper.

Saxenian, A. (2001). The Silicon Valley-Hsinchu Connection: Technical Communities and Industrial Upgrading. *Berkely Planning Journal*, 15(1): 3–31.

Saxenian, A. (2005). From Brain Drain to Brain Circulation: Transnational Communities and Regional Upgrading in India and China. *Studies in Comparative International Development*, 40(2): 35–61.

Shastri, R. K. & Sinha, A. (2010). The Socio-Cultural and Economic Effect on the Development of Women Entrepreneurs (with Special Reference to India). *Asian Journal of Business Management*, 2(2): 30–34. doi:10.1177/0149206304272151.

Sinha, K. (2003). Citizenship Degraded: Indian Women in a Modern State and a PreModern Society. *Gender and Development*, 11(3): 19–26. doi:10.1080/741954366.

Smallbone, D. & Welter, F. (2012). Entrepreneurship and Institutional Change in Transition Economies: The Commonwealth of Independent States, Central, and Eastern Europe and China Compared. *Entrepreneurship and Regional Development*, 24(3–4): 215–233. doi:10.1080/08985626.2012.670914.

Straubhaar, T. (2000). International Mobility of the Highly Skilled: Brain Gain, Brain Drain or Brain Exchange. 88. HWWA Discussion Paper. Hamburg.

Svejenova, S., Mazza, C. & Planellas, M. (2007). Cooking up Change in Haute Cuisine: Ferran Adrià as an Institutional Entrepreneur. *Journal of Organizational Behavior*, 28: 539–561.

Tung, R. L. & Lazarova, M. (2006.) Brain Drain versus Brain Gain: An Exploratory Study of Ex-Host Country Nationals in Central and East Europe. *The International Journal of Human Resource Management*, 17(11): 1853–1872. doi:10.1080/09585190600999992.

Venturini, A. (2008). Circular Migration as an Employment Strategy for Mediterranean Countries. 2008/39. CARIM Analytic and Synthetic Notes – Circular Migration Series.

Warnecke, T. (2013). Entrepreneurship and Gender: An Institutional Perspective. *Journal of Economic Issues*, 47(2): 455–464. doi:10.2753/JEI0021-3624470219.

Welter, F. (2004). The Environment for Female Entrepreneurship in Germany. *Journal of Small Business and Enterprise Development*, 11(2): 212–221.

Wijers, G. D. M. (2013). Contributions to Transformative Change in Cambodia: A Study of Returnees as Institutional Entrepreneurs. *Journal of Current Southeast Asian Affairs*, 32(1): 3–27.

Wong-MingJi, D. J., Sullivan, S. E. & Brush, C. G. (1999). Women Entrepreneurs: Moving beyond the Glass Ceiling. *The Academy of Management Review*, 24(3): 585–589.

World Economic Forum. (2015). *The Global Gender Gap Report 2016 Insight Report.* Vol. 25. World Economic Forum.

Wright, M., Liu, X., Buck, T. & Filatotchev, I. (2008). Returnee Entrepreneurs, Science Park Location Choice, and Performance: An Analysis of High-Technology SMEs in China. *Entrepreneurship: Theory and Practice*, 32(1): 131–155.

Yin, R. K. (2009). *Case Study Research: Design and Methods.* 4th edition. Thousand Oaks: Sage Publications Inc.

7 How Will the Service Actor and the Related Activities in Tourism Improve Women's Empowerment in the World?

Ceyhun Çağlar KILINÇ and Gülsün YILDIRIM

Introduction

With the development of communication tools, especially the internet, technology provides us with a number of advantages in accessing information. There are an increasing number of applications created with recently developed technologies and there are several activities that can be carried out via the internet (Özdemir, 2008: 890). In the media of popular science, technology promises robots, the conquest of space, infinity etc. for a golden era of humanity in the future. Recently, continuously developing technology has brought along significant changes in the living habits of society. Technopolythene culture has affected everyday language, and concepts like interface, feedback and outcome have begun to be used commonly among people (Kuban, 2004: 313). The integration of mass communication tools and the internet have become more widespread and have brought along an evolution in the conventional media. With this evolution, computer-based systems and technologies like mobile creativity have contributed to the dissemination of social media components (Köseoğlu, 2006: 152; Yavuz, 2017: 171). Especially, the number of people using smart phones which have become indispensable in today's world is continuously increasing. Besides, social media, the most important platform to emerge with the use of the internet has created positive changes in people's behavior and ideas about creativity.

People began to write more creative messages and content to become popular and catch the attention of target groups. There are many tools in social media and they are generally categorized as wikis, blogs, microblogs, content sharing sites, professional networks, podcasts, forums, social bookmarking sites etc. (Vural and Bat, 2010: 3356). In the light of all these developments, enterprises have begun to transfer their marketing activities onto internet-based platforms and carry out these activities in a digital environment and reach more target masses. The traditional information and technology production factors have affected the labor force and natural resources. With the information age and the increase in education levels, concepts like compulsory education were introduced; the number of educated women increased and the women benefiting from the equality of opportunities between men and women thanks to social transformation began to contribute more to the economy and employment. The purpose of the present study is to find out how much women can be empowered by supporting their marketing activities with essential marketing knowledge and how women's empowerment will be achieved by the support of the service sector activities from the point of tourism knowledge.

The Place and the Importance of Women in the Labor Force and the Problems They Experience

Making up the half of the world population, the female labor force represents nearly half of the potential labor force that is not sufficiently mobilized. Women generally remain outside professional life because of the obstacles associated with their gender (Gedik and Gürbüzer, 2017: 422). The studies investigating the culture theory indicate that women face some obstacles due to company policies, procedures or working styles (Ramgutty-Wong, 2000: 184). With the economic, social and cultural changes occurring in society as a result of globalization, there has been an increase in women's employment rate. Women employees began to take part in professional life due to such needs as additional income, having economic independence and advancing themselves. Whereas women used to be assigned mostly housework and manual labor until the Industrial Revolution, their status in society has changed considerably since (Deane, 1994: 18; Nayır, 2008: 634; Günday, 2011: 11).

In parallel to the changes in the conditions of agricultural production with the Industrial Revolution, women began to be employed in sectors other than agriculture, mainly in the service industry. During this time, especially the production in large-scale textile companies that did not require a highly skilled labor force increased which gave women the opportunity to give up unpaid family work or agricultural labor (Çolak, 2003: 1; Küçük, 2015: 3). However, the female workforce which was called 'unqualified' at that time was only considered as a substitute for male work force because of long working hours and low wages (Yılmaz et al., 2008: 91).

In the new world order that has changed with the development of information technologies, the number of educated women and, accordingly, women's employment rate have increased. Today, women have begun to take part in almost all professional areas and in all aspects of professional life (Narin et al., 2006:67). The number of women in the labor force as well as the number of working couples has increased. There are also single mothers who provide for their family. For instance, 25–33% of companies in the formal economy are owned by women (Schindehutte et al., 2003: 94). In another study carried out in the Middle East, it was found out that 13% of 4,000 company owners were women (Prifti et al., 2008). As it has been demonstrated, women are employed or set up their businesses especially in the service industry or in education, textile and nutrition etc. because of having mostly the skills associated with their gender roles (Gürol, 2000: 25; Hisrich and Brush, 1984; Hisrich and Öztürk, 1999; Ufuk and Özgen, 2001; Welsh et al., 2014).

There are some international conventions about the equality of men and women in social, economic and other areas (Güzel, 2009: 34–35). These are:

- The UN Convention on the Elimination of all Forms of Discrimination Against Women (CEDAW)
- The UN – Beijing Declaration
- Treaty of Rome
- Maastricht Treaty
- Treaty of Amsterdam

Both the problems that women experience in the employment stage and professional life and their entrepreneurship have been investigated in several studies in the literature. In a study carried out on 3,500 male and female employees in England, the participants were asked to describe their bosses and what type of a boss they wanted to have. The results of the study indicated that the participants mostly preferred to work with female bosses (Örücü et al., 2007: 121–122).

Across all economies, there are examples of female entrepreneurs making significant contributions to innovation, employment and growth (Brush et al., 2009). To give an example, more than 10 million out of approximately 16 million employers are self-employed women according to the estimations in European countries. Similarly, it has been found out that 6.4 million out of 9.2 million people are self-employed women in the USA. Both examples demonstrate the importance of working women in the economy (Delmar, 2003: 14).

When the studies on women entrepreneurs and women employees are examined, it is seen that entrepreneur women are mostly aged 25–55 (Welsh et al., 2014; Ufuk and Özgen, 2001; Hisrich and Öztürk, 1999). The approaches reflecting women's perspective argue that the role that is assigned to women is not natural, but it shaped by the society and can be changed (Özar, 2000: 157). In the study carried out by Hisrich and Brush (1989), women entrepreneurs evaluated their skills for developing new ideas and products as "excellent" in their self-evaluation of "managerial skills". It was also demonstrated that women were "very good" at human relations, management, development and education, marketing and marketing researches whereas they were "good" at technical areas such as inventory, production etc. However, it was concluded that women were "relatively insufficient" in finance and the use of capital. Besides, the personal, social and professional obstacles they encounter in their lives might result in their avoiding taking risks (Welsh et al., 2014). The principal problems that women face in setting up or managing a business can be summarized as follows: the provision of capital resources, lack of information, competence in business management, social norms, business-life conflict, participation in professional business networks, bureaucratic operations, coping with problematic clients and employees, working with family members etc. (Vita et al., 2014).

Gül and Gül (2018) aimed in their study to find out the qualifications and general profiles of women entrepreneurs working in the food sector in Balıkesir province as well as the problems they experienced before and after setting up their business. They obtained data from 60 women entrepreneurs who received funds from the Small and Medium Enterprises Development Organization (KOSGEB) in Balıkesir in 2012–2017. Interviews were carried out and survey forms were used for data collection. As a result of the study, it was concluded that the most important entrepreneurship characteristics of women entrepreneurs were being self-confident, successful and having economic independence. It was also found out that they received the greatest support from their husbands but still experienced problems finding the capital and the workplace as well as facing bureaucratic obstacles in starting their business. They also indicated that finding qualified personnel, building a balance between business and family and finding customers were the hardest problems they faced after opening their workplace.

Küçük (2015) investigated the problems that women faced most in their business lives and in the society according to employers in different branches of the private sector. In line with the aim of the study, semi-structured question forms prepared using qualitative research methods were employed. In this regard, in-depth interviews (based on eight questions) were carried out with 45 women in 11 different sectors. The participants indicated that the actions taken by the bureaucracy and the government were insufficient and unfriendly in resolving the problems experienced by women. On the other hand, one of the most significant expectations that women generally indicated in the study was their desire to become powerful. They also indicated that they needed a fair salary system, an improvement in the working conditions, the right to early retirement, the elimination of prejudices against women in society, respect towards the freedom of individuals as well as being given more space on social platforms.

Erdem (2014) aimed to find out the stress level that women working at a public institution in Turkey had and its outcomes. For this purpose, 12 women participants were chosen randomly as the sample group out of the personnel responsible for counting tickets. Face-to-face interviews were carried out with the participants and the problems they experienced while working and their effects on their family lives were investigated. During the interview, it was aimed to find out whether there was an inequality between male and female personnel in terms of promotion and whether there was pressure in the working environment as well as finding out about their relationship with their colleagues, the problems experienced at the workplace, the relationship they had with their superiors and its outcomes. As a result of the study, it was concluded that there was not an inequality between male and female personnel at the public institution but the working conditions had some negative effects on the employees among which were headache, stress, lack of motivation, the disturbance of peace in the family due to work-related stress, not paying enough attention to children, inefficiency at work, quick temper etc. It was indicated that it would be wrong to categorize these negative effects because the stress that people can suffer in their business or private lives can result from many factors such as the environment they are in, their personalities, physical or psychological characteristics etc.

Cömert (2014) carried out a parallel study to find out the opinion of students studying in their final year at the tourism management department; to discover whether the gender factor is important in their preferences, and the opinion of students about the gender factor in employment and promotion in the tourism sector. The study was carried out with 126 students studying in their fourth year at the Tourism Management Department of Gazi University. The data collected with a participation rate of 76.54% were analysed using the SPSS Statistics package program. As for the analyses, the average scores of the Likert scale relevant to gender discrimination were used while t-test and Chi-square tests were employed for evaluating the employment preferences in independent groups. The study results demonstrated that the majority of the students considered working at 4 or 5-star urban hotels whereas working at food and beverage companies was the least popular option. It was also determined that front desk, human relations and marketing were the three most common areas that students preferred to work in hotels whereas housekeeping became the least popular area.

Türeli and Dolmacı (2014) aimed to carry out a field survey on the academic and administrative female personnel working at Isparta Süleyman Demirel University by handling the topics of discrimination and mobbing against women in business life. The study group consisted of the academic and administrative female personnel working at Isparta Süleyman Demirel University. In this regard, a survey form was sent to 600 female personnel by e-mail while it was also administered to 130 personnel on a face-to-face basis. In total, 278 female personnel (108 being administrative and 170 being academic personnel) returned the survey forms. The obtained data were analysed using SPSS analysis program. The results of the study indicated that there was a significant relationship between being exposed to discrimination at the workplace and being woman. As for the victimization associated with "mobbing" at the workplace, the participants indicated that they were not precisely aware of instances that constitute "mobbing".

Dedeoğlu (2009) investigated how the gender equality policies put into effect during the harmonization process within the EU affected women's employment and non-functional efforts of women in Turkey, with a critical perspective. It was shown that the amendments that were put into effect with regards to the right to fair wages, equal treatment, maternal leave, parental leave etc. were effective for only some women while most women could not benefit from them. It was concluded in the study that such practices affected potential women's employment negatively and resulted in discrimination against both working women and those remaining outside the labor force while reinforcing the traditional gender roles which caused the majority of women to stay at home as housewives or offer their efforts in return for low wages in the informal market.

Özkan and Özkan (2010) aimed to find out the factors that affect the amount of female workers' wages and test whether gender constitutes a discriminative criterion with regards to their wage. In line with the purpose of the study, a scale was developed to obtain accurate data and the study was limited to the province of Gaziantep. The data were collected through random sampling method. In order to find out whether there was wage discrimination in Gaziantep, face-to-face interviews were carried out with 257 employees and managers. The sample of the study constituted 15% of the whole study population. While determining the sample, attention was paid to choose companies working with female personnel. With the factor analysis administered on the obtained data, it was attempted to determine the dimensions of the wage discrimination and as a result, three factors were specified: discriminative factors, objective factors and selective factors. Besides gender discrimination, political, religious and cultural factors and kinship with the employer etc. played a role in determining the amount to be paid to female workers. However, duties, skills and the educational background of female workers were the most important factors that determined their wages.

Karcıoğlu and Leblebici (2014) studied the relationship between career obstacles and the glass ceiling syndrome among female executives. In line with the purpose of the study, they investigated the place of women in the business life in Turkey and in the world besides the scope of the career obstacles for women and the concept of a glass ceiling. In order to find out whether there was a glass ceiling syndrome in the banking sector, a survey was administered to 40 female and 40 male personnel working at the branches of public and private banks. As a result of the analysis of the survey, women's taking on multiple roles, their personal choices and perceptions, organizational culture, organizational policies, the lack of a mentor, not being able to participate in informal communication networks and occupational segregation were handled separately as the reasons for women's failure to make progress in their careers. These variables handled as the dimensions of the concept of a glass ceiling were analysed according to the gender, age, marital status, educational background, status and professional experience of the participants in the survey and it was concluded that "Glass Ceiling Syndrome" played a role in women's failure to make progress in the banking sector. The researchers also indicated that there were very few senior female executives in the banking sector, as in other sectors, and they mostly concentrated in the positions of mid-level management. Besides, female executives seem to believe that they can be a good wife, mother and a successful executive at the same time, whereas male executives are hesitant about it. Thus, it was concluded that conventional ideas about the roles of women have not changed completely in today's world.

Berber and Eser (2008) aimed to demonstrate the current status of women's employment in Turkey. For this purpose, they investigated the situation of women in the labor market from different perspectives, in line with the data provided by the Turkish Statistical Institute. In the study, the distribution of women's employment in Turkey according to sectors as well as the status of women in the labor market were evaluated. The sectoral analysis of women's employment was carried out across Turkey, in general in the first place and then according to different regions. It was found that women's employment rate in Turkey started to decline as of 2002. When viewed according to different sectors, it was seen that the employment rate of women in agriculture fell over the last year although women are still employed mostly in this sector whereas their number has significantly increased in the service industry. In parallel to these changes, it was determined that women's status in the working life changed in general but still varies according to the development levels of regions.

The so-called "glass ceiling" does not allow women to occupy top administrative levels in organizations. Such policies and practices that lead to these obstacles in working life against women limit their career opportunities although they do not seem to be real obstacles (Jerris, 1999: 62). In the 1970s women began occupying administrative positions, challenging the idea that women are not eligible for these positions (Reskin, 1992: 344). Women working as executives indicated that they did not have examples that they could take as role models, so they had reached their current position by trial and error (Jelinek and Adler, 1988: 14). In addition, women in society are seen only as mother, seductive, domestic (Gupta and Sharma, 2003: 610); in the professions where men are dense the success of women is attributed to chance as well as their talents (Lyness and Judiesch, 1999: 159). According to today's traditional perspective, female personnel do have a place among potential executive candidates (Selmer and Leung, 2002: 348).

Ufuk and Özgen (2001) suggested in their study that female entrepreneurs generally planned their time according to their job and families but did not spare enough time for themselves. As a result of this situation, many women indicated that having to assume several roles at the same time affected their life satisfaction negatively and led to stress. They also pointed out that entrepreneurial activities have been effective in helping them realizing their potential and contributing to society.

It is necessary that there is a good relationship between many factors besides the developments in the service industry so that the female labor force can increase (Koray, 1999: 182). These factors can be summarized as follows:

- Increasing the number of laws and practices that protect and support working women across the world
- Demographic developments
- Increasing education opportunities
- Creating and disseminating non-standard types of working

- Marginalization of the family concept and the popularity of nuclear families
- Decline in rates of marriage and increase in divorce rates
- Positive changes in the attitude towards working women in the society
- Improvement in childcare and other services.

In order for women to take their place more actively in the economy, political and social life above all their employability should be increased. In this regard, changes are necessary in education and non-formal education, and active employment measures should be applied for women who have not received formal education. The women who cannot benefit from education opportunities sufficiently have very limited options in the labor force outside the agricultural sector. However, those having the opportunity to get education can work in many professions requiring specialization (Günday, 2011: 35).

According to a study carried out by Krishnan and Park, (2005: 1712), only 3.9% of 4,341 executives working at 825 companies and earning high salaries are women. In another study, it was found out that the minimum salary of female CEOs listed in Fortune 500 was $4.3 million while the maximum rate was $13.7 million. It was also found that male and female personnel working at the same position did not earn the same salary (Ackah and Heaton, 2003: 134–138).

Women experience many problems at their workplaces. The most common of these problems is gender discrimination. This refers to being treated more negatively or positively compared to men, and adversely affects their career (Acar et al., 1999: 5). As a result of this, women generally concentrate in entry or mid-level positions in their working lives. They are given jobs that require few skills and responsibilities and thus they have difficulty in getting a promotion or end up getting lower salaries compared to men (Dalkıranoğlu and Çetinel 2008: 279). Besides the discrimination they are subject to at work, women also face obstacles in making career progress under the same conditions as men and reaching top administrative positions because of their responsibilities associated with family, children and other duties (Akcan and Başaran, 2009).

In another study, women indicated that one of the most important reasons for their quitting a job was the lack of a person to provide assistance and their not being included in social communication networks (Ackah and Heaton, 2003: 140). As a result of this, it was indicated that prejudices took root in the organization culture which caused an inequality in salaries because of the stereotypes and other factors arising from patriarchal culture (Ramgutty-Wong, 2000: 184).

Female Labor Force in Tourism

Providing for one out of ten jobs across the world, tourism is a labor-intensive industry that creates job opportunities at all skill levels, with its role as the value chain in many sectors such as agriculture, construction, production, handcrafts, financial services or information and communication technologies

(Kaya, 2017: 7). It is also one of the sectors that create the most job opportunities in the world. According to the data of World Travel and Tourism Council (WTTC), the tourism and travel sector provided direct and indirect job opportunities to 267 million people across the world, in 2013. This rate accounts for 8.7% of the total employment in the world (Uguz and Topbaş, 2014: 497). Because it requires large quantities but low-skilled labor, a high number of informal employees, low salaries in return for long working hours, and a low rate of unionization and coverage of collective labor agreements, the tourism sector fails to promote an effective social dialogue (Kaya, 2017: 6).

In the tourism sector, the lack of people who provide guidance and assistance to women is one of the most important reasons why female personnel leave their jobs (Ackah and Heaton, 2003: 140). The female personnel being promoted to significant positions in hotels indicated that the presence of mentors at the enterprise was considerably important for their career, whereas the top female executives indicated that it did not matter so much because they did not improve their career with the help of a mentor themselves (Brownell, 1994: 114). Another problem experienced by female personnel working in the tourism sector is the work and family balance. This adversely affects the career development especially of female personnel working in the hospitality industry (Brownell, 1994: 102). This is because women feel as if they have to make a choice between career and family and thus they delay their plans for having children (Ackah and Heaton, 2003: 136).

When we have a look at the economy in general, it is seen that tourism has a larger share in terms of women's employment compared to other sectors, providing twice as much employment than in other sectors (*Global Report on Women in Tourism*, 2011; Dinçer et al., 2016: 382) which makes it an effective means to support gender equality and women's empowerment in working life (Kaya, 2017: 5). The tourism industry where women are largely employed provides 10% of the GDP (WTTC, 2015; Kaya, 2017: 6). The *Global Report on Women in Tourism 2010* commissioned by UNWTO and UNIFEM (now UN Women) drew attention to the potential of tourism in providing opportunities for women to have paid work and be empowered (Kaya, 2017: 3).

Another report was prepared within the scope of the G20 Summit held in Antalya with the participation of heads of state and heads of government of different countries (G20 Turkey, 2015). According to this report, the countries indicated that they agreed on working in line with the determined targets and indicators in order to support gender equality in the work conditions in tourism.

There is also the concept of a "woman's job" that is used in industrial tourism. This is because women are mostly employed for cleaning and housekeeping jobs that do not require qualifications and are hardly seen in administrative positions in tourism (Kinnaird and Hall, 1994; Skalpe, 2007). It is known that they concentrate in entry-level jobs (Burgess, 2003: 50; Uguz and Topbaş, 2014: 498). This structural characteristic is definitely determining for women employed in this sector. A significant share of the work carried out in tourism industry – catering, reception, housekeeping and cleaning – is considered as an extension of the housework done by women. For this reason, tourism is seen as a "women-intensive" sector as well as being labor-intensive (Akoğlan 1996: 17; Cave and Kılıç 2010: 285; Elmas 2007; Uğuz and Topbaş, 2016; Kaya, 2017: 6). Besides, women often work both as an unpaid worker for the family and as a seasonal worker at hostels, providing cleaning, cooking and housekeeping services (Kaya, 2017: 3).

In several studies, researchers describe the tourism sector as feminine, unqualified, low-paying and unstable (Baum 2013; Cave and Kılıç, 2010; Costa et al. 2011; Elmas 2007; Fernandez et al. 2009; Hemmati 2000; Kaya, 2017: 6). Thus, women experience a lot of problems both at entry-level and administrative positions and even as business owners (Dinçer et al., 2016: 383). They are mostly employed in front-desk, human relations, marketing and catering (Doherty and Manfredi, 2001) and only one third of women employed at hotels are in administrative positions (Soehanovic et al., 2000: 270) whereas men generally occupy general manager, branch manager or supervisor positions (Doherty and Manfredi, 2001: 68). UN Women indicated with statistics that women performing 66% of the labor and producing 50% of the food needed in the world earned 10% less than men and owned only 1% of property across the world (UN Women, 2013). The rate of women's employment increased from 41.1% in 1995 to 61.5% in 2015. (ILO, 2016: 22). In the service industry women's employment rate reached 55.5% in 2016 from 55.1% in 2015 (Çakır et al., 2017: 468).

As well as the problems arising from external factors in tourism, women's own psychology and roles in this sector constitute problems for employment in this sector (Li and Leung, 2001: 191; Dinçer et al., 2016: 383). For example, the number of seasonal female workers dismissed in Ireland is more than that of seasonal male workers (Breathnach et al., 1994) which indicates that employers tend to dismiss female workers while keeping male workers at times of economic crisis (Kaya, 2017: 8–9). To give an example of women in business, when men went into the military during World War II, women helpers were called in order to maintain the economic balance; women responded positively to this call and they created labor (Greenwood et al., 2002: 4, Günday, 2011: 18). As an example for women's successful work in the tourism sector, tourism activities in rural areas allow women to acquire new roles beyond the traditional female roles and duties. In rural tourism, women are both producers and sellers of products, thus creating jobs for women and supporting social development in this direction.

It is known that the disparity of the wage policies applied in the tourism sector (Olalı and Timur, 1998: 290) creates serious bottlenecks in the sector and when wages of women and men working at the same level are compared, women earn about 2/3 of the wages that the men receive (Krishnan and Park, 2005: 1712). Female employees also think that women will have a constant wage differential with men throughout their careers and that this difference will be quite large (Iverson, 2000: 43).

Conclusion

When analyzed historically, although women have always worked, they have never fully received what they deserved for their labor. In recent years, women have been actively involved in the labor force, this has brought economic and social experiences of women to a more efficient and effective form. Considering that women contribute significantly to economic development, and constitute approximately half of the world population, the participation of women in the workforce and its activities are considered as very important for the progress of a country. Female labor force creates additional employment and savings. During World War II when men were conscripted, women were called to help in order to maintain economic balance, and women responded positively to this call (Günday, 2011: 18). This is an indication of what women can do when given the opportunity. They are also able to turn the judgments on gender discrimination in favor of women. In addition, while trying to be successful in their professional lives, women try not to disrupt their role as women and this requires double responsibility. Impoverishment of women around the world is directly related to the employment of women and obstacles to the labor market. The poverty rate being higher among women and women's being clustered around ill-paid, irregular and unsafe jobs especially in developing countries is a result of inefficiency of the labor and social security laws on women's rights (Günday, 2011: 18).

Women's labor keeps the economy moving, however, women do not take enough share of the income to which they highly contribute. Tourism becomes a crucial and effective means of supporting social gender equality and empowering women in work life because of the fact that employment rate for women is two times higher in the tourism industry than in other sectors. Women's employment being at a sufficient level in tourism sector especially in a service-driven and human-sensitive area will be fruitful in terms of increasing the success of the sector and customer satisfaction through ensuring qualified service besides better publicising of the relevant destination. For this reason, there need to be efficient and useful policies to promote and develop opportunities for women to work in the tourism sector. It is proposed that women will positively contribute to the acceleration of economic growth through higher women participation in the labor force in both private and public sectors on condition that the legal regulations and policies regarding women's rights are put into action.

References

Acar, F., Ayata, A. G. & Varoğlu, D. (1999). *Cinsiyete Dayalı Ayrımcılık: Türkiye'de Eğitim Sektörü Örneği*, Cem Web Ofset: Ankara.

Ackah, C. & Heaton, N. (2003). Human Resource Management Careers: Different Paths for Men and Women? *Career Development International*, 8(3).

Akcan, M. & Başaran, R. (2007). İş Yaşamında Kariyer. Retrieved from: https://schola r.google.com.tr/scholar?hl=tr&as_sdt=0%2C5&scioq=Akcan%2C+Ba%C5%9Faran

+&q=%C4%B0%C5%9F+Ya%C5%9Fam%C4%B1nda+Kariyer+M+Akcan%2C
+R+Ba%C5%9Faran+-+2007&btnG=

Akoğlan, M. K. (1996). Konaklama Endüstrisinde Kadının Konumu. *Anatolia Turizm Araştırmaları Dergisi*, 7(3–4).

Baum, T. (2013). International Perspectives on Women and Work in Hotels, Catering and Tourism. Printed by the International Labour Office, Geneva, Switzerland Bureau for Gender Equality and Sectoral Activities Department GENDER Working Paper 1/2013, SECTOR Working Paper No. 289.

Berber, M. & Eser, B. Y. (2008). Türkiye'de Kadın İstihdamı: Ülke Ve Bölge Düzeyinde Sektörel Analiz. *ISGUC (The Journal of Industrial Relations and Human Resources)*, 10(2).

Breathnach, P., Henry, M., Drea, S. & O'Flaherty, M. (1994). Gender in Irish Tourism Employment. In: *Tourism: A Gender Analysis*. Wiley, UK, pp. 52–73. ISBN 0471948330

Brownell, J. (1994). Women in Hospitality Management: General Managers' Perceptions of Factors Related to Career Development. *International Journal of Hospitality Management*, 13(2).

Brush, C. G., Bruin, A. & Welter, F. (2009). A Gender-Aware Framework for Women's Entrepreneurship. *International Journal of Gender and Entrepreneurship*, 1(1).

Burgess, R. G. (Ed.). (2003). *Field Research: A Sourcebook and Field Manual*. Routledge.

Cam, E. (2006). Çalışma Yaşamında Stres ve Kamu Kesiminde Kadın Çalışanlar. *Journal of Human Sciences*, 1(1).

Cave, P. & Kılıç, S. (2010). The Role of Women in Tourism Employment with Special Reference to Antalya, Turkey. *Journal of Hospitality Marketing & Management*, 19(3).

Costa, C., Carvalho, I. & Breda, Z. (2011). Gender Inequalities in Tourism Employment: The Portuguese Case. *Revista Turismo & Desenvolvimento*, 15.

Cömert, M. (2014). Turizm Eğitimi Alan Öğrencilerin Sektörde Çalışmak İstedikleri Alanlar Ve Sektördeki İstihdamda Cinsiyet Ayrımcılığıyla İlgili Düşünceleri. *Gazi Üniversitesi Turizm Fakültesi Dergisi*, 1(1).

Çakır, P. G., Barakazı, M. & Barakazı, E. (2017). Turizm Sektöründe Çalışan Kadınların Karşılaştıkları Sorunları Değerlendirmeye Yönelik Bir Araştırma. *The Journal of Academic Social Science Studies*, 61, 461–474.

Çolak, Ö. F. (2003). *Sanayileşme ve Kadın İşgücü*. İstihdam Kadın İşgücü ve Yeni İş Kanunu Sempozyumu: Muğla.

Deane, P. (1994). *İlk Sanayi İnkilabı*. Çeviren: Tevfik Güran, Türk Tarih Kurumu Yayınevi: Ankara.

Dedeoğlu, S. (2009). Eşitlik mi Ayrımcılık mı? Türkiye'de Sosyal Devlet, Cinsiyet Eşitliği Politikaları ve Kadın İstihdamı. *Çalışma ve Toplum*, 2(21).

Delmar, F. (2003). Women Entrepreneurship: Assessing Data Availability and Future Need. Workshop on Improving Statistics on SMEs and Entrepreneurship, OECD Headquarters, Paris.

Dinçer, F. İ., Akova, O., Ertuğral, S. M. & Çifçi, M. A. (2016). Woman Labour in Tourism Industry in Turkey: Opportunities And Barriers. *Eurasian Academy of Sciences Social Sciences Journal*, 1.

Doherty, L. & Manfredi, S. (2001). Women's Employment in Italian and UK Hotels. *International Journal of Hospitality Management*, 20(1).

Elmas, S. (2007). *Gender and Tourism Development: A Case Study of the Cappodoccia Region of Turkey, Tourism and Gender: Embodiment, Sensuality and Experience*, A. Pritchard, N. Morgan, I. Atelyevic (Eds), Cambridge, MA: CABI Publishing.

Erdem, M. (2014). The Level of Quality of Work Life to Predict Work Alienation. *Educational Sciences: Theory and Practice*, 14(2): 534–544.

Fernandez, M., Pena-Boquete, Y. & Pereira, X. 2009. Labor Conditions in the Spanish Hotels and Restaurants Industry. *Tourism Analysis*, 14(3).

G20 Turkey. (2015). G20 Leaders' Communiqué agreed in Antalya. G20 Turkey. Retrieved from http://g20.org.tr/g20-leaders-commenced-the-antalya-summit/

Gedik, H. & Gürbüzer, G. B. (2017). Girişimcilik Ve Pazarlamada Kadın İş Gücünün Artan Önemi. *The Journal of Academic Social Science Studies*, 63.

Global Report on Women in Tourism. (2011). UNWTO/UN Women. Facts & Figures on Women, Poverty & Economics, Poverty & Employment. Retrieved from: http://www.unifem.org/gender_issues/women_poverty_economics/facts_figures.php#2

Greenwood, J., Seshadri, A. & Yörükoglu, M. (2002). Engines of Liberation. *Economie d'Avant Garde Research Reports* 2.

Gupta, N. & Sharma, A. K. (2003). Gender Inequality in the Work Environment at Institutes of Higher Learning in Science and Technology in India. *Work, Employment and Society*, 17(4).

Gül, M. & Gül, K. (2018). Balıkesir İlinde Kadın Girişimci Profili ve Sorunları: Yiyecek Sektöründe Bir Uygulama. *Dumlupinar University Journal of Social Science*, (56).

Günday, P. D. (2011). *Ekonomik Kalkınmada Kadının Önemi ve Katkısı, Yüksek Lisans Tezi*. T.C. Dokuz Eylül Üniversitesi, Sosyal Bilimler Enstitüsü. İzmir.

Gürol, A. (2000). *Türkiye'de Kadın Girişimci ve Küçük İşletmesi: Fırsatlar, Sorunları, Beklentiler ve Öneriler*. Atılım Üniversitesi yayını 2: Ankara.

Güzel, B. (2009). *Kadın Çalışanların Kariyer Engellerinin Örgütsel Bağlılık Üzerine Etkisi: Dört ve Beş Yıldızlı Otel İşletmelerinde Bir Uygulama* (Doctoral dissertation, DEÜ Sosyal Bilimleri Enstitüsü).

Hemmati, M. (2000). Women's Employment and Participation in Tourism. *Sustainable Travel & Tourism*, 1(5).

Hisrich, R. D. & Brush, C. (1984). The Woman Entrepreneur: Management Skills and Business Problems. *Journal of Small Business Management*, 52(2): 286–305.

Hisrich, R. D. & Öztürk, S. A. (1999). Women Entrepreneurs in a Developing Economy. *Journal of Management Development*, 18(2).

Hisrich, R. D. & Brush, C.G. (1989). *The Women Entrepreneur. Starting, Financing and Managing a Successful Business*. Lexington Books, USA.

ILO. (2015). *Women in Business and Management: Gaining Momentum*. ILO Publications: Geneva.

ILO. (2016). *Women at Work*. ILO Publications: Geneva.

Iverson, K. (2000). The Paradox of the Contented Female Manager: An Empirical Investigation of Gender Differences in Pay Expectation in the Hospitality Industry. *International Journal of Hospitality Management*, 19(1).

Jelinek, M. & Adler, N. J. (1988). Women: World-class Managers for Global Competition. *Academy of Management Perspectives*, 2(1).

Jerris, L. A. (1999). *Human Resources Management for Hospitality*. Pearson.

Karcıoğlu, F. B. & Leblebici, Y. (2014). Kadın Yöneticilerde Kariyer Engelleri: Cam Tavan Sendromu Üzerine Bir Uygulama. *Ataturk University Journal of Economics & Administrative Sciences*, 28(4).

Kaya, Ş. (2017). Turizmde Kadın Emeği. *KARATAHTA İş Yazıları Dergisi*, Sayı: 9/ Aralık 2017.

Kinnaird, V. & Hall, D. R. (Eds.). (1994). *Tourism: A Gender Analysis*. Belhaven Press.

Koray, M., Demirbilek, S. & Demirbilek, T. (1999). *Gıda İşkolunda Çalışan Kadınların Koşulları ve Geleceği.* KSGM: Ankara.

Köseoğlu, Ö. (2006). *Bilgi İletişim Teknolojileri ve Yansımaları,* İçinde: Bilgi iletişim Teknolojilerinin Pazarlamaya Etkisi, Z. B. Akıncı Vural (ed.), Nobel Yayın Dağıtım: Ankara.

Krishnan, H. A. & Park, D. (2005). A Few Good Women – on Top Management Teams. *Journal of Business Research,* 58(12).

Kuban, B. (2004). *Teknoloji ve Toplumsal Denetimi, Teknoloji.* Türk Mühendis ve Mimar Odaları Birliği: Ankara.

Küçük, M. (2015). Çalışma Hayatında Kadınlar ve Karşılaştıkları Sorunlar: Bir İşverene Bağlı Olarak Çalışan Emekçi Kadınlara İlişkin Bir Araştırma. *Ekonomi Bilimleri Dergisi,* 7(1).

Küçük, M. (2015). Çalışma Hayatında Kadınlar Ve Karşılaştıkları Sorunlar: Bir İşverene Bağlı Olarak Çalışan Emekçi Kadınlara İlişkin Bir Araştırma. *Ekonomi Bilimleri Dergisi,* 7(1): 1309–8020.

Li, L. & Leung, R.W. (2001). Female Managers in Asian Hotels: Profile and Career Challenges. *International Journal of Contemporary Hospitality Management,* 13(4).

Lyness, K. S., ve Judiesch, M. K. (1999). Are Women More Likely to be Hired or Promoted into Management Positions? *Journal of Vocational Behavior,* 54(1).

Narin, M., Marşap, A. & Gürol, M. A. (2006). Global Kadın Girişimciliğinin Maksimizasyonunu Hedefleme: Uluslararası Arenada Örgütlenme ve Ağ Oluşturma. *Gazi Üniversitesi İİ BF Dergisi,* 8(1).

Nayır, D. Z. (2008). İşi ve Ailesi Arasındaki Kadın: Tekstil ve Bilgi İşlem Girişimcilerinin Rol Çatışmasına Getirdikleri Çözüm Stratejileri. *Ege Akademik Bakış,* 8(2).

Olalı, H. & Timur, A. (1998). *Turizm Ekonomisi.* Ofis Ticaret Matbaacılık Şti: İzmir.

Örücü, E., Kılıç, R. & Kılıç, T. (2007). Cam tavan sendromu ve kadınların üst düzey yönetici pozisyonuna yükselmelerindeki engeller: Balıkesir ili örneği. *Yönetim ve Ekonomi,* 14(2), 117–135.

Özar, Ş. (2000). İstihdamda Toplumsal Cinsiyet Ayrımının Uluslararası Karşılaştırmalı Bir Çözümlemesi, Kadın İstihdamı. T.C. Başbakanlık Devlet İstatistik Enstitüsü Yayını: Ankara.

Özdemir, G. (2008). *Destinasyon Pazarlaması,* Detay Yayıncılık: Ankara.

Özkan, G. S. & Özkan, B. (2010). Kadın Çalışanlara Yönelik Ücret Ayrımcılığı ve Kadın Ücretlerinin Belirleyicilerine Yönelik Bir Araştırma. *Çalışma ve Toplum,* 1(24).

Prifti, C., Simantiraki, S. & Wagner, J. H. (2008), *Middle East Local and Regional Woman Entrepreneurship.* Centre for Mediterranean and Middle Eastern Studies, Edit: A. Vassiliou, www.idis.gr (12.11.2008).

Ramgutty- Wong, A. (2000). CEO Attitudes toward Women Managers in Corporate Mauritius. *Women in Management Review,* 15(4).

Reskin, B. F. & Ross, C. E. (1992). Jobs, Authority, and Earnings among Managers: The Continuing Significance of Sex. *Work and Occupations,* 19(4).

SchindehutteM., M. Morris, M. Lord& C. Brennan (2003). Entrepreneurs and Motherhood: Impacts on their Children in South Africa and the United States. *Journal of Small Business Management,* 41(1).

Selmer, J. & Leung, A. S. (2002). Career Management Issues of Female Business Expatriates. *Career Development International,* 7(6).

Skalpe, O. (2007). The CEO Gender Pay Gap in the Tourism Industry—Evidence from Norway. *Tourism Management,* 28(3), 845–853.

114   *Ceyhun Çağlar KILINÇ, Gülsün YILDIRIM*

Soehanovic, J., Zougaj, M., Krizoman, D. & Bojanic-Glavica, B. (2000). Some Characteristics of Women Managers in the Hotel Industry. *International Journal of Contemporary Hospitality Management*, 12(4).

Dalkıranoğlu, T. & Çetinel, F. G. (2008). Konaklama İşletmelerinde Kadın ve Erkek Yöneticilerin Cinsiyet Ayrımcılığına Karşı Tutumlarının Karşılaştırılması, Dumlupınar Üniversitesi. *Sosyal Bilimler Dergisi*, 20.

Türeli, N. Ş. & Dolmacı, N. (2014). İş Yaşamında Kadın Çalışana Yönelik Ayrımcı Bakış Açısı Ve Mobbing Üzerine Ampirik Bir Çalışma. *Muğla Sıtkı Koçman Üniversitesi İktisadi Ve İdari Bilimler Fakültesi Ekonomi Ve Yönetim Araştırmaları Dergisi*, 2(2).

Ufuk, H. & Özgen, Ö. (2001). Interaction between the Business and Family Lives of Women Entrepreneurs in Turkey. *Journal of Business Ethics*, 31.

Uguz, S. Ç. & Topbaş, F. (2014). Turizmde Kadın İstihdamı ve Ücret Ayrımcılığı: Karşılaştırmalı Bir Analiz. *Anatolia: Turizm Araştırmaları Dergisi*, 27(1).

Vita, L.D., Mari, M. & Poggesi, S. (2014). Women Entrepreneurs in and from Developing Countries: Evidences from the Literature. *European Management Journal*, 32.

Vural, A.B. & Bat, M. (2010). Yeni Bir İletişim Ortamı Olarak Sosyal Medya: Ege Üniversitesi İletişim Fakültesine Yönelik Bir Araştırma. *Journal of Yasar University*, 20(5).

Welsh, D.H.B., Memili, E., Kaciak, E. & Miyuki, O. (2014). Japanese Women Entrepreneurs: Implications for Family Firms. *Journal of Small Business Management*, 52(2).

World Travel & Tourism Council (WTTC). (2015). *Economic Impact of Travel and Tourism*. Retrieved from: https://zh.wttc.org/-/media/files/reports/economic-impact-research/ regional-2015/world2015.pdf

Yavuz, C. (2017). Meslek Yüksekokulları Halkla İlişkiler Programı Öğrencilerinin Sosyal Medya Kullanımı Alışkanlığı: Ordu Üniversitesi Örneğinde. *Manas Sosyal Araştırmalar Dergisi*, 2(6).

Yılmaz, A., Bozkurt, Y. & İzci, F. (2008). Kamu Örgütlerinde Çalışan Kadın İşgörenlerin Çalışma Yaşamlarında Karşılaştıkları Sorunlar Üzerine Bir Araştırma. *Eskişehir Osmangazi Üniversitesi Sosyal Bilimler Dergisi*, 9(2).

8 Eliminating Economic Violence against Women for Gender Equality

Empowering Women through Human Rights Based Approach

Altın Aslı ŞİMŞEK

Introduction

Economic violence experienced by women is not as visible as physical, sexual, or psychological violence both in law and policy. Futhermore, it is not explicitly described in studies on violence against women. Accordingly, economic violence is a sort of violence hardly taken into consideration both at national and international level. While eliminating violence against women, it is necessary to understand the self-reinforcing, interconnecting and intersectional structure of different types of violence. Economic violence against women (EVAW), which is a type of discrimination against women, is a kind of human rights violation. There is a need to define and name EVAW as a women's rights issue according to feminist critical legal thinking for understanding the gendered structure of human rights.

This perspective entails studying violence experienced by women as a type of discrimination and human rights violation through the transformative, holistic and gender-specific approach of the Convention on the Elimination of All Forms of Discrimination against Women (CEDAW). The International Covenant on Civil and Political Rights (ICCPR) and the International Covenant on Economic, Social and Cultural Rights (ICESCR) clearly show the obligation of State Parties to provide for the equal rights of both men and women to enjoy human rights; however, only recognising the formal approach to equality (*de jure* equality) does not guarantee women can enjoy their right to equality. The *de facto* equality by means of gender equality is the core principle to respect, protect and fulfill women's human rights. In 2011, as a result of being blind to women's experiences both in public and private power relations, a regional but still empowering legal instrument came on the scene: The Council of Europe Convention on Preventing and Combating Violence Against Women and Domestic Violence (Istanbul Convention).

This chapter aims to explore the definition and nature of EVAW and to show the relation between gender inequality and EVAW in the first instance. Hence, women's experiences and real life difficulties both in private and public socio-economic life are going to be taken into consideration according to the human rights based approach. This approach helps us to link women's civil and political rights with their economic, social and cultural rights. Another aim of this article is to address *sine qua non* structure of women's socio-economic rights for eliminating EVAW, considering the specific focus on subordination of women's experience in policymaking and marginalization of socio-economic rights in law.

In this respect, two main risks against achieving full enjoyment of women's socio-economic rights are going to be highlighted: (i) During the economic policy process, the goal of growth/economic development is often privileged over the enjoyment of human rights, especially socio-economic rights. This impact of economic policy is much more harmful in the times of economic crisis and gender-blind and rights-blind thinking of the neoliberal decision-making process; (ii) Women are generally victimized or seen as a vulnerable group, which is assumed as a group lack of self-determination and this reinforces the subordination of women. The third aim of this chapter is to start a conversation about empowering women against economic violence by strengthening their socio-economic rights in terms of international, regional and national legal instruments. To achieve this, the legal framework of the CEDAW and Istanbul Convention and the decisions and comments of the international monitoring bodies will be analyzed. Therefore the focus is "seeing injustice in law" (Uygur, 2013) built by EVAW and discovering how to contest it with a special focus on Turkish legal experience and way of thinking in policymaking.

The chapter proceeds as follows: the first part presents the conceptual framework by defining and naming EVAW according to feminist critical legal thinking. The second part assesses the legal framework concerning the obligations of the state with a focus on human rights law, which contests or reinforces EVAW. The third part explains the legal framework where the emphasis is on the relation between EVAW, gender inequality and the violations of women's human rights. The fourth part asserts the significance of women's socio-economic rights for eliminating EVAW. In the fifth part the challenges and opportunities for eliminating EVAW and empowering women's socio-economic rights are considered and the positions of human rights law when coping with gender inequality or the courts when interpreting EVAW are discussed.

The Definition and Nature of EVAW

In the movie *Pleasantville* (Ross, 1998), George Parker, father of the house comes back home from work and when he enters the house calls to his wife "Honey, I'm home!" There, the mother of the house, Betty Parker, as an obedient "house"wife to her husband, is waiting for him, setting the dinner table and cooking the meal. This scene shows the gendered division of household labour in an American nuclear family living in a suburban neighbourhood (Gómez Galisteo, 2009, p. 66). This is also the representation of the patriarchal approach to the family, everyday life and family economics which also shows the expected performance of men's and women's duty in public and private sphere:[1] Men are visible working in the public sector, making important decisions about politics and economics; women are responsible for domestic duties and caring for all family members. Like in *Pleasantville*, which pictures "the perfect nuclear family, the perfect house, and the perfect life" in black and white shaped by 1950s conservatism (Dickinson, 2006, p. 212), the same gendered division of household labour is observed in the Turkish nuclear family today with two different dimensions; first not in black and white, but in colour, and second not in the 1950s, but in the 2000s. So not only in the 1950s but also in the 2000s the rise of right wing conservatism shapes and reinforces stereotypes about women and men. When these stereo-types turn into laws, then this type of law prevents women from fully enjoying human rights. Considering the subject of this chapter, stereotypes about women cause an invisible type of violence against women. This type of vio-lence is economic violence and the gendered division of household labour based on stereotypes is a form of it (Memiş, 2014, p. 174).

Why is economic violence invisible compared to other kinds of violence against women? There are many studies and empirical data both in Turkey and in the world about violence against women in psychological, physical and sexual aspects. A recent global report declares that lifetime prevalence of physical and/or sexual intimate partner violence among women who reported having experienced one or more acts of physical or sexual violence, or both by a current or former intimate partner at any point in their lives in different regions is as follows: "Africa 36.6%, Americas 29.8% Eastern Mediterranean 37.0%, Europe 25.4%, South-East Asia 37.7%, and Western Pacific 24.6%" (World Health Organization, 2013, p. 17). According to a report prepared by the Turkish public institute working on statistics, lifetime prevalence of phy-sical and/or sexual intimate partner violence among women is 41.9% in Turkey (Turkish Statistical Institute (TUIK) Report, 2008). Yet there is not enough data to see the catastrophic consequences of EVAW. Therefore an analysis through a human rights based perspective of this kind of abuse is crucial, especially in countries dealing with poverty, particularly women's poverty. Although some of the international human rights treaties cover EVAW as a form of violence against women, none of them defines the term. For this reason feminist legal scholarship has taken the first steps to name, define and contest EVAW.

As in that scene of *Pleasantville* mentioned above, the division of house-hold labour regarding gender is one of the most important components of EVAW. However, what else should be added to this component to see a clear definition of EVAW? First, there are different financial issues related to EVAW besides gendered division of household labour. Secondly not only housewives face EVAW; there are working women who suffer from this kind of violation and this matter is closely related to women's choice about work-ing or not working after a marriage/intimate partnership. TUIK's report also shows three aspects of EVAW related with the above two points. These are: making a woman quit her job or preventing her from working, not giving money for daily domestic needs, and depriving a woman of her income. Thirdly, EVAW is not as visible as physical wounds; so initially it is harder to recognise it as a women's rights violation. This matter is closely connected to the secondary status of socio-economic rights in both international law and the national laws of many countries (Barak-Erez and Gross, 2007, p. 4). The more socio-economic rights are ignored by both the United Nation's human rights system and national, regional and international non-governmental organizations working on human rights, the more EVAW, a sort of socio-economic injustice faced by women becomes invisible. Since not recognised as full legal rights, women's socio-economic rights must be empowered by feminist legal theory and practice to eliminate EVAW.

So if there is a need to make a list of EVAW causing violations of women's rights, it must be highlighted that violence against women is a type of violation of women's rights. In order to define EVAW, we need the concept of "women's rights are human rights". The three dimensional human rights obligations (to respect, to protect and to fulfil) of the states indicate that a state or a third party can cause a women's rights violation. According to the international human rights obligations framework, states have a duty "to refrain from interfering with the enjoyment of the right (respect) and prevent others from interfering with the enjoyment of the right (protect) and to adopt appropriate measures towards the full realization of human rights (fulfil)" (The Committee on Economic, Social and Cultural Rights (CESCR) General Comment No. 3). As presented in the "Courts and the Enforcement of Economic Social and Cultural Rights: Comparative Experiences of Justiciability" Report (Courtis, 2008), for expressing obligations of "to respect, protect and fulfil" the term "tripartite classification" is used. This classification offers a fruitful way for removing the obstacles to the justiciability of socio-economic rights. When there is a violation of women's rights caused by EVAW, this means the state does not implement this framework properly. Therefore we can observe EVAW by examining women's rights violations, and socio-economic rights in particular.

In this context there are two types of violations related to EVAW's broader meaning determined in literature: (i) EVAW committed by the state: Caused by public policies and laws. Laws regarding unequal pay for work, limited access to cash and credit resources, discriminatory rules about inheritance and property rights, low maintenance after divorce or widowhood are the main examples of EVAW committed by the state (Fawole, 2008, p. 169). (ii) EVAW committed by third parties, particularly by family members or employers: This is both seen in private life and work life. Thus, EVAW is a form of discrimination, namely economic discrimination.

In addition, the lack of laws fighting against poverty is a cause of EVAW. The concept of the feminization of poverty shows how women become powerless on financial issues without noticing they are poor or not. On the one hand, poverty affects both men and women all over the world, on the other hand, women live in poverty more than men and usually there is no direct connection between women's poverty and the income of the household. Women usually have limited control over the money in the family and they do not have the power to decide on how it should be spent, even if they and their children have a comfortable and luxurious life (Fawole, 2008, p. 169). According to field research in Turkey (Bora and Üstün, 2005, p. 30), in some cases the father leaves his daughter penniless even if she has no job and lives with him or the husband takes his wife's bankcard without permission to have her salary. If women resist against this behaviour, then the man who is a family member or shares the same home batters the women. Thus, feminization of poverty is a control mechanism over women. As is seen by the women's experiences in this field research, women are forced to obey a culture of "men make houses, women make homes". The home made by the woman is actually her cage. Since she cannot enjoy freedom sufficiently in two ways: (i) being free *from* something and (ii) being free *to* something (Şenol Cantek, 2001, p. 103).

According to Fawole (2008, p. 169) "economic violence is when the abuser has complete control over the victim's money and other economic resources or activities"; it is a type of domestic violence. In a broader sense EVAW is a type of violence which gained attention in the world with the rise of neo-liberal economics and right wing conservatism and is both a reason for and a consequence of women's poverty. The concept of EVAW has grounds in gender stereotypes and links to socio-economic rights of women and economic discrimination. For women it results in the lack of decision-making on financial issues related to herself and/or family. Therefore it is necessary to determine what legal instruments do and how to prevent or combat EVAW as a human rights violation.

The Legal Framework: Transnational and Regional Perspectives on EVAW

As a human rights violation, EVAW still does not have a formal definition in legal instruments. These legal instruments are international human rights conventions, which are also criticized by feminist legal theory and practice for not considering gender issues. Before examining the legal framework, I am going to summarize the gendered nature of women's disadvantage, the substantive notion of equality that recharacterizes human rights and the approach delivered by CEDAW.[2]

Gender disadvantage is formed by (i) gendered barriers to economic participation like unpaid or low-paid work for women; (ii) poverty itself as explained above; (iii) gender based violence; (iv) lack of the power to control vital decisions in one's life; (v) restricted access to socio-economic goods shaped by the gendered character of social institutions, containing customary, traditional, cultural and legal factors (Fredman, 2013, pp. 218–223).

In order to eliminate these barriers a substantive notion of equality should be implemented to human rights law. "It is not sufficient simply to extend rights to women" and this is what formal equality offers. "If the gender-specific factors causing women's disadvantage are fully to be addressed, human rights must be infused with substantive gender equality" which allows to take into account women's experiences in socio-economic life and aims for real change in male-oriented social structures (Fredman, 2013, pp. 223–224).

To sum up, CEDAW's approach constitutes:

- A transformative approach, linking equal rights, social support and socio-cultural elements;
- A holistic approach, linking civil, political, social and economic rights;
- A gender-specific approach to equality and non-discrimination.

(Hellum and Aasen, 2013, p. 2)

This approach was shaped by the UN Committee on the Elimination of Discrimination against Women (the CEDAW Committee) recommendations and decisions, and helps to understand how to implement the convention in national legal systems. The CEDAW Committee's General Recommendation No. 19 (1992) shows that:

The Convention in article 1 defines discrimination against women. The definition of discrimination includes gender-based violence, that is, violence that is directed against a woman because she is a woman or that affects women disproportionately. It includes acts that inflict physical, mental or sexual harm or suffering, threats of such acts, coercion and other deprivations of liberty. Gender-based violence may breach specific provisions of the Convention, regardless of whether those provisions expressly mention violence.

(para. 6)

The CEDAW Committee also defines gender-based violence as follows:

Gender-based violence, which impairs or nullifies the enjoyment by women of human rights and fundamental freedoms under general international law or under human rights conventions, is discrimination within the meaning of article 1 of the Convention.

(para. 7)

CEDAW does not mention EVAW directly. The CEDAW Committee did not class EVAW when defining discrimination against women, but refers to "coercion" and "deprivation of liberty". These elements are acknowledged as inherent to EVAW in recent studies. In the V.K. v. Bulgaria decision,[3] the complainant gives a concrete description and the Committee sites it as following:

...she was not allowed to work despite her education and qualifications. He alone decided on the spending of the family's income and provided the author with money only for the basic needs of the family. She had no additional money for herself and was not allowed to spend money given to her for purposes other than those strictly specified; nor was she informed about how the rest of her husband's income was spent. As a result, she was economically entirely dependent on her husband.

(para. 2.2)

In the same decision, the complainant claims are about non-recognition of EVAW as a type of domestic violence by public authorities and courts:

...[the] judicial system refused to recognize her status as a victim of domestic violence despite the evidence gathered and support from different non-governmental organizations. Therefore, she was in an even more vulnerable position and in greater danger than before initiating court proceedings, as the State party had failed to afford her with protection following the end of the court proceedings relating to the protection order. Free from any State intervention in his "private matters", her husband behaved even more aggressively towards her. In addition, he was constantly threatening her financial stability, pressuring her to agree to his proposal to leave the children with him and to give up most of the family property.

(para. 3.5)

In 1993, the Declaration on the Elimination of Violence against Women (DEVAW) was adopted by the UN General Assembly. Despite setting a clear international standard for addressing violence against women, DEVAW does not have the power to force states to obey norms constructed in the Declaration. Edwards (2010, p. 20) mentions that UN's DEVAW[4] internalizes the approach to "violence against women" by reference to "gender-based violence". Eighteen years after DEVAW, a definition similar to DEVAW's – a regional human rights treaty – including economic violence was given in the Istanbul Convention, but again the concept remains undefined.

The decisions of the European Court of Human Rights declares that all states of the Council of Europe are party to CEDAW and the European Convention on Human Rights. In the Opuz v. Turkey decision[5] the Court made a clear reference to CEDAW. In this decision, the Court found violation of Article 14 (prohibition of discrimination) as the gender-based violence suffered by Nahide Opuz and her mother. This was the very first time in a domestic violence case. Here the Court determined that domestic violence mainly affected women and that it was encouraged by discriminatory judicial passivity. Therefore, it was realised that special attention needs to be paid in combatting this violation of women's rights. So the Istanbul Convention has revealed.

The fundamental principles of the Istanbul Convention's triple structured approach of prevention, promotion and prosecution are as follows:

- The convention embodies the eradication of violence against women and domestic violence while accomplishing *"de jure"* and *"de facto"* equality through applying a gender perspective.
- Women are not helpless victims, but they can rebuild their own lives. It is about the states parties' positive obligations according to "due diligence" principle.
- There are other victims of domestic violence, such as LGBTI individuals and prevention of domestic violence covers both civil marriages and partners living together.
- Measures should be taken to prevent violence and support victims while dealing with the needs of vulnerable individuals and prohibit discrimination, towards migrants, refugee women, women asylum seekers, women with disabilities and girls.
- State parties should implement comprehensive and coordinated policies including government agencies, NGOs and national, regional and local authorities.

The Istanbul Convention defines "violence against women" as follows:

> a violation of human rights and a form of discrimination against women and shall mean all acts of genderbased violence that result in, or are likely to result in, physical, sexual, psychological or economic harm or suffering to women, including threats of such acts, coercion or arbitrary deprivation of liberty, whether occurring in public or in private life.

The Istanbul Convention also uses the terminology of "gender" and "gender based violence against women". According to the Convention's Article 3/c gender is: "the socially constructed roles, behaviours, activities and attributes that a given society considers appropriate for women and men." The Convention's Article 3/d provides that: "'genderbased violence against women' shall mean violence that is directed against a woman because she is a woman or that affects women disproportionately." By defining these terms what the Istanbul Convention has done is to codify the hidden meaning that the CEDAW Committee pointed at in General Recommendation No. 19.

The Convention also recognises EVAW as a form of "domestic violence" as follows:

> 'domestic violence' shall mean all acts of physical, sexual, psychological or economic violence that occur within the family or domestic unit or between former or current spouses or partners, whether or not the perpetrator shares or has shared the same residence with the victim.

The Istanbul Convention notably contains economic harm of suffering in both definitions of violence against women and domestic violence. By taking into account the gendered nature of violence, the Convention shows that sex based or gender based EVAW is a human rights violation of women. This perspective severs itself from the claim about the neutrality of traditional human rights instruments. Otto (1993, p. 161) argues this new perspective by examining DEVAW and states that "inequalities in power are the fundamental problem, and the struggle to maintain male privilege results in world-wide systemic violence against women". In order to understand systemic violence against women, not only power relations between state and individual, but also power relations between individuals – power relations between women and men – should be taken into consideration. At this point simply recognising civil liberties and meeting the "respect" duty is not enough to achieve equal rights for women. For this reason a weak understanding of socio-economic rights comparing them to civil liberties is not enough to accomplish preventing or ending EVAW (Otto, 1993, p. 161; Edwards, 2010, p. 21). Edwards also notes that unlike the Istanbul Convention, DEVAW recognises neither violence against women as a violation of human rights nor EVAW as a kind of violence against women.

Within the Istanbul Convention there is a second and backdated regional treaty, adopted in 2003, the Protocol to the African Charter on Human and Peoples' Rights on the Rights of Women in Africa (PRWA) which articulates economic harm as a kind of violence against women. PRWA's Article 1/b defines "violence against women" as follows:

> ...all acts perpetrated against women which cause or could cause them physical, sexual, psychological, and economic harm, including the threat to take such acts; or to undertake the imposition of arbitrary restrictions on or deprivation of fundamental freedoms in private or public life in peace time and during situations of armed conflicts or of war.

Therefore, unlike transnational conventions, two of the regional conventions recognise EVAW particularly in the definitions of violence against women.

After the Istanbul Convention, EVAW has started to get attention by legal professionals about its meaning, scope and nature. In his speech at the Meeting of the Parliamentary Network "Women Free from Violence" of the Council of Europe, Truchero (2013) mentions the unclearness of EVAW's boundaries: "economic violence or economic harm refers to a conduct directed to depriving the victim of all or any of its economic or financial resources."

These interpretations of EVAW are not *numerus clausus* and will increase and be varied in time. Hence legal interpretations and definitions are important for seeing the relation between EVAW and women's rights issues. So it is essential to conceptualize the relation between gender inequality and EVAW in order to see injustice in legal instruments and the interrelating discriminatory judicial passivity in the face of violence against women.

The Relation between Gender Inequality and EVAW

As summarized by Edwards (2010, pp. 58–59), human rights discourse is unable to name complex power relations and also ignores these relations. This ignorance has its grounds in the subordination of economic, social, and cultural rights to civil and political rights and causes structural inequalities for women. Like prioritization of civil and political rights (Charlesworth and Chinkin, 1993, p. 70), formal equality is also used for interpretation of right to equality. The human rights discourse also focuses on the individual and thereby women can prove a certain kind of violation of their rights; even so a major change in the lives of women in general is not going to happen (Smart, 2002, p. 145). This kind of interpretation prevents seeing injustice built by new human rights issues like poverty, globalization and lack of economic independence. These issues are main areas where we observe EVAW. Subordination of economic, social, and cultural rights creates the attitude of underestimating social, economic and cultural reasons for women's rights violations (Charlesworth et al., 1991, p. 635).

Regarding EVAW as a lack of full enjoyment of socio-economic rights, neither global poverty nor traditions and customs that damage human dignity of women are judicially contested. For this reason, as highlighted by Barak-Erez (2007, p. 397), the struggle for women's freedom has always involved the aim to realize economic independence and has usually been structured by the right to equality which is positioned as a fundamental principle for political and civil rights in liberal legal theory. As it is seen in the different waves of feminism defending political and civil rights is only the starting point of women's rights movements, as with the Suffragettes. Barak-Erez (2007) mentions that:

> The ability to own property and earn a living independently is a preliminary condition for personal freedom, and therefore constitutes a crucial first step on the long way towards the equality of women.
>
> (p. 397)

Moreover, this can be managed by substantive equality, which considers gendered disadvantage and gender-specific factors causing women's disadvantage. Nevertheless the formal equality idea of liberal legal theory is a gender-blind approach which does not offer women a solution to combat socio-economic inequalities. In addition, socio-economic inequalities cause a specific type of discrimination which is economic discrimination. So discrimination exists when distributing the benefits or positions between sexes arbitrarily or irrationally in a society (Kymlicka, 2001, p. 379). In this regard, EVAW is considered as a type of economic discrimination to women and a violation of their socio-economic rights.

Rethinking Women's Socio-economic Rights for Eliminating EVAW

The subordination of socio-economic rights creates the attitude of under-estimating social, economic and cultural reasons for women's rights viola-tions. This subordination goes side by side with EVAW. Therefore rather than Darwinist ideas regarding an "every man for himself" type of competition, and "male" oriented individualist liberal rights discourse, feminism defends the right to freedom of occupation and the right to property for women in the light of distributive justice (Barak-Erez, 2007, p. 399). Barak-Erez continues as follows:

> Feminism illuminates the importance of the right to freedom of occupa-tion not for the sake of promoting business competition free from gov-ernment regulation, but rather as an expression of the natural right to make a living, and the role of the right to property as a source of perso-nal freedom, and not merely as a tool for protecting the wealthy from taxation.
>
> (p. 399)

Due to this feminist perspective, independent economic activities of women cannot be guaranteed unless the correlation between women's socio-economic rights and EVAW is understood. There are two main risks against achieving full enjoyment of women's socio-economic rights. These are: (i) Privileging economic growth/economic development over the enjoyment of human rights, particularly socio-economic rights, especially in times of economic crisis and neoliberal decision-making process; (ii) Victimization of women as a vulner-able group, which is assumed as a group lack of self-determination, thus reinforcing the subordination of women.

The first risk turns women into easy-to-direct, cheap, and unionized work-ers in labour-intensive manufacture industries, which are affected by globali-zation and structural adjustment policies. In addition to that, women became the precursors of the new types of labour of which the majority are part-time and home-centered workers doing piecework, self-employed workers within the informal sector, or small entrepreneurs supported by micro credits, com-posed and shaped by a neoliberal developmentalist discourse (Ecevit, 2013). Secondly victimizing women leads to patriarchal approaches in social politics and digresses from a human rights based approach.

Socio-economic rights are listed in international and regional legal instru-ments widely. Some of these rights are directly connected with EVAW and in some cases, lack of these rights intersects with other kinds of oppression. In this context prominent socio-economic rights are rights to social security, a right to education, the right to social protection, the right to adequate stan-dard of living, rights to decide freely to accept or choose work, to fair wages and equal pay for equal work, to leisure and reasonable limitation of working hours, to safe and healthy working conditions, and land rights. Therefore, to empower women against economic violence, socio-economic rights must be reconsidered and fully implemented through the CEDAW and Istanbul Convention's approaches.

Empowerment of Women through Socio-economic Rights: Challenges and Opportunities

In society, the recognition of socio-economic rights is important for diverse groups, especially for groups that are economically vulnerable. For example, this is more important for people working in low-paid jobs, unprofessional jobs or the informal sector. Women are one of these groups who share these common aspects, as other disempowered groups like minorities, people with disabilities, refugees and immigrants. Challenges for women in the socio-economic area are: lower working rates than men, usually working in part-time jobs regarding their domestic role, spending little time in the labour market because of gender stereotypes, not valued economically, working in the casual employment sector, being in poverty (especially single mothers face this risk), not getting equal pay for equal work (Barak-Erez, 2007, p. 399).

Taking the responsibility of the domestic sphere, women are thought of as self-sacrificing altruists and the housework is related to their love and care. This perspective combines with unspecific working hours and lack of formal shifts of the housework. The housework also is done in an unremarkable way in daily life (Memiş and Özay, 2011, p. 252). Accordingly gendered division of household labour is still not legally recognised as a type of economic violence. In opposition to that, most conservative politics encourage women quitting their jobs and becoming housewives. This kind of policy-making also leads to not recognising domestic labour as "real job" like the other jobs in the market.

There are also changes in policy-making strategies and these changes are promoted globally. The UN has started a policy on gender mainstreaming which aims at applying gendered techniques to evaluate the impact of particular policies and programmes on women and men respectively. This means changing the perspective from victimization to empowerment by determining the particular effect of all human rights laws, policies, and programmes on women and their communities, and to guard against the negative or unintended consequences of them. This also means the change from formal equality to substantive equality (Edwards, 2010, p. 54).

There are examples of this kind of empowerment approach in the Istanbul Convention. The Istanbul Convention Article 18/3 codifies the obligation of the state to protect and support and to "aim at the empowerment and economic independence of women victims of violence" while taking "necessary legislative or other measures to protect all victims from any further acts of violence."

Furthermore, the Istanbul Convention Article 33 regulates substantive law against psychological violence. Substantive law covers not only necessary legislative measures but also "other measures" like administrative practices, policies, socio-economic conditions to realise substantial justice. Despite the fact that Article 33 does not mention EVAW explicitly, it refers coercion or threats through which a person's psychological integrity is seriously impaired. In addition, the Istanbul Convention's Article 3 highlights "coercion or arbitrary deprivation of liberty" as acts causing a violation of human rights and a form of discrimination against women when defining violence against women. New studies focus on "coercive control" or "coercion and control" to determine the abusive characteristics of the intention behind the perpetrator's behaviour. This is a useful pattern to discover the invisible and hardly recognisable structure of economic violence compared to other kinds of violence against women.

According to key studies, which link mind control and other forms of victimization as opposed to separate physical incidents, domestic violence is a powerful non-physical process. In these studies coercive control is a part of domestic violence in which the focus is on non-physical abuse that makes the totality of women's experiences understandable in a better way (Pitman, 2017, p. 145).

Stark (2007, p. 171) describes the concept of coercive control as typically a sum of "frequent, but often minor, assaults with tactics to intimidate, isolate, humiliate, exploit, regulate, and micromanage women's enactment." This concept helps to see injustice built by coercive control that ends with socioeconomic inequality for women. Regardless of whether coercive control contains physical violence, Stark's (2007) focus is on these tactics, which rarely are named as abuse and have no legal status (Pitman, 2017, p. 146).

The coercive control involves both psychological and economic violence in a fashion that interconnects domination through isolation, psychological terrorization and deprivation. It also includes physical assault which has an influence on the autonomy, independence and dignity of the person who is exposed to violence, and which constitutes her ability to make decisions to break the circle of violation (Truchero, 2013). It is the deprivation of the resources she needs – such as money, friends and transportation – to have autonomy. In the end the victim loses her own perspective (Tickle, 2017).

In a legal system which generally focuses on physical violence, the concept of coercive control is a step forward in the struggle to recognise EVAW. Some examples of coercive control are forcing women to quit their jobs or preventing them from working, throwing mother and children out of the house, refusing to put a woman's name on the house deeds, monitoring her mail/e-mail, scrutinising her bank statements and tampering with her phone (Tickle, 2017). Contrary to popular belief, coercive control is not a "soft" form of abuse (Tickle, 2017), but the perception of legal professionals, public authorities and even victims is that if it is softer, then it can be negligible when compared to physical violence.

According to the Istanbul Convention, there should be integrated policies to accomplish a human rights based approach and this is emphasised repeatedly (Preamble, Article 3, Article 12, Article 16, Article 18, Article 49, Article 66). Especially obligations regulated in the "Prevention" chapter express the women empowerment approach clearly. This chapter provides promoting changes in "customs, traditions and all other practices which are based on the idea of the inferiority of women or on stereotyped roles for women and men" (Article 12), awareness-raising (Article 13), education on "issues such as equality between women and men, non-stereotyped gender roles, mutual respect, non-violent conflict resolution in interpersonal relationships, gender-based violence against women and the right to personal integrity" (Article 14), strengthening "appropriate training for the relevant professionals dealing with victims or perpetrators" (Article 15).

Moreover, the Istanbul Convention clearly and directly correlates empowerment and the economic independence of women. Article 18 obligates state parties to "aim at the empowerment and economic independence of women victims of violence" when organising protection and support mechanisms. The meaning of this statement expressed in Explanatory Report of the Istanbul Convention (2011) is as follows:

> ...all measures to aim at the empowerment and economic independence of women victims of such violence...means ensuring that victims or service users are familiar with their rights and entitlements and can take decisions in a supportive environment that treats them with dignity, respect and sensitivity. At the same time, services need to instil in victims a sense of control of their lives, which in many cases includes working towards financial security, in particular economic independence from the perpetrator.
>
> (para. 118)

Despite having enough legal documents to name, contest and eliminate EVAW, change is not as fast as expected. More data is needed about women's experiences and disadvantages intersecting with different types of oppression such as disabilities, migration, and xenophobia to see the injustice built by public authorities and jurisprudence. In order to collect the necessary data and turn it into integrated policies according to a human rights based approach, the concept of "the law in books and the law in action" (Pound, 1910) is a starting point for further research; especially when patriarchal customs and traditions are advocated by government-organized, non-governmental organizations (GONGOs) (Hasmath-Hildebrandt and Hsu, 2016) against achievements of feminist NGOs about gender stereotypes in law. Furthermore, only recognizing the international human rights conventions is not sufficient for a state to eliminate violence against women and to achieve full enjoyment of women's rights. This is the case in the Turkish legal system. Despite having proper legal instruments, the segregationist speeches of public authorities against women, portraying women as wives and mothers when making public policies, and making the divorcing process unmanageable and difficult for women, not showing necessary efforts to stop early marriages and ignorance of women's rights by legal practitioners are the topics determined and found threatening for women in the CEDAW Committee's seventh periodic report on Turkey. Moreover, women in Turkey do not have adequate instruments to access information about their rights and job opportunities, especially women who have double disadvantages like women with disabilities, women living in poverty, refugee women, trans women who do not have equal access to job market, health, education and justice.

Conclusion

Considering the literature and positive law, EVAW contains complete control over the victim's money and other economic resources or activities which is named as coercive control. Gender-based violence also needs special attention to name EVAW in such cases including domination through intimidation, isolation, degradation, lack of independence, independence, all of which affect women's ability to make decisions to escape from subjugation.

In order to break the circle of violence it is essential for women to gain economic independence. In order to change the hierarchical power relations between women and men that subordinate women, a strengthening of socioeconomic rights in the light of international, regional and national legal instruments is necessary. Making EVAW visible will help naming and contesting violence against women. Despite having enough legal tools for eliminating EVAW, there is a need for changing the attitudes of public authorities' unwillingness to implement a human rights-based approach in the place of stereotypical perspectives on women. Moreover, there should be a transformation in human rights discourse to prevent subordination of socio-economic rights to civil and political rights.

Recognising socio-economic rights as full legal rights helps to improve women's empowerment. It is necessary for legal professionals and policy makers to understand and implement the transformative, holistic and gender-specific approach of the CEDAW's additional values. The CEDAW's perspective contests with gender stereotypes that violate women's human rights. Furthermore, the Istanbul Convention's progressive approach to EVAW promotes tripartite responsibilities of the states' parties to combat violence against women and domestic violence.

Notes

1 By saying "men" and "women's" duty, my intention is not to exclude same-sex relationships. Therefore, it is important to express here that "same-sex relationships end up following the heterosexual model of one partner having primary responsibility for bringing in income and the other for childcare and household work and management." Therefore, gender norms have a wider influence, which goes beyond the determination of roles of different biological sexes (Nedelsky, 2012, p. 17).
2 UN General Assembly Resolution 34/180 of 18 December 1979. Entry into force 3 September 1981.

3 V.K. v. Bulgaria, Comm. 20/2008, U.N. Doc. CEDAW/C/49/D/20/2008 (CEDAW, July 25, 2011).
4 Declaration on the Elimination of Violence against Women (DEVAW); http://www. un.org/documents/ga/res/48/a48r104.htm
5 Opuz v. Turkey, Application no. 33401/02, Council of Europe: European Court of Human Rights, 9 June 2009.

References

Barak-ErezD. (2007). *Social Rights as Women's Rights, Exploring Social Rights: Between Theory and Practice*, Barak-Erez, D., & Gross, A. (Eds.). Bloomsbury Publishing.
Barak-Erez, D., & Gross, A. (Eds.) (2007). Introduction: Do We Need Social Rights? Questions in The Era of Globalisation, Privatisation, and the Diminished Welfare State, *Exploring Social Rights: Between Theory and Practice*. Bloomsbury Publishing.
Bora, A. & Üstün, İ. (2005). *'Sıcak Aile Ortamı' Demokratikleşme Sürecinde Kadın ve Erkekler*. Istanbul: Tesev Yayınları.
CEDAW Committee General Recommendation No. 19 (1992). 11th Session, Violence Against Women. Retrieved from: https://www.un.org/womenwatch/daw/cedaw/recommendations/recomm.htm
CESCR General Comment No. 3. (1990). The Nature of States Parties' Obligations (Art. 2, Para. 1, of the Covenant), Adopted at the Fifth Session of the Committee on Economic, Social and Cultural Rights, Contained in Document E/1991/23. Retrieved from: https://tbinternet.ohchr.org/_layouts/treatybodyexternal/Download.aspx?symbolno=INT%2fCESCR%2fGEC%2f4758&Lang=cn
Charlesworth, H. & Chinkin, C. (1993). The Gender of Jus Cogens, *Human Rights Quarterly*, 15(1): 63–76.
Charlesworth, H., Chinkin, C. & Wright, S. (1191). Feminist Approaches to International Law, *The American Journal of International Law*, 85(4): 613–645.
Courtis, C. (2008). *Courts and the Enforcement of Economic Social and Cultural Rights: Comparative Experiences of Justiciability Report*, International Commission of Jurists, Geneva.
Dickinson, G. (2006). The Pleasantville Effect: Nostalgia and The Visual Framing of (white) Suburbia, *Western Journal of Communication*, 70(3): 212–233.
Ecevit, Y. (2013). For a Feminist Strategy Against Poverty, *Amargi*, 6. Retrieved from: http://www.amargidergi.com/yeni/?p=455#more-455
Edwards, A. (2010). *Violence Against Women under International Human Rights Law*. New York, USA: Cambridge University Press.
Explanatory Report to the Council of Europe Convention on Preventing and Combating Violence Against Women and Domestic Violence Council of Europe (2011). Treaty-Series, No. 210, Istanbul, 11.V.
Fawole, O. I. (2008). Economic Violence to Women and Girls: Is It Receiving The Necessary Attention? *Trauma, Violence & Abuse*, 9(3): 167–177.
Fredman, S. (2013). *Engendering Socio-Economic Rights. CEDAW in International, Regional and National Law*, Hellum, A. and Sinding Aasen, H. (Eds.), United Kingdom: Cambridge University Press, pp. 217–242.
Gómez Galisteo, M. C. (2009). Certain Things Have Become Unpleasant: Pleasantville, far from Heaven and American Society in the Fifties, *The Grove: Working Papers on English Studies*, 16: 63–85.

Hasmath, R., Hildebrandt, T. & Hsu, J. (2016). Conceptualizing Government-Organized Nongovernmental Organizations, Paper Presented at Association for Research on Nonprofit Organizations and Voluntary Action Annual Conference (Washington D.C., USA), pp. 17–19 November.

Hellum, A., & Aasen, H. S. (2013). Introduction. *CEDAW in International, Regional and National Law*, Hellum, A. and Aasen H. S., H. (Eds.), Cambridge University Press, pp 1–25.

Kymlicka, W. (2001). *Contemporary Political Philosophy: An Introduction*, Second Edition, Oxford: Oxford University Press.

Memiş, E. (2014). Ekonomik Şiddet Kapsamında Karşılıksız Emek, *Kadınların ve Kız Çocuklarının İnsan Hakları: Kadına Yönelik Şiddet ve Ev-içi Şiddet*, Kaya, F., Özdemir, N. and Uygur, G. (Eds.), Ankara: Savaş Yayınevi, pp. 167–179.

Memiş, E., & Özay, Ö. (2011). Eviçi Uğraşlardan Iktisatta Karşılıksız Emeğe: Türkiye Üzerine Yapılan Çalışmalara İlişkin Bir Değerlendirme, *Birkaç Arpa Boyu: 21. Yüzyıla Girerken Türkiye'de Feminist Çalışmalar (Prof. Dr. Nermin Abadan Unat'a armağan)*, Sancar, S. (Ed.), Cilt 1, Koç Üniversitesi Yayınları, Istanbul.

Nedelsky, J. (2012). The Gendered Division of Household Labor: An Issue of Constitutional Rights, *Feminist Constitutionalism: Global Perspectives*, Baines, B., Barak Erez, D. & Kahana, T. (Eds.), Cambridge University Press, pp. 15–48.

Otto, D. (1993). Violence Against Women: Something Other Than a Violation of Human Rights, *Australian Feminist Law Journal*, 1: 159–162.

Pitman, T. (2017). Living with Coercive Control: Trapped within A Complex Web of Double Standards, Double Binds and Boundary Violations. *The British Journal of Social Work*, 47(1): 143–161.

Pound, R. (1910). Law in Books and Law in Action, *American Law Review*, 44(12): 12–36.

Ross, G. (Director). (1998). *Pleasantville* [DVD]. USA: New Line Home Video.

Şenol-Cantek, F. (2001). "Fakir/Haneler": Yoksulluğun "Ev Hali", *Toplum ve Bilim*, 89: 102–131.

Smart, C. (2002). *Feminism and the Power of Law*. USA and Canada: Routledge. .

Stark, E. (2007). *Coercive Control: The Entrapment of Women in Personal Life (Interpersonalviolence)*. New York: Oxford University Press.

Tickle, L. (2017). Coercion and Control: Fighting Against the Abuse Hidden in Relationships. *The Guardian*. Retrieved from: https://www.theguardian.com/society/2017/may/20/coercion-and-control-fighting-against-the-abuse-hidden-in-relationships

Truchero, J. (2013). Economic Violence, a Form of Domestic Violence, *The Economic Dimensions of Violence Against Women*. Retrieved from http://assembly.coe.int/Communication/Campaign/DomesticViolence/Newdefault_EN.asp

Turkish Statistical Institute (TUIK) Report. (2008). *Kadına Yönelik Aile İçi Şiddet Istatistikleri*. Retrieved from: https://biruni.tuik.gov.tr/kadinasiddetdagitim/kadin.zul

Uygur, G. (2013). *Hukukta Adaletsizliği Görmek*. Ankara: Türkiye Felsefe Kurumu Yayınları.

World Health Organization Report. (2013). *Global and Regional Estimates of Violence Against Women: Prevalence and Health Effects of Intimate Partner Violence and Non-Partner Sexual Violence*. Retrieved from: https://www.who.int/reproductivehealth/publications/violence/9789241564625/en/

9 Women's Empowerment with Physical Activity and Sports

Gözde ERSÖZ

Introduction

Sports is an activity that has been given various meanings and served various purposes throughout time. While it was a sign of the laziness and extravagance of the upper class, with advancing technology it has become a life quality increasing event that is open to a wide section of a community. As the interest in sports grows larger, the prizes for high performances and financial gains have increased as well. As a result, more complex structures have started to be shaped within sports. Though sport is associated with its many benefits, it also includes negative sides such as doping, over loading, alienation to one's own body as a sportsman, and alienation to real life problems as a viewer, and aggressive behaviour. The high personality of the elite athletes, who had won championships and degrees, remains outdated. Nowadays, the image of a "higher morality" of professionals has been damaged by hooliganism, violence, racism, aggression and sexism, and elite sport and mass sport that is used to achieve the physical standards of today's society even though it neglects health ideas stand out (Fişek, 2003).

The negativity in sports is generally overlooked due to the popularity of sports; however, these drawbacks peak when it comes to women in sports. It is known that physical activity and participation in sports helps physical, cognitive and psycho-social developments in people. Nonetheless, some women try hard to participate "correctly" in sports, and to be "actively" involved in them. In this context, the differences between women and men in sports are also sexist, hierarchical divisions of labor. It is shocking that sport, said to be universal and examined as a scientific discipline, was and is under the influence of hierarchical sexist beliefs and tendencies (Yaprak & Amman, 2009).

Throughout history, in every society, women and men have lived by the socially constructed norms that are based on biological factors. Gender roles have created a hierarchical structure that is beyond natural differences, and this hierarchical structure suggested that women should be controlled by men as they are "inferior" (Koca, 2011). According to Theberge (1993), the fact that physical power is an essential factor in performances caused the gender roles to be visible in sports. This situation carries messages about being manly and womanly, especially in competitive sports where performance stands out, and causes sports to be seen as a manly activity that require manly gender roles. That sport is seen as a manly activity as it is associated with the athletic structure of man is a result of an understanding that accepts man as the standard norm. The patriarchal society structure that assigns men and women different roles and participation of women and men in sports and their experiences are closely related. When historically examined, it is observed that women athletes are not tolerated that much.

Historical Development of Women and Sports in the World

The sporting activities that women do have differed in every culture from Ancient Greece to Europe until the 19th century. Women were granted opportunities in sports as seen in wall paintings in Ancient Egypt where there are female figures playing ball and doing acrobatic moves and in musical-aesthetic components that are visible in the body culture of Ancient Greece starting from 1600 BC (Bandy, 2000). In the Ancient Era, on the other hand, women were not allowed in Olympic games for the first 500 years, and they were only given opportunity to do sports in the Hera games which consisted only of women (Pfister, 2000). Unlike Greek societies, in Sparta, women were given sporting education so as to give birth and raise healthy and strong children due to military needs.

In Ancient Rome the image of women changed with the Etruscans; women took care of their bodies, and took part in sporting events and gymnastics from a very young age, becoming more visible in Hellenistic Rome starting from around 200 BC. A woman is known to have won horse chariot races in the Olympics in 84 BC. In the Medieval Era there were no activities aimed at women's physical development due to intense religious beliefs. Women participated in folk festivals either as a viewer or a participant during the Renaissance and the Reformation periods. With America's declaration of independence in the 18th century, women's sports developed in a short period of time (Bandy, 2000). However, in Europe, women were hardly involved in sports even in the 19th century. In 1896, women were not allowed to participate as athletes in the Modern Olympic Games which were started by Pierre de Coubertin. With some women's movements led by female athletes, women achieved the opportunity to attend the Olympics in 1900 in Paris though Coubertin suggested that "sports is against women's nature". The leader of the women's right to participate in sports movement, Frenchwoman Alice Milliat, led institutional and organizational efforts in the first quarter of the 20th century to gain an increase in women's participation in sports and women's branches of sports in every culture until today (Memiş & Yıldıran, 2011).

The Historical Development of Women and Sports in Turkey

In periods of societal change, social, cultural and economic signs change too. When looking into Turkey's history, there were three main periods of societal changes: Before Islam, After Islam (Ottoman Period), and the Turkish

Republic. In these periods when societal changes occured, the place of women in society also changed and their sporting activities changed as well (Atalay, 2007).

There are several documents that prove that among ancient Turks, women were involved in sports starting from the first ages before Islam compared to Ancient Greek and Europe. For example, Hittite embossments show that women were involved in athleticism (Hiçyılmaz, 1995). Yıldız (2002), citing Soy-Wer the ancient Chinese writer, points out that in Central Asia there were sports festivals and women and men shot arrows and played ball games together, including one called "Tepuk" in old Turkish and known as football today. It is also known that in Gokturks, women and men rode horses, shot arrows, wrestled together and competed with each other. Grave paintings found in Qurciola, Corneto also show women and men doing sports together. The Dada Gorgud epic also supports this information. In *Divan-i Lugat-it Turk* by Kashgarli Mahmud, there are some sayings pointing out how strong Turkish girls are and how well they wrestle (Yıldız, 2002). Turkish women and men doing sports together and participating in competitions continued in public until the rising period of the Ottoman Empire. Among ancient Turks men and women also practised a sport where equestrian skills were essential (Memiş & Yıldıran, 2011).

Turkish society adopted Islam in the 8th century, and since then, under the influence of Islam, the social status of women has changed drastically in a negative direction (Atalay, 2007). The theocratic structure of the Ottoman Empire brought restrictions to the social order of women. According to Guven (2001), before Islam there was absolute equality between men and women in Turkey however, with Islam, the Arabic culture's effect and migration, the social order where women were modern was turned into a traditional conservative ideology where women were assigned the roles of a mother and a wife, and these identities have been actualized in women's bodies. Plain and unpretentious dresses and being stuck between the child and the husband have determined the place of women in Islam. With the Tanzimat Reform Era and II. Constitutional Era in Ottoman Empire, women's freedom of movement was started in 1913 and physical education was granted to girls in Girls High Schools (Atalay, 2007).

With the Turkish Republic reforms, Mustafa Kemal Ataturk emphasized that the greatest aim in the modernization process was equality between men and women and he tried to include women in many institutions (Atalay, 2007). Within the first years of the Turkish Republic, women's social status was increased and sports were a part of this attempt. In 1926, women started to take part in athleticism and they managed to participate in the 1928 Olympic Games. In rowing, women started to appear starting in 1927. In those years, women also participated in tennis and swimming disciplines (Atabeyoğlu, 1981). In the same years, due to a loophole in regulations, a female athlete trained with males in Fenerbahçe Men's Volleyball Team and became a champion with this team. Women wrestling along with men also started to appear in this period. In 1935, in order to promote sports in the life of women, radio was used (Yıldız, 2002). Gymnastic moves were broadcast and women were asked to repeat the exercises from the radio. In the 1936 Berlin Olympics, Turkish women were participants for the first time (Atabeyoğlu, 1981). With the incentives of Mustafa Kemal Ataturk, to train physical education teachers, a female PE teacher was brought from Switzerland and Turkish women who were successful in this trainee program were sent to Europe to advance themselves (Yıldız, 2002).

Despite all the initiatives of Mustafa Kemal Ataturk, an understanding that sees women and men as equals could not be developed in Turkey. Even Selim Sirri Tarcan, an intellectual who is known for his contributions to sports in Turkey during the establishment of the Turkish Republic, emphasized that while men should always be ready to hold a gun or come to close quarters with a strong and muscular body, women should only have strong stomach and thighs as their sole and foremost aim is to be mothers (Bora, 2012).

Gender and Sports

Whereas people's biological, physiological and genetic sexes are defined either as man or woman (Bayhan, 2013), gender is a concept that is socially constructed to divide two sexes with the roles assigned to them and it projects the cultural perspectives in women's or men's behavior (Ecevit, 2011). One of the areas where gender norms are most strict and meticulous is sport (Talimciler, 2015). Most individuals choose sports appropriate to their gender, and it is common that interests and abilities are overlooked or are considered secondary; in other words, men and women choose manly or womanly sports (Koivula, 1995).

Gender norms in sports were first defined by Metheny (1965) who classified acceptable and unacceptable sports branches into three categories; sports branches that are not appropriate for women, sports branches that are partially appropriate for women and sports branches that are appropriate for women (Riemer & Visio, 2003). In this classification competitive sports that require physical contact, boxing, barbell, pole jumping, long distance races and team sports other than volleyball are listed as inappropriate for women. Mild degree sports such as short distance races, long jump, shot put, javelin throwing and gymnastics are listed as partially appropriate. On the other hand, sports that make the body look aesthetic and sports where there are obstacles between competitors or tools that are designed to help a certain movement be carried out or mildly applying force or where there are physical obstacles during competition such as artistic ice skating, skiing, golf and tennis, bowling, volleyball, swimming or diving are listed as completely appropriate for women. In society, while men are directed to sports branches that require firmness, durability and stability, such as boxing, wrestling, karate or football, women are directed to branches that require aestheticism and grace. Whenever any gender chooses to continue with a branch that is seen as inappropriate for their gender, they are outcast (Sancar, 2013). Women athletes who take part in sports considered outside their gender norms are labeled as "manly" or "lesbian" and are exposed to negative comments from society (Kavasoğlu & Yaşar, 2016).

Research in gender context has shown that there is a relation between participation in sports and manly or womanly attributes (Chalabaev et al., 2013; Koca et al., 2005; Emir et al., 2015). In these studies, gender roles are divided into three categories of womanly, manly and neutral; and these categories are found to be essential determinants in sports and physical activity preference of any gender. In the study conducted by Koca and Demirhan (2005) in Turkey, gymnastics, pilates, step-aerobic, volleyball, swimming, ice-skating, tennis and hiking are listed as appropriate for women; and football, basketball, boxing, wrestling and barbell are listed as appropriate for men. Gender ideas, which have a long history, have differentiated the rates of women as judges in sports, being participants in sports or having a vocation related to sports while influencing the way men and women see sportive practices.

Women in Sports Administration in Turkey

Restricting women from some vocations or naming some vocations as inappropriate for women within the scope of gender roles given by society is discrimination based on gender. Also treating women more poorly than men only because of their gender is discrimination towards women. These forms of discrimination are seen as an important issue in today's organizations and actions to block this sexist discrimination which is a huge obstacle for women are being carried out (Kara & Yıldıran, 2011). In sports, the basis for gender equality is the ability to benefit from opportunities offered to men and women equally. In Turkey, there are only a limited number of studies that look at the place of women in sports administration. A study of the attitudes of employees towards women administrators in the General Directorate of Sport (GDS) by Arslan (2007) revealed that male employees do not support the advancement of women in their careers and they do not have a positive attitude towards women administrators. In the same study, Arslan (2007) stated that the reason why women are not judges or in decision making mechanisms in sports is that "women are not supported enough" and "women have responsibilities towards their families". Aycan (2004), who suggests that women are rarely offered administration positions in Turkey, explained the reasons for this with individual and environmental factors. Aycan (2004) emphasized that self-reliance, motivation for success, determinism and focusing on career are effective as individual factors, and highlighted the importance of family support, as women have trouble entering social and societal networks in patriarchal communities, as environmental factors.

The issue of whether people can benefit from sports opportunities equally can be measured with the equal representation of men and women in decision-making mechanisms. In this context, the representation of women in decision-making mechanisms is essential for equality in sports (Koca, 2011). Two of the decision-making mechanisms of sports in Turkey are the GDS under The Ministry of Youth and Sports and the Sports Federations. The Ministry of Youth and Sports located in Ankara, the capital of Turkey, regulates sports centrally in coordination with Provincial Directorates. There are also Federations for 63 branches of sports. Sports Federations, and even though they were made independent in 2004, they are not entirely autonomous in decision-making and have to rely for financial assistance on the government. Another institution that has a say in sports administration in Turkey is the Turkish Olympic Committee (TOC) which is a non-governmental, non-profit organization working for the good of society with voluntary employees. The most extensive study that explains the representation of women in the above-mentioned sports organizations in Turkey with numerical data was conducted by Koca (2011) and this study displayed the number of women in sports organizations in Turkey. The following tables illustrate numerical data regarding men and women working at GDS, Federations and TOC.

The GDS consist of two units, one of which is the center located in Ankara, and the other unit formed by the provincial offices of 81 cities in Turkey. In Table 9.1, the distribution of the employees working in the GDS in the central and provincial centers is shown. It is classified according to gender. The percentage of female workers (9.0%) employed in provincial organizations has been found to be lower than the number of female employees (31.6%).

The distribution of GDS management levels according to gender shows that there are no women in the positions of general manager ot assistant general manager. Only one of the 18 branch managers in the GDS central organization is held by a woman. The provincial directorates of the GDS provincial organizations in 81 provinces outside the center are all male. When the total number is studied, it is found out that only 1% of the GDS management levels are occupied by women (Table 9.2).

Women constitute 3.3% of the presidents of the federations and 4% of the vice presidents, who are considered to be the senior management positions of the sporting federations. It is seen that 11.7% of those who have performed the general secretary role having a middle level management positions are female and 88.3% are male; 5.4% of the total board members are women. In all, 5.5% of upper and mid-level managerial positions of sport federations are held by women.

The total number of employees in the Turkish Olympic Committee (TOC) which has a say in the management of sports in Turkey as a voluntary foundation is 52, 7.7% of which is formed by women and 92.3% by men. All TOC senior executives are male. 11.8% of TOC's mid-level management positions are women.

As a result, when the total number of employees working in all three institutions (5,971) is analyzed by gender, it is seen that the women constitute 14% (833) of the total number of employees while men constitute 86% (5,138).

Table 9.1 Gender distribution of employees working in central and provincial organizations in GDS

Organization Type	Female		Male		Total	
	n	%	n	%	n	%
Central Organization	239	31.6	517	68.4	756	100
Provincial Organization	417	9.0	4211	91.0	4628	100
Total	656	12.2	4728	87.8	5384	100

Table 9.2 Gender distribution at management level in GDS

Line Management	Female		Male		Total	
	n	%	n	%	n	%
General Director	-	-	1	100	1	100
Assistant General Manager	-	-	4	100	4	100
Departmental Manager	1	5,6	17	94.4	18	100
Provincial Director	-	-	81	100	81	100
Total	1	1.0	103	1.0	104	100

Table 9.3 Gender distribution at management level in sports federations

Line Management	Female		Male		Total	
	n	%	n	%	n	%
President	2	3.3	58	96.7	60	100
Vice President	6	4.0	145	96.0	151	100
Secretary-General	7	11.7	53	88.3	60	100
Executive Board Members	38	5.4	662	94.6	700	100
Total	53	5.5	917	94.5	970	100

Table 9.4 Gender distribution at management level in TOC

Line Management	Female		Male		Total	
	n	%	n	%	n	%
President			1	100	1	100
Vice President			2	100	2	100
Secretary-General	1	100			1	100
Executive Board Members	1	9.1	10	90.9	11	100
Total	2	11.8	13	88.2	15	100

There are eight women (3.7%) in total senior management positions of all three institutions and 48 women (5.5%) in total middle management positions. Of the total management levels (1,090), 94.9% are men and 5.1% are women (Koca, 2011). It is especially important to regulate gender equality in sports organizations. Sports organizations are organizations that aim to direct people to both professional and recreational sports, control policies and mainstream sports in the society. That organizations that control policies and implement those policies have gender equality within them is closely related to equal participation of men and women in every branch of sports.

Women Athlete and Trainer Rates in Turkey

According to Koca (2006a), women participate more and more in sporting activities every year; however, women also quit more and more in sporting activities every year. Amman (2006) suggests that with economic development, the life style and the upbringing of women who come from rural areas that are led by traditions, women who live in small villages, women living in suburbs and women living in cities all differ greatly and this difference is reflected in sports as well.

When the athlete numbers published on the GDS's website are examined, it is seen that women athlete numbers increased the most in 2016 (44%) and reached their lowest level in 2008. When the latest athlete numbers in 2017 are examined, it is seen that the sports branches that have the highest numbers of athletes in order are as follows: chess (815,078), taekwondo (406,185), volleyball (271,316), athleticism (214,550), basketball (213,500), kick box (202,427) and karate (201,258). The sports branches where women athletes outnumber men athletes are as follows: volleyball (61.39%), folklore (59.37%), gymnastics (62.39%), and dance sports (59.64%). The sports branches where women athletes are the least are as follows: automobile sports (601), amputee sports (1,060), visually impaired sports (1,214), triathlon (1,439), rowing (1,474) and motorcycling (1,582) (http://sgm.gsb.gov.tr/Sayfalar/175/105/İstatistikler Date accessed: 11.11.2018).

Some differences rooted in Turkey's culture are also visible in women's participation in sports for that country. In a study by Fasting and Pfister (1999) that examines the participation of women in Turkey, factors such as social status and place of residence, family relations, the importance of school success, the idea that sports is a manly activity, the harsh working conditions, the importance of family, that women do not perceive sports to be fun, the perception of body and beauty and coverage affect the participation of women in sports negatively.

Though Muslim men and women in Turkey do not think that their religion hinders them from participating in sports (Fasting and Pfister, 1999), religious factors play a great role in Islamic countries concerning participation especially of women and their lack of representation in sports organizations (Grant, 2007). The restrictions religion imposes on men and women especially

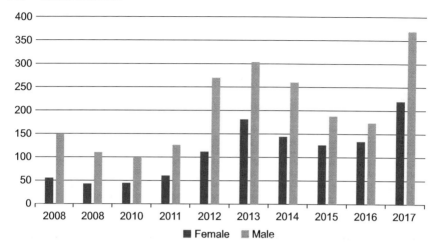

Figure 9.1 The number of female and male athletes by year
Source: own illustration

Table 9.5 The number of female and male athletes by year

Years	Female	%	Male	%
2008	54671	26	151790	74
2009	42315	28	109682	72
2010	43419	30	99988	70
2011	60535	32	125925	68
2012	111293	29	268650	71
2013	182561	38	304053	62
2014	142924	36	258627	64
2015	126623	40	188365	60
2016	134284	44	173004	56
2017	218629	37	368606	63

in clothing are among the greatest obstacles that stand in the way of participation in sports. At this point, it should be emphasized that even though every individual is a Muslin, not everyone necessarily has the same degree of religious sensitivity. Therefore, it is possible for different ideas and attitudes towards sporting activities and/or the concept of sports. However, building the sports facilities in a manner that both genders can easily use or arranging programs accordingly may increase the participation of women in sports (Yüksel, 2014).

When the number of trainers are examined according to the distribution of sports branches and genders, it is seen that 82% of all trainers are men (70,479) while 18% of them are women. When women trainers are examined closely, the branches they are most prominent in are as follows: swimming

(12.8%), basketball (11%), volleyball (10.2%) and step-aerobic (9.8%). When the gender distribution within the sports branches is examined, the branches where women trainers outnumber men trainers are as follows: step-aerobics (79.5%), softball (66.7%), fencing (58.7%) and artistic ice-skating (55.2%) (Koca, 2011).

In a study conducted with students that study in departments related to sports, Yaprak and Amman (2006) found that women have the idea that "women trainers have to be more manly in order to find jobs". This idea signals that in Turkey, sport is still seen as a manly activity. In a study conducted with 80 volleyball players and volleyball trainers 48% of whom are male while 51% are female, Şallı et. al. (2006) showed that in occupations such as trainers, lawyers and doctors, the first gender that comes to mind is male by 84%. In another study where basketball referee's profiles were looked into in 2006, it was found that while there are only 90 female referees, there are 371 male referees (Ekmekçi, 2006).

The Reasons for and Obstacles to Women Participating in Physical Activities and Exercises

In societal and cultural areas where womanhood and manhood are determined, one of the areas where women can resist their secondary position in society is leisure time activities (Bulgu et al., 2007). Childcare, housework etc. the kind of traditional roles brought by the patriarchal system are huge obstacles to women's participation in leisure time activities (Green et al., 1990). According to studies, the secondary and unequal position of women in society also exists in sports, physical activities and exercise environments where women have lower rates of participation. That housework limits the time of women and puts them in an unequal position in their daily lives is proven in the studies (Kelly, 1995; Rapoport & Rapoport, 1995). In a study examining the exercising habits of women, the reasons why they participate in exercises and what obstacles they face, Şahin et al. (2014) found that 52.4% of women exercise for their physical appearance at the ages of 20–29; they exercise for health at the ages of 30–19 (66.6%) and at the ages of 40–49 (56%); and women mainly choose walking or step-aerobics. Out of 517 women participating in the study, 15.6% were physically active, 81.7% were inactive and 2.5% had quit exercising. This study and some other studies in Turkey have found that exercise habits increase with age (Koçak & Özkan 2010; Şahin et. al., 2014). The studies conducted among university students mainly proves that youth is physically inactive (Savcı et al., 2006).

In Turkey's general population, according to data from the Turkish Ministry of Health, only 3.5% of all the population do regular exercises (Turkish Ministry of Health, 2004). Studies, though, show that physical activity and exercises have an important place in women's lives and these activities help women both physically and psychologically. Henderson et al. (1989) stated that participation in leisure time activities can help a woman's development of identity and help her with the problems occurring in daily life (Wearing,

1998). In this context, Henderson sees leisure time activities as a way of expressing oneself and having a certain freedom; and thinks that they are a tool to free women from the gender roles that restrict them and a maturation process in their own lives. Other studies conducted on the same topic show that physical activity, exercises and leisure time activities help women to raise their awareness of their own body, feel better and more energetic, gain self-confidence, create time for themselves, express themselves and socialize (Bulgu et al., 2007; Hacisoftaoğlu & Bulgu, 2012). According to Markula (1995), physical activity, exercise and fitness are not only tools to strengthen and achieve freedom, they also offer an action towards the ideal body and reproduce the articulation of gender roles. At this point, the quality of the exercise environment is one of the determinants (Elmas et al., 2016).

A recent study (Yılmaz & Mehmet, 2016) examines the reasons women in Turkey participate in physical activities; these are to be healthy, to have a fit body, to gain relief from stress, to be happy and to have fun, to make friends and have the experience of being in a group. The obstacles, on the other hand, are categorized into two areas, one physical and another environmental. Among the physical obstacles there short and insufficient walking areas, insufficient sports equipment, lack of knowledge of how to use machines, closeness to traffic and work places; environmental obstacles include curious eyes and closeness to male only coffee houses. In another study conducted among working women about their physical activity and leisure time, Bulgu et. al. (2007) found that women's housework limits their leisure time and places them in an unequal position in their daily lives. In some societies, as in Turkish society, cultural conditions are the biggest obstacle to participation in physical activity, as emphasized by Babakus and Thompson in 2012. Their study found that especially North Asian women living in families cannot find time to participate in physical activities as they have more house work.

Elmas et al., (2016) whose study examined women's physical activity experiences from the perspective of gender and socio-ecological models stated that women experience trouble participating in physical activities due to issues such as mixed exercise groups where men are also included compared to all-women exercise groups. Women felt that being in mixed groups together with men brings along power relations based on gender from the patriarchal society, too (for example, being observed by the men) (Collins, 2002; Markula, 1995; Brudzynski & Ebben, 2010). Therefore, it is understood that women tend to participate in all-women's physical activity groups to be able to move better and more freely, feel better, have fun, relax and socialize (Bulgu et al., 2007; Hacisoftaoğlu & Bulgu, 2012).

Gender Roles in Turkish Folklore

Turkish culture is rich in terms of folklore diversity. Folklore types differ in regions in Turkey. In folklore, role models are traditionally based on the people living in the area they are performed in, and when performances are watched, it is possible to perceive the gender roles especially of women in traditional costume. When these dances are examined from gender perspectives, a patriarchal dance culture is seen (Ötken, 2011). Demirsipahi (2006) expresses his dissatisfaction with the patriarchal tendency in our folklore as follows: "There are many things wrong with our folklore which could not display itself due to reactions. But the most important thing is that it is deprived of women's grace and aesthetic and it is exposed to men's clumsiness and roughness." Also pointing out that women are not involved in traditional folklore due to regressive societal understanding, Demirsipahi suggests that "köçeklik" (a man wearing woman's clothes and dancing with woman's steps) in Turkish culture was created due to lack of women in that area (Ötken, 2010).

In traditional folklore, it was not possible for a woman and a man to dance together because of societal, cultural values and religious beliefs. Starting from 1950s, women and men appeared together in folklore. First, they were on the same stage but the dances were separated as women's dances and men's dances. Later on, they started dancing together in mutual dances. In this period, the image of a passive woman was kept during the first stages. In 1990, though, folklore was started to be seen as a performing art and the image of a passive woman started to change. In this period, the number of women dancers increased, women came into prominence in folklore and especially in solo dances, and they started to appear more on the stage. And so the 1960s when there were hardly any women dancers gave way to the 1990s when women and men were dancing together (Ötken, 2010).

In the 2000s, woman's image on the stage again changed. With the advent of professional folk dances based on beauty and grace, the beauty of women's body started to be displayed and dances that project the strength within the women's body began to be chosen. According to Illich (1996), women use manly figures more than men use womanly steps when dancing. This is because women wish to get rid of the secondary position that is assigned to them both behind the scenes and in daily life. In the staging of folk dances jobs such as choreographers, art directors, design and stage technicians are mostly occupied by men. In groups of professional folk dancers such as Sultans of the Dance and the Shaman Dance Theater, founded in the early 2000s, the woman's body was emphasized on the stage, and women were firstly assessed by their bodies instead of their dance performance (Ötken, 2010).

Even though the passiveness of women was eschewed in folk dances in Turkey, it is still valid in the natural environments where folk dances are performed. As well as the passiveness or activeness of women in folk dances, women standing out with their sexuality in modern folk dance groups is another issue that should be examined from a gender perspective.

Gender Relations in PE Courses

Gender is also considered by researchers in the field of education so as to see the societal inequality that exists in schools. Physical Education (PE) courses in schools are seen as one of the areas where gender ideologies are most prominent. They are one of the environments in which inequality between men and women is most visible when considering biological differences. As standards of success in sports are mainly set by the male students, female students are seen as less able, less strong and less competitive (Koca, 2006a).

Ennis (1999) considers that no other programs in the PE field are as effective as mixed and multiple-activity sports classes in the alienation and restriction of female students, and some researchers suggest that traditional sports-based PE programs should be reformed because of this reason (Gorely et al., 2003). In a recent study, Koca (2006a) found that the number of students that prefer separate PE classes is more than the number of students that prefer mixed PE classes, yet, there are individual differences between those who prefer separate or mixed classes. Therefore, recent studies suggest using a strong theoretical frame that includes race/societal, class/societal, relation between gender and ability in order to demonstrate the complex structure of the relation of gender in physical activities in PE classes (Wright, 1999; Azzarito & Solmon, 2005). Koca and Demirhan (2006) conducted research on this issue and examined how gender roles are reproduced in PE and sports as a societal area by looking three elementary schools taken to represent different social classes. Studies in PE in Turkey demonstrate that PE classes and sporting activities play an important role in the making of manhood while female students and male students that do not conform to hegemonic manhood norms try to exist as silent, invisible bodies (Koca, 2006b; Koca, 2004).

Women in Turkish Sports Media within the Scope of Gender

The representation of womanhood and a woman's body in the media has a great effect on gender roles in sports. Much research in sociology, psychology and sports emphasizes that it is essential for women and men to coexist equally in issues related to sports. While the visuals and representations in the media affect the participation rates in sports and the spreading of sports branches, what the media does not say also affects the preferences of individuals (Koca & Bulgu, 2005). Two topics stand out in media and sports interaction: one is the fact that less news is broadcast about female athletes; and the other one is the fact that when female athletes are reported on, rather than their sporting success, their womanly features are mentioned.

The situation in Turkey of less news reporting on women's sports when compared to men's sports is similar to that of sports media around the world (Özsoy, 2008). In a study focusing on the situation in Turkey, Arslan and Koca (2006) examined 2,103 pieces of sports news in popular newspapers in August 2004 and found that 79.98% of all news was about male athletes and only 8.56% about female athletes. News about female basketball players was analyzed by Kırılmaz (2015) who found that male basketball players were covered more in the news than female basketball players; and news articles about females were not illustrated with photographs while those concerning males were. The reason why female sports news is less in the media and gender norms are mentioned in sports news about females might be because the media is controlled by males, that there are not enough female employees in media institutions and the few women who do work there are in lower positions where responsibility and participation in decisions is less (Arslan & Koca, 2006). This situation is also mentioned by Özsoy (2008) in the analysis of sports and media. It is shown in a study on the quality of sports media employees in Turkey that active sports reporters are 96% males. The Turkey Sports Writers Association, which is the greatest non-governmental organization of sports reporters in Turkey, has 980 members all over Turkey (as of July 2009). Only nine of those members were women. In 2007, all over Turkey, 25 women worked in sports media; seven of them are reporters in written media, five of them are writers, one is an administrator and 12 of them are reporters in television. There are also five female sports reporters that work as photo-reporters (Özsoy, 2008).

According to feminist approaches, mass media is an important tool in the creation of manhood and womanhood descriptions that are based on patriarchal values (Koca & Bulgu, 2005). In the book *Feminism and Sporting Bodies* by Ann Hall (1996), it is said that the most effective and the most visible tool that helps the creation of gender norms in sports is the media, and that the true function of media is to normalize and naturalize the differences between female and male athletes.

Many incidents that prove such connotations have occurred in Turkish newspapers and television broadcasts. In a study by Arslan and Koca (2006), it is stated that in 20% of sports news about women athletes statements about gender norms (generally heterosexuality) exist clearly. In the Turkish sports media it is also seen that female volleyball players are defined by their physical features. "If Fenerbahçe passes the tour, I will wear a bikini on the show", a comment by a former referee and a football commentator, reflects the patriarchy ruling over football and the prejudice against women. In Turkey, football is a "boys club" and any utterance, sign or implication associated with womanhood is seen as humiliating by men. This sexist view is very common and effective in the football world today. In the Turkish sports media where the woman is seen solely as a "body", it is obvious that women are placed to be "passive images". In a popular football commentary program, three male football commentators discussed the games to be played that week, while the female presenter in the program was only following the comments and talking only when she was given the opportunity to speak. The presenter, who was placed where the camera could get the best view of her, could be present "physically" in a program that was mostly watched by men. In another football commentary program with a famous football player and a female football commentator, the player said to the commentator: "I will not discuss football with you. Football is a man's game... " (Akkaya & Kaplan, 2014).

According to radical feminists; any kind of interaction in daily life such as non-verbal communication, the ways to listen to someone, not giving an opportunity to speak, cause women to feel uncomfortable in public and contribute to societal gender inequality. According to radical feminists, commonly accepted ideas regarding beauty and sexuality are imposed on women by men to create a certain type of "femininity". This situation is also stated in many studies conducted abroad. Female identities referred to in the media completely overlap with a sexuality defined by patriarchal statements. These statements cause women to be passive and easily ruleable while turning them into sexual objects. Therefore, women receive "ideal" women ideas that are demanded of them while watching their fellow women and they are given the message to be an "ideal" woman (Saktanber, 1990).

Conclusion

Before modernism, people needed sport in order to run to survive, practice to jump better, wrestle and punch to defend themselves, then with the advance of technology, to shoot arrows and use swords and guns, to ride horses and row for transportation. Mankind used sport to prepare for battle and also as a tool to maintain peace, for instance as in Ancient Greece. The policies of societies have influenced sport and sport has influenced the policies of societies, mutually throughout history. Sport has been an important training method over time, as well as an indicator of dignity. It is seen that sport, that is affected by the societal structure, has a patriarchal structure and has existed under the influence of men from the earliest ages until today. While transforming from the most basic movement of humans to a structure with rules, how can sport influenced by men be explained by the existence of gender roles.

Inequality between men and women has naturally been observed in Turkey, as well as in every society throughout history. Societal behavioral patterns that differ with the values and traditions of that society construct the societal gender norms in that area. Turkey has a cooperative structure and is a country where family relations are strong under the influence of Islam. Although the country is affected by some transformations such as secularization and individualization in line with relations with the West, it does not contain these features. The inequality between men and women is changing in a positive direction due to several factors as a result of the interaction between Turkey and the West. In addition, relations with the West are getting more intense every day. With this interaction, it can be observed that attitudes and behaviors regarding societal gender roles have changed and softened, even in the most conservative areas. As not all individuals are affected by these changes equally, gender differentiation has become problematic. Furthermore, religion has influence in matters related to gender and policies of the political system support the solidarist structure and put pressures onto differences. Therefore, deviations from the behavior of the general public can cause conflicts.

There is a right-ethical concept in the world for the development of policies on sports and physical activities. In its International Condition for Physical Training and Sports, the United Nations Education, Science and Culture Organization (UNESCO) has defined the right to physical activity and sports as follows: "Everybody should be free in developing his physical, intellectual and ethical powers and access to physical training and sports should be ensured for all people" (UNESCO, 1978). "The Millennium Targets" published by the United Nations also emphasized remedying social inequalities in sport, which is a social right, and increasing the access of women and female children to sports (International Year of Sport and Physical Education, 2005). Today in Turkey significant developments are observed in women's participation in sports even though it is still not close to the level of men. It is observed that the consciousness of women on physical activity and participation in sports has started to change. Women started to compete against men, and be visible in sports that were once controlled solely by men. In Turkey, it is now possible to see women in many sports branches that were only available for men. Consciousness on the subject increases day by day along with the increasing number of studies on societal gender and sports.

References

Akkaya, C. & Kaplan, Y. (2014). Women in Sports Media in the Context of Gender. *International Journal of Science Culture and Sport*, 2(Special Issue 2), 177–182.

Amman, M.T. (2006). *Social Dynamics of Mass Sports*. Istanbul: Çamlica Yayinlari.

Arslan, B. (2007). Determination of the Attitudes and Gender Role Trends towards Women's Work Roles in General Directorate of Sport, (Bachelor Project), Başkent University.

Arslan, B. & Koca, C. (2006). An Examination of Female-related Articles in Daily Newspapers with Gender Perspective. The 9th International Sports Sciences Congress, 3–5 November, Muğla, Turkey.

Atabeyoğlu, C. (1981). *Ataturk and Sport*. Hisarbank Kultur Yayinlari.

Atalay, A. (2007). Westernization Movements in Sports during the Ottoman Empire and Early Republican Turkey. *Spor Yönetimi ve Bilgi Teknolojileri*, 2(2), 24–29.

Aycan, Z. (2004). Key Success Factors for Women in Management in Turkey. *Applied Psychology: An International Review*, 53(3), 453–477.

Azzarito, L. & Solmon, M.A. (2005). A Reconceptualization of Physical Education: The Intersection of Race, Gender, and Social Class. *Sport, Education and Society*, 10, 25–47.

Babakus, W.S. & Thompson, J.L. (2012). Physical Activity among South Asian Women: A Systematic, Mixed – Methods Review. *International Journal of Behavioral Nutrition and Physical Activity*, 9(1):150.

Bandy, S.J. (2000). Women & Sport from Antiquity to the 19th Century. *Olympic Review*, 31 (Feb./March), 18–22.

Bayhan, V. (2013). Body Sociology and Gender Role. *Doğu-Bati*, 16(63), 147–164.

Bora, A. (2012). Sport and Women as a National Duty. *Hacettepe Journal of Sport Sciences*, 23(4), 220–226.

Brudzynski, L.R. & Ebben, W. (2010). Body Image as a Motivator and Barrier to Exercise Participation. *International Journal of Exercise Science*, 3(1), 14–24.

Bulgu, N., Koca-Aritan, C. & Aşçi, F.H. (2007). Daily Life, Women and Physical Activity. *Hacettepe Journal of Sport Sciences*, 18(4), 167–181.

Chalabaev, A., Sarrazin, P., Fontayne, P., Boiché, J. & Clément-Guillotin, C. (2013). The Influence of Sex Stereotypes and Gender Roles on Participation and Performance in Sport and Exercise: Review and Future Directions. *Psychology of Sport and Exercise*, 14, 136–144.

Collins, H.L. (2002). Working Out the Contradictions: Feminism and Aerobics. *Journal of Sport and Social Issues*, 26(1), 85–109.

Demirsipahi, C. (2006). Conventionalism and the Art of Game. *Folklor Edebiyat*, S. 45, Ankara.

Ecevit, Y. (2011). The Beginning of the Sociology of Gender. In Y. Ecevit & N. Karkiner (Eds.). *Within the Sociology of Social Gender*, pp. 2–30. Eskişehir: Anadolu University.

Ekmekçi, R. (2006). Turkiye'deki Basketbol Hakemlerinin Genel Profili. 9. Uluslararasi Spor Bilimleri Kongresi, Muğla.

Elmas, S., Hacisoftaoğlu, I. & Aşçi, F. H. (2016). Kadinlara Özgu Mekânlarda Egzersiz Yapmak: Sosyal-Ekolojik Model. *Turkiye Klinikleri Journal of Sports Sciences*, 8(2), 76–86.

Ennis, C.D. (1999). Creating a Culturally Relevant Curriculum for Physically Disengaged Girls. *Sport, Education and Society*, 4, 31–49.

Emir, E., Karaçam, M.Ş. & Koca, C. (2015). Kadin Boksörler: Boks Ringinde ve Ringin Dişinda Surekli Eldiven Giymek. *Hacettepe Journal of Sport Sciences*, 26(4), 136–153.

Fasting, K. & Pfister, G. (1999). *Opportunities and Barriers for Women in Sport: Turkey*. Las Vegas: Women of Diversity Productions Inc.

Fişek, K. (2003). Sport Management in World and Turkey with the Perspective of Goverment Policy and Social Structure. *YGS Yayinlari*, 1. Istanbul: Basim.

Gorely, T., Holroyd, R. & Kirk, D. (2003). Muscularity, the Habitus and the Social Construction of Gender: Towards A Gender-relevant Physical Education. *British Journal of Sociology of Education*, 24(4), 429–448.

Grant, J. (2007). *Sport, Culture and Society: An Introduction*. London: Routledge.

Green, E., Hebron, S. & Woodward, D. (1990). *Women's Leisure, What Leisure?* London: McMillan.

Guven, I. (2001). Development of Women's Education from Tanzimat Period to Republication Period in Turkey. *Ankara University Journal of Education Science*, 34 (1), 61–70.

Hacısoftaoğlu, I. & Bulgu, N. (2012). Women and Exercise: Contradictory Meanings of Aerobic Exercise. *Hacettepe Journal of Sport Sciences*, 23(4), 177–194.

Hall, M. A. (1996). *Feminism and Sporting Bodies: Essays on Theory and Practice*. Human Kinetics Publishers.

Henderson, K.A., Bialeschki, M.D., Shaw, S.M. & Freysinger, V.J. (1989). *A Leisure of One's Own: A Feminist Perspective on Women's Leisure*. Venture Publishing Inc.

Hiçyılmaz, E. (1995). *Sport in Turkey*. Istanbul: Yeni Yuzyil Kitapliği.

Illich, I. (1996). *Gender*, Çev. A. Fethi, Ankara: Ayraç Yayinlari, pp. 165–175.

International Year of Sport and Physical Education (2005). *A Year of Sports*. Retrieved from: http://www. un.org/sport2005/a_year/mill_goals.html.

Kara, F.M. & Yıldıran, I. (2011). Perception of the "Other": Gender Biases and Discriminationin Sports Sector Perceived by the Women. *Gazi Journal of Physical Education and Sport Science*, 16(1), 3–13.

Kavasoğlu, I. & Yaşar, M. (2016). The Athletes beyond Gender Norms. *Hacettepe Journal of Sport Sciences*, 27(3), 118–132.

Kelly, J. (1995). *Leisure and the Family*. C. Critcher, P. Bramham, A. Tomlinson (Eds.), *Sociology of Leisure: A Reader*, pp. 44–54. London: E&FN Spon.

Kirilmaz, E.D. (2015). Investigation of the First Women Basketball Team in Republic of Turkey via Oral History Interview, Institute of Social Science, Master Thesis, Adviser: Assoc. Prof. Birsen Talay Keşoğlu.

Koca, C. (2011). Analysis of the General Directory of Youth and Sport and Turkish National Olympic Committee with Regard to Gender Equity Perspective, Project number: 109K358, Ankara.

Koca, C. & Bulgu, N. (2005). Sport and Gender: An Overview. *Toplum ve Bilim*, 103. 163–184.

Koca, C. (2004). Boys' Bodies, Hegemonic Masculinity and Physical Education. 9. European Sport Science Congress, Clermont-Ferrand, France.

Koca, C. (2006a). Gender Relations in Physical Education and Sport. *Hacettepe Journal of Sport Sciences*, 17(2), 81–99.

Koca, C. (2006b). Social and Cultural Reproduction in the Field of Physical Education and Sport. Doctorate Thesis. Adviser: Prof. Dr. Gıyasettin Demirhan, Institute of Medical Science, Hacettepe University, Ankara.Koca, C. (2011). Women Representation in Managerial Positions of Sport Organisation. *Hacettepe Journal of Sport Sciences*, 22(1), 1–12.

Koca, C. & Demirhan, G. (2005). Gender Reproduction Process in the Field of Physical Education and Sport. *Hacettepe Journal of Sport Sciences*, 16(4), 200–228.

Koca, C. & Demirhan, G. (2006). The Place of Sport and Physical Activity in Turkish Young People's Lives and Their Positions within the Field of School PE. International Association of Physical Education in Higher Education (AIESEP), 5–8 July, Jyvaskyla, Finland.

Koca, C.Aşçi, F.H. & Kirazci, S. (2005). Gender Role Orientation of Athletes and Non-athletes in a Patriarchal Society: A Study in Turkey. *Sex Roles*, 52(3–4), 217–225.

Koçak, F.U. & Özkan, F. (2010). Physical Activity Levels and the Quality of Life in the Elderly. *Turkiye Klinikleri Journal of Sports Sciences*, 2(1), 46–54.

Koivula, N. (1995). Ratings of Gender Appropriateness of Sports Participation: Effects of Gender-based Schematic Processing. *Sex Roles*, 33(7/8), 543–557.

Markula, P. (1995). Firm but Shapely, Fit but Sexy, Strong but Thin: The Postmodern Aerobicizing Bodies. *Sociology of Sport Journal*, 12(4), 424–453.

Metheny, E. (1965). *Connotations of Movement in Sport and Dance*. Dubuque, IA: Wm. C. Brown.

Memiş, U.A. & Yıldıran, I. (2011). The Historical Development of Women's Involvement in Sports in Western Cultures. *Gazi Journal of Physical Education and Sport Science*, 16(3), 17–26.

Ötken, N. (2010). Woman and Woman Body Image in the Staging of Folk Dances Over Traditional and New Applications. *Dokuz Eylul University Journal of Faculty of Fine Arts*, 4, 49–54.

Ötken, N. (2011). Women in Folk Dances from the Gender Aspects. *International Journal of Human Science*, (1).

Özsoy, S. (2008). Female Sports Journalists in Turkey. *Hacettepe Journal of Sport Sciences;* 19(4), 201–219.

Pfister, G. (2000). The Role of Women in Traditional Games and Sports. *Olympic Review*, 31 (Feb/March), 38–45.

RapoportR. & Rapoport, R. (1995). Leisure and the Family Life-cycle. In C. Critcher, P. Bramham, A. Tomlinson (Eds.). *Sociology of Leisure: A Reader*, pp. 66–70. London: E & FN Spon.

RiemerB.A. & VisioM.E. (2003). Gender Typing of Sports: An Investigation of Metheny's Classification. *Research Quarterly for Exercise and Sport*, 74(2), 193–204.

Şahin, G., Özer, M.K., Söğutçu, T., Bavli, Ö., Serbes, Ş., Yurdakul, H.Ö. & Gözaydin, G. (2014). Regular Physical Activity Habits in Women. *International Refereed Academic Journal of Sports, Health & Medical Sciences*, 10(4).

Saktanber, A. (1990). Woman in Turkish Media: Free or Available Woman Good Wife, Devoted Mother. In Ş. Tekeli, (Ed.) *Woman's Perspective on Turkey in 1980s*, pp. 198–210. Istanbul: İletişim.

Şallı, A., Çetinkaya, M., Çotuk, M. & Çotuk, B. (2006). Voleybol Bayan ve Erkek Takım Antrenörlerinin Cinsiyet Ekseninde İncelenmesi. 9. International Sport Science Congress, Muğla.

Sancar, S. (2013). Masculinity. In Y. Ecevit & N. Karkiner (Eds.). *Within Social Gender Studies*, pp.168–191. Eskişehir: Anadolu University.

Savci, S., Özturk, M., Arikan, H., İnce, D.İ. & Tokgözoğlu, L. (2006). Physical Activity Levels of University Students. *Journal of Turkish Cardiology Association*, 34, 166–172.

Talimciler, A. (2015). *Sociology of Sports, Sport of Sociology* (2. Baski). Istanbul: Bağlam.

Theberge, N. (1993). The Construction of Gender in Sport: Women, Coaching, and the Naturalization of Difference. *Social Problems*, 40(3), 301–313.

Turkish Ministry of Health (2004). General Directorate of Primary Health Care. Let's Eat Healthily Protect, Project Research Report, Ankara, p. 23.

UNESCO (United Nations Educational, Scientific and Cultural Organization) (1978). The International Charter of Physical Education and Sport. Adopted by the General Conference at its twentieth session, 21 November. Paris, France.

Wearing, B. (1998). *Leisure and Feminist Theory*. London: Sage.

Wright, J. (1999). Changing Gendered Practices in Physical Education: Working with Teachers. *European Physical Education Review*, 5(3), 181–197.

Yaprak, P. & Amman, M. T. (2009). Women in Sports and their Problems. *Turkish Kick Box Federation Journal of Sport Science*, 2(1), 39–49.

Yıldız, D. (2002). *Çağlarboyu Turkler'de Spor*. Istanbul: Telebasim Yayincilik.

Yılmaz, A. & Mehmet, U. (2016). Making Goals Physical Activity of Women and Challenges Faced in Recreational Areas. *Hacettepe Journal of Sport Sciences*, 27(3), 101–117.

Yüksel, M. (2014). Gender and Sport. *Tarih Okulu Dergisi*, 7(19), 663–684.

10 Women's Empowerment and Women's Poverty

Mehmet ŞENGÜR

Introduction

The basic aim of economics is to meet the unlimited needs of people with scarce resources. All economic units and resources are used most effectively to meet these needs. As a result of the stages following the inclusion of resources into the production process, the formation of the final goods and services to be offered to the consumers is completed. A value or income is created by the presence of the goods and services produced. With this income created, distribution arises as a new problem for people in society. Distribution, the way in which the economic cycle will be sustained continuously, is also a subject of curiosity. It is possible to make numerous theories and explanations about distribution, however, in its simplest form; we can say that this distribution will be among those who produce.

Whoever is more involved in the production process, their share of the income will be higher. Therefore, considering women in terms of gender, if they are less involved in the production process than men, the income they receive in this case will be less. If everyone in society gets an equal share of income, there is no problem and a fair distribution of income will be achieved. However, the realization of this seems quite difficult for today's economies. Therefore, we encounter income inequality and along with it social inequalities. The economy is not only composed of mere numbers, but also closely related to socio-cultural areas. It is also clear that labor, which is one of the basic elements of economic production, does not just consist of the efforts of men. Women's gaining a place in economic life will contribute to them not only in the economic sense but also in the social sense.

In traditional societies around the world, women have been pushed back in economic and social life. Therefore, the visibility of women in economic and social areas is lower than men. Women constantly face gender discrimination and oppression in a negative way. In addition, they are exposed to physical, sexual and economic violence by their spouses or someone else in the family. In terms of basic criteria such as education, health, shelter and income, women have worse conditions than men. It will again be women who will be most affected by the poverty created by the income inequality. Women and children are the groups experiencing poverty most severely.

With the increase in women's labor force participation rates in economic terms, their visibility in different areas of social life will increase. Women do not adopt the gender-based role that society gives them, and they are becoming more and more effective in all areas of life. With this phenomenon that is changing day by day, there is an increase in educational levels and visibility of women in economic life. In time, women have taken part in social life with their free will and started to make their own decisions. There are national and international institutions that support women's efforts in this direction. In Turkey and other countries, a number of policies and practices are being developed with regard to women's poverty, social exclusion, gender discrimination and women's empowerment.

This study examines the different dimensions and reasons for female poverty in terms of women's empowerment in Turkey. First of all, the concepts of poverty, women poverty and social exclusion are discussed and then information on women's participation in the labor force, participation in social life, levels of happiness, equality of opportunity in the field of education and the rates of violence against women in Turkey are given. In the last section, a number of socio-economic factors affecting women's poverty in Turkey are interpreted with the findings obtained from established models and various suggestions are made for the empowerment of women.

Concept of Poverty and Basic Poverty Types

What is Poverty?

The Turkish Statistical Institute (TUIK) defines poverty as an inability of individuals to meet their needs in general (TUIK, 2018a). Poverty, in its simplest sense, is the deprivation of income so as to ensure the continuity of life. But poverty is not simple enough to be explained by a single sentence or a single definition. The extent and scope of poverty is very deep. There is more than one concept and definition of poverty in terms of depth and multidimensionality.

Poverty is also defined as a deprivation of welfare. This traditional perspective links welfare primarily to having dominance over goods. It is the situation where poor people do not have a minimum level of consumption. This view focuses on poverty in more monetary terms. However, poverty may also arise due to a particular type of consumption. For example, it may be in the form of domestic poverty, food poverty or health poverty (Haughton and Khandker, 2009, pp. 1–2). According to the dictionary, poverty refers to the individual who does not have enough money and cannot reach a number of basic tools. In addition to this situation, the word "poverty" is a state of deprivation of necessary means (possibilities) for life (Aktan, 2002, p. 1). For the poor working people, the main area of effort is to worry about how to build up their lives or how to earn the income needed to survive. Poverty is defined in many ways as a multidimensional concept. This multidimensionality also includes some of the following:

- Access to income in order to meet basic needs,
- Access to the most basic human development criteria such as education, health and longevity,
- Poor people's access to civil, political, economic and social rights,
- Poor people's access to their citizenship rights and being able to emerge in matters that affect their works and lives.(Chen et al., 2005, p. 15)

For these reasons, it is difficult to study poverty from a single point of view as it is not possible to make a single definition for it. The way people perceive poverty will vary according to multiple factors. These can be divided into two groups, mainly individual and social factors. Poverty should be studied from a multidimensional perspective, whether it depends on the individuals themselves or on the community in which they live. As a result of this natural situation, the inadequacy of the mere concept of income poverty was questioned and more than one poverty definition was made.

The views on poverty appear basically in two approaches. The first one argues that poverty is only a result of income. The other approach emphasizes the importance of income for poverty, but also the need for tools to enable individuals to demonstrate their socio-cultural potential (UNDP, 2004, p. 31). Even if poverty is defined only by economic criteria, it can be seen as a broad view covering many important variables (Şenses, 2001, p. 62).

Identifying and measuring poverty should have several objectives. Otherwise, determining the number or rate of the poor does not have any meaning on its own. So, answering the questions such as "Who are the poor?" and "What is the rate of the poor in the population?" should have specific objectives.

Haughton and Khandker (2009) explained the main objectives of defining and measuring poverty in four headings.

Why Should We Measure Poverty

Keeping the Poor on the Agenda

Determining the framework of poverty is an extremely powerful tool for attracting the attention of policy makers to the living conditions of the poor. The lack of any numerical data can lead to poverty being ignored. However, when poverty measures keep the issue politically and economically on the agenda, it indicates the need for poverty research (Haughton and Khandker, 2009, pp. 3–4). Thus, it will not be possible for public institutions and governments to ignore the poverty revealed by the figures.

Being Powerful for Appropriate Interventions by Defining Poor People Correctly

Measurement and identification of poverty are also important in terms of focusing on the targets. If a person or any institution will help someone, they will be able to do it by getting to know that person well (Haughton and Khandker, 2009, p. 4). This objective will help the breakdown of multidimensional poverty. It will be possible to choose the right targets in order to be able to intervene after the break down. In this way, it will be possible to implement the correct interventions as a result of the correct determination of poverty.

Monitoring and Evaluating Projects and Policies for Poor People

Another reason for measuring poverty is to estimate and evaluate the impact of policies and programs designed for the poor. These policies, which are seen as new opportunities for the poor, seem good in theory. However, when it comes to the application phase, this sometimes does not work as expected. It is necessary to establish a control group in order to evaluate and see the effects of the policies on the poor. The outputs of the control group should be handled mutually. Then, in order to develop the projects and programs as a result of analysis, those who do not comply with the objectives and do not work need to be sorted to be organized (Haughton and Khandker, 2009, p. 5). It is possible to develop a number of numerical plans for the poor. Economic policy and plans include stages such as diagnosis, selection of appropriate tools and implementation. Similarly, in any plan developed to combat poverty, a failure in one of these stages will result in the failure of the result. Therefore, the policies selected within the framework of the plan to be implemented should be carefully monitored and evaluated.

Evaluating the Efficiency of Institutions' Objectives to Help Poor People

Helping the evaluation of the effectiveness of institutions is also one of the reasons for poverty measurement and identification. If governments do not have numbers and consistent information, we cannot say that the government has good political authority to fight poverty. Apart from national governments, the same is true for international institutions. World Bank (WB) and similar international institutions should make necessary measures and identifications related to poverty for a lasting and professional solution (Haughton and Khandker, 2009, pp. 5–6). Knowing the success or failure of the institutions in achieving their goals will benefit the poor. If there is a failure in the target or practice of an institution, it will not be possible for the institution to contribute to the poor. Appropriate methods and targets will guide the institutions to enter into action on time.

Basic Types of Poverty

As with the multiple definitions of poverty, poverty types are also examined under different headings. Among the definition of many types of poverty, the most common ones are absolute poverty, relative poverty, objective poverty, subjective poverty and human poverty. Apart from these, there are many definitions such as urban poverty, rural poverty and income poverty.

The measurement of poverty is generally based on the provision of resources necessary for needs. If a person or his/her family cannot access the resources required for their needs, then that person is poor (Foster, 1998, p. 335). Considering an assessment of the impacts of policies aimed at preventing poverty in a timeframe, or an estimate of the impact of projects developed to combat poverty, absolute poverty will be the basis for these (Haughton and Khandker, 2009, p. 45). Types of poverty are also very different, as are many dimensions and determinants of poverty. Absolute poverty shows only the number of the poor. On the other hand, relative poverty shows the income distribution among the different income percentages. It is generally explained by the Lorenz curve and the Gini coefficient (Khusro, 1999. p 51). Gini coefficient has a value between "0" and "1". If perfect equality is ensured in society, the coefficient value will be "0". In contrast, if the Gini coefficient is "1", this indicates the situation of total inequality, i.e. that the total income is in the hands of only one person.

The relative definitions of poverty are all based on the comparative life-level comparisons in the studied population. Thus, the required expenditure and consumption items can be examined for individuals. A person who does not have enough income to spend on the cost of living in society will be considered as poor (Dixon and Macarov, 2002, pp. 7–8). For relative poverty, it is essential that a person not only meets the basic needs of his or her life, but also reaches the average welfare level of society. Therefore, the person who is below the average quality of life in society will be considered relatively poor.

Khander expresses that in some way and for any reason, sometimes we can take into account poor people who make up a certain percentage of society. This is the poorest part of the society that constitutes one fifth or two fifths of the society. In addition, these groups are composed of "relatively" poor individuals. As a result of such an identification, it is clear that poverty is always with us. Definition of relative poverty and identifying the poor will also contribute to the effectiveness of policies to combat poverty (Haughton and Khandker, 2009, pp. 43–44, 67–68). Here, the exact determination of the percentages of income from the income groups would allow for the precise identification of the gap between the poor and the other. The individuals and their communities in the UNDP (United Nations Development Program) Turkey Human Development Report published in 2004 took an important place. The report emphasizes that individuals are social entities. The minimum level of consumption and the standard of living required for self-reproduction are defined as relative poverty (UNDP, 2004, p. 31).

It is possible to obtain comprehensive information about poverty in any country or region by examination of relative poverty in that country or region. It is necessary to apply relative poverty in terms of determining the differences between the population or groups, such as income and quality of life. However, it is important that analyses of poverty are carried out not only at the national level but also at the international level. Since the determination of absolute poverty is made with objective criteria, it is the main source of national and international studies.

In addition to concepts such as poverty and income inequality, concepts such as "human development" and "human poverty" have become new areas of discussion. The main source of discussions on this issue is the definition of human poverty, which was developed by the UNDP. Human poverty is also a multidimensional concept, as it is impossible to address poverty and income inequality from a single viewpoint. Human poverty and dimensions are measured primarily by the "human poverty index", which includes criteria such as life expectancy, education and a good standard of living.

Women's Poverty

Women's Poverty, Causes and Combating Poverty

Between 1950 and 1970, almost 2/3 of the poor were women in the United States. Although the labor force participation rate of women has increased steadily in the labor market, the economic situation of women has deteriorated continuously. As a result of this situation, the concept of women's (female) poverty or feminization of poverty was first used by Diane Pearce in 1978 (Pearce, 1978). Women's poverty is a multidimensional concept, as there are different dimensions of poverty. The basic unequal role between women and men in society makes women's poverty more diverse than other groups (Bradshaw and Linnekar, 2003). The relationship of inequality between individuals and groups in the society is experienced more unevenly among women and men. In traditional societies, this inequality becomes more evident as the roles of men and women are determined very strictly.

In theory, the concept of "feminization of poverty" was used for the first time to explain the situation of women living in the United States in the 4th World Women's Conference Action Plan. The changes in the family structure, the increase of divorce rates, the increase in the number of children out of wedlock, and the fact that the care of children is carried out by women are among the factors that deepen women's poverty. The concept of female poverty and its causes are explained by studies that show that women living alone in the US and living with their children are poorer (McLanahan and Kelly, 2006). Goldberg and Kremen made statements about the situation in different countries regarding "feminization of poverty", i.e. women's poverty. Women's poverty is explained by the fact that most of the poor are women or their families (Goldberg and Kremen, 1990). Roles such as motherhood and housewife imposed on women by the society deepen the poverty of women. With women becoming more visible in economic and social life, the effects of poverty on women will also be reduced.

Women's poverty should be considered as both multi-dimensional and multi-sectoral. Women experience poverty in different social areas at different times. In spite of institutionalized discrimination, women participate in many social areas as in the labor market. Social norms and expectations in the society determine the gender relations and their roles. This structural disparity in society relatively differentiates the feeling of poverty between men and women (Bradshaw and Linnekar, 2003, p. 9). As a result of the relative poverty difference between men and women, men play a more active role in economic and social life than women. As a result of this unequal relationship shaped by the influence of the social structure, the return of women to the labor market is also quite low compared to men.

The feminization of poverty should now be treated as a legitimate foreign policy issue. Women play an important role in the economy as both mother and head of the household. Increasing female poverty also slows down global economic growth rates. Moreover, environmental factors and population growth for women in poor countries are disadvantaged by the factors that feed the circle of poverty (Buvinić, 1997). The individual poverty of women is observed to pose negative effects both at national and international level. Women's poverty, which leads to economic contraction and loss of income within the country, also affects the income through trade globally.

Goldberg and Kremen have listed the status of the labor market and some demographic factors as the main reasons for deepening women's poverty. Some of these factors are low wages, marriage, divorce, motherhood, responsibility for the family alone, lack of any financial support, and the unequal distribution of welfare in society (Goldberg and Kremen, 1990, pp. 4–7). The two main factors affecting women's poverty are women's position in the labor market and access to education opportunities. Statistics show that women are far behind men in terms of their share of welfare despite their abilities. According to global literacy rates in 1990, 74 women were literate compared to every 100 men. Compared to 52 million boys of primary school age throughout the world, 77 million girls remained out of school. The vast majority of women work for low wages. The reason for this is that women are constantly discriminated against in terms of employment and wages. Demand for women's labor, particularly in poorer countries, in women's participation in the labor market is in the form of low-paid services, agriculture, small-scale trade and family businesses (Buvinić, 1997).

There are two different approaches for struggling with poverty. One of the approaches aims at direct struggle with poverty and the other approach is to adopt policies that indirectly select targets to reduce poverty. There is no consensus on the success or failure of these different policy propositions. It will be more meaningful to decide which approach will be preferred along with the economic policy objectives to be adopted in general. The indirect approach to combating poverty aims at reducing the effects of poverty through the realization of economic growth and development. The underlying idea of this approach lies in the belief that if economic growth is achieved in an economy, poverty and inequality will decrease. In fact, there are some arguments that suggest that poverty cannot be reduced through economic growth. Another approach applied in the combat against poverty is the preference of direct combat policies. Radical reform, public spending and poverty alleviation programs are among the policies that will be implemented directly in the fight against poverty. Since poverty is a multidimensional concept, there are multiple factors affecting poverty. The direct and indirect aspect of poverty alleviation policies and the impact of the factors affecting poverty appear in a similar way. Many factors such as population, quality of life, education level, inflation, economic growth, political stability, globalization, labor market situation and informal economy are the factors affecting poverty.

A decrease in income and an increase in number of children in families have negative effects on women and children. Moreover, the more they work the less they have leisure time This situation, which negatively affects the working hours of women, does not cause any change for men. If women have more children than they are able to take care of on their own, then the responsibility of care is assigned to the older daughter of the family, if there is one. As a result of this situation, the education of the girls will be pushed into the background and women's poverty will be transferred from generation to generation (Buvinić, 1997). In such a case, the phenomenon of the feminization of poverty will turn into a vicious cycle. Getting out of this vicious circle depends only on women's empowerment and greater inclusion in social and economic spheres.

Social Exclusion, Women's Poverty and Women's Empowerment

Social exclusion, a relatively new concept, spread rapidly in the 1990s. The concept of social exclusion was first used by sociologists to explain the social problems that emerged during the socio-economic transformation of France in the 1980s. It refers to the economic weakness, transition to mass society and deterioration of social cohesion as a result of increasing inequality in the growing population.Social exclusion is not only related to lack of material wealth but also to symbolic lack of participation in terms of social institutions (Silver, 1994).

The concept of empowerment has different meanings in different socio-cultural and political contexts and does not easily translate to all languages. Exploring local terms about empowerment around the world always leads to a lively debate. These terms can be listed as individual power, control, one's own preference, the individual's dignity in accordance with his own values, the ability to fight for one's rights, ability to implement one's own decisions and freedom (Narayan et al., 2002, p. 13). The concepts of social exclusion and empowerment become more meaningful together. It is an inevitable result that poor people and especially women are more likely to feel social exclusion. It is very crucial for poor women to have a louder voice in social areas and to be free in economic decisions.

Empowerment in the broad sense means to increase the freedom of a person while taking actions and choices that will shape his or her life. What we want to emphasize here with freedom is actually the control over resources and decisions. For the poor, this freedom is restricted by their silence and lack of power. This limitation is mostly related to the state and markets. There is an important gender inequality, including in the household. Because poverty is a multi-dimensional concept, poor people need a number of capacities at individual and collective levels. Whereas at the individual level education is required for health and shelter, at the collective level it is necessary to solve problems collectively and be organized. For the empowerment of poor men and women, the formal and informal institutional barriers that limit their choices and actions to improve community welfare should be removed. Here, the official institutions with a key role are state-regulated laws and rules which are approved by markets, civil society and international institutions. On the other hand, informal institutions include social solidarity, sharing, social exclusion and corruption (Narayan et al., 2002).

The new forms of poverty, along with mass powerlessness and long-term unemployment, have led to concerns of social polarization between the highest income group and the lowest income group. All countries will be faced with a lack of social definition for millions of people in the future of developing globalized economies, when the need for labor decreases or becomes obsolete. The emerging global economy is characterized by strong tendencies towards the fragmentation of social structure and professional structure. The most important question here is how to ensure social integration with a large marginalized society in the name of economic efficiency and flexibility (Bhalla and Lapeyre, 2016).

There are thousands of empowerment approaches initiated by governments, civil society and the private sector to empower poor people. The success of efforts to empower the poor and their increasing freedom of movement and choice in different contexts depend on four elements: (Narayan et al., 2002, p. 18)

- Access to information.
- Inclusion and participation.
- Accountability.
- Local organization capacity.

Women's Poverty and Empowerment of Women in Turkey

In Turkey and the world, the part of the society that feels more poverty is women and alongside children. There are many factors affecting women's poverty. The situation in the labor market, income, education and gender equality are those that stand out among these factors.

Female Labor Force Participation in Turkey and OECD Countries

In Turkey, while the labor force participation rate of males aged 15 years and over in 2007 is 69.2%, the labor force participation rate of the same age female group is 23.6%. The difference between female and male labor force participation rates was approximately three times in 2007. Labor force participation rate for men was 70.1% in 2008, 70.6% in 2009, 70.8% in 2010, 71.7%

in 2011, 71.7% in 2011, 71% in 2012, 71.5% in 2013, 71.3% in 2014, 71.6% in 2015, 72% in 2016 and 72.5% in 2017. However, female labor force participation rate was 24.5% in 2008, 26% in 2009, 27.6% in 2010, 28.8% in 2011, 29.5% in 2012, 30.8% in 2013, 30.3% in 2014, 31.5% in 2015, 32.5% in 2016, and rose up to 33.6% in 2017. The labor force participation of women has increased relatively between the years of 2007–2017, but the difference between men and women has not completely closed. As of 2017, the difference of labor force participation rate between men and women was still doubled.

Labor force participation rates in OECD (Organization for Economic Co-operation and Development) member countries, including Turkey, and some non-member countries are given in Table 10.2. As Table 10.2 illustrates, the least difference in the labor force participation rate between men and women is Finland with 3.5% in 2007. The second least difference between the labor force participation rates is Sweden with 4.6%. It is followed by Norway with 5.9% in the third place, then Lithuania with 6.4%, Denmark with 7.3%, Iceland with 8%, Canada with 8.2%, Estonia with 8.7%, Slovenia with 9.2% and France with 9.8%.

In 2007, the difference between the labor force participation rate of men and women in other OECD countries apart from the mentioned countries is 10% or more. The biggest difference among the countries in the table belongs to Turkey, which has increased by 3 times in 2007. The second country that has the most significant difference in labor force participation rate is Mexico, which has increased by 2 times. In 2007, women's labor force participation in Chile was approximately 31% less than that of men. After Chile, it is seen that the difference between Italy and Greece is approximately 24%. Amongst the non-OCED countries, it c seen that in 2007 and 2008, the difference between women's and men's labor force participation rates was highest in India

Table 10.1 Labour force participation rate for people by sex, 2007–2017 (15+ years)

Year	Total	Male	Female
2007	46.2	69.8	23.6
2008	46.9	70.1	24.5
2009	47.9	70.6	26.0
2010	48.8	70.8	27.6
2011	49.9	71.7	28.8
2012	50.0	71.0	29.5
2013	50.8	71.5	30.8
2014	50.5	71.3	30.3
2015	51.3	71.6	31.5
2016	52.0	72.0	32.5
2017	52.8	72.5	33.6

Source: TurkStat, Household Labour Force Survey, 2007–2017

Table 10.2 Labour force participation rate by sex and age group (15–64 years)

Country	Sex	2007	2008	2009	2010	2011	2012	2013	2014	2015	2016
Australia	Men	83.0	83.0	82.6	82.9	82.8	82.5	82.4	82.1	82.7	82.3
	Women	69.4	70.0	70.1	70.0	70.5	70.4	70.5	70.5	71.2	71.6
Austria	Men	80.0	80.0	80.0	80.0	79.9	80.2	80.4	80.0	80.1	80.7
	Women	67.1	67.8	68.7	68.9	69.3	70.0	70.7	70.8	70.9	71.7
Belgium	Men	73.6	73.3	72.8	73.4	72.3	72.5	72.7	72.4	72.2	72.3
	Women	60.4	60.8	60.9	61.8	61.1	61.3	62.3	63.0	63.0	62.9
Canada	Men	82.4	82.6	81.7	81.4	81.4	81.3	81.4	81.3	81.8	81.8
	Women	74.2	74.2	74.2	74.3	74.1	74.3	74.7	74.2	74.2	74.4
Chile	Men	78.5	79.3	78.6	77.8	78.6	78.0	78.1	77.6	77.7	77.4
	Women	47.6	50.2	51.1	51.8	53.9	54.6	54.9	55.7	55.8	56.1
Czech Republic	Men	78.1	78.1	78.5	78.6	78.7	79.5	80.5	81.2	81.4	82.2
	Women	61.5	61.0	61.5	61.5	62.2	63.5	65.1	65.6	66.5	67.6
Denmark	Men	83.7	84.3	83.6	82.6	82.3	81.4	80.6	81.1	81.6	82.6
	Women	76.4	77.0	76.8	76.0	76.1	75.8	75.6	75.0	75.3	77.2
Estonia	Men	77.5	78.1	77.5	76.7	78.2	78.5	78.6	79.3	80.4	81.7
	Women	68.8	70.3	70.5	71.0	71.4	71.3	71.7	71.2	72.9	73.1
Finland	Men	77.4	78.1	75.8	76.7	77.5	77.3	76.0	77.1	77.4	77.9
	Women	73.9	74.0	73.5	72.5	72.7	73.4	73.5	73.8	74.4	74.1
France	Men	74.7	74.7	75.0	74.9	74.6	75.3	75.5	75.4	75.5	75.6
	Women	64.9	65.2	65.7	65.8	65.7	66.3	66.9	67.4	67.6	67.9
Germany	Men	81.8	82.1	82.2	82.4	82.7	82.5	82.6	82.5	82.1	82.2
	Women	69.4	69.7	70.4	70.8	71.9	71.9	72.6	72.9	73.1	73.6

(Continued)

Table 10.2 (Cont.)

Country	Sex	2007	2008	2009	2010	2011	2012	2013	2014	2015	2016
Greece	Men	78.4	78.4	78.5	78.3	77.2	76.9	76.9	76.0	75.9	76.2
	Women	54.8	55.0	56.5	57.5	57.5	58.3	58.3	59.0	59.9	60.4
Hungary	Men	68.6	68.0	67.7	67.8	68.4	69.6	71.0	73.4	75.3	76.9
	Women	54.9	54.7	55.0	56.3	56.6	58.0	58.6	60.7	62.2	63.5
Iceland	Men	91.6	90.9	88.4	88.2	87.8	87.6	88.8	89.1	90.3	91.8
	Women	83.6	82.5	82.0	82.7	82.4	83.3	84.3	84.2	85.5	86.2
Ireland	Men	81.6	81.0	79.3	77.4	76.7	76.7	77.2	77.1	77.6	77.7
	Women	63.5	63.3	62.8	62.3	62.3	62.2	63.2	62.5	62.8	64.1
Israel	Men	77.0	76.8	76.1	76.3	75.9	75.9	76.0	76.1	76.1	75.6
	Women	65.5	65.3	66.3	66.4	66.1	67.1	67.3	68.4	68.3	68.6
Italy	Men	74.3	74.3	73.5	73.1	72.8	73.7	73.3	73.6	74.1	74.8
	Women	50.6	51.6	51.1	51.1	51.4	53.4	53.6	54.4	54.1	55.2
Japan	Men	85.2	85.2	84.8	84.8	84.4	84.3	84.6	84.9	85.0	85.4
	Women	61.9	62.2	62.9	63.2	63.0	63.4	65.0	66.0	66.7	68.1
Korea	Men	77.6	77.3	76.9	77.1	77.4	77.6	77.6	78.6	78.6	78.9
	Women	54.8	54.7	53.9	54.5	54.9	55.2	55.6	57.0	57.9	58.4
Latvia	Men	77.9	78.3	76.6	75.3	75.8	77.1	76.6	77.8	78.9	78.8
	Women	67.8	70.3	70.7	70.8	70.1	72.0	71.6	71.6	72.8	74.0
Lithuania	Men	71.3	71.6	71.7	72.0	73.5	73.7	74.7	76.0	75.8	77.1
	Women	64.9	65.5	67.6	68.6	69.4	70.1	70.3	71.6	72.5	73.9
Luxembourg	Men	75.0	74.7	76.6	76.0	75.0	75.9	76.3	77.2	76.0	75.1
	Women	58.9	58.7	60.7	60.3	60.7	62.8	63.2	64.2	65.6	64.7
Mexico	Men	83.8	83.4	82.7	82.4	82.4	82.7	82.4	82.2	82.0	81.8
	Women	45.4	45.2	45.8	45.6	46.2	47.3	47.4	46.6	46.8	47.0

Country	Sex	2007	2008	2009	2010	2011	2012	2013	2014	2015	2016
Netherlands	Men	83.8	84.8	84.6	83.8	83.6	84.2	84.7	84.6	84.6	84.4
	Women	70.4	71.7	72.3	72.6	73.1	74.3	74.6	74.0	74.7	75.0
New Zealand	Men	84.9	84.4	83.9	83.6	83.7	83.1	83.1	84.1	84.2	85.0
	Women	71.5	71.7	71.8	71.6	72.1	72.4	73.0	74.1	74.1	74.9
Norway	Men	81.8	82.9	81.4	80.8	80.1	80.7	80.4	80.2	80.5	80.3
	Women	75.9	77.4	76.5	75.6	75.8	75.9	76.1	75.9	76.2	75.9
Poland	Men	70.0	70.9	71.8	72.1	72.6	73.3	73.9	74.6	74.8	75.7
	Women	56.5	57.0	57.8	58.5	58.9	59.7	60.1	61.1	61.4	62.0
Portugal	Men	79.2	79.2	78.2	77.8	78.0	77.3	76.5	76.7	76.7	77.2
	Women	68.7	68.9	68.9	69.7	69.5	69.7	69.8	70.0	70.3	70.5
Slovak Republic	Men	75.8	76.4	76.3	76.0	76.6	77.1	77.2	77.6	77.5	78.3
	Women	60.7	61.4	60.6	61.3	60.8	61.7	62.4	62.8	64.3	65.3
Slovenia	Men	75.8	75.8	75.6	75.4	73.9	73.7	74.2	74.3	75.4	74.5
	Women	66.6	67.5	67.9	67.4	66.5	66.9	66.6	67.2	67.9	68.6
Spain	Men	82.6	82.8	82.0	81.8	81.5	81.2	80.9	80.7	80.9	80.5
	Women	62.8	64.5	66.0	67.1	68.3	69.3	69.7	69.8	70.0	70.2
Sweden	Men	81.4	81.6	81.3	81.8	82.4	82.6	83.3	83.6	83.5	83.9
	Women	76.8	77.0	76.4	76.2	77.4	77.9	78.8	79.3	79.9	80.2
Switzerland	Men	88.2	88.0	87.8	87.2	87.8	87.8	87.6	87.6	87.8	88.2
	Women	75.0	76.6	77.1	75.3	76.3	76.7	77.1	78.1	78.6	79.5
Turkey	Men	74.4	74.8	75.2	75.4	76.4	75.8	76.3	76.6	77.0	77.6
	Women	25.7	26.7	28.4	30.2	31.5	32.3	33.7	33.6	35.0	36.2
United Kingdom	Men	83.3	83.5	83.2	82.5	82.5	83.1	82.9	83.1	82.8	83.4
	Women	69.8	70.2	70.2	70.2	70.4	70.9	71.6	72.1	72.5	73.0

(Continued)

Table 10.2 (Cont.)

Country	Sex	2007	2008	2009	2010	2011	2012	2013	2014	2015	2016
United States	Men	81.7	81.4	80.4	79.6	78.9	78.8	78.7	78.5	78.5	78.8
	Women	69.1	69.3	69.0	68.4	67.8	67.6	67.2	67.1	66.9	67.3
OECD – Average	Men	80.4	80.4	79.9	79.6	79.5	79.6	79.6	79.6	79.7	80.0
	Women	60.9	61.3	61.6	61.6	61.8	62.2	62.5	62.8	63.0	63.6
Non-OECD Economies Brazil	Men	84.9	85.1	85.1		83.5	83.3	82.8	83.5	82.4	
	Women	62.8	62.9	63.5		60.8	60.8	60.7	62.4	61.1	
China (People's Republic of)	Men				84.3						
	Women				70.3						
Colombia	Men	82.6	82.8	84.5	84.9	85.6	86.0	85.5	85.7	85.8	85.4
	Women	54.2	54.8	58.5	60.5	61.5	63.0	62.8	62.9	63.7	63.6
Costa Rica	Men	84.2	82.9	81.8	80.5	79.7	81.9	81.3	82.0	80.4	79.2
	Women	49.7	50.4	50.8	50.2	49.6	55.6	54.9	54.6	53.9	50.4
India	Men		84.5		82.4		81.4				
	Women		32.5		30.3		28.5				
Indonesia	Men	85.6	85.5	85.6	85.8	85.9	86.3	85.4			
	Women	52.1	53.1	52.9	53.7	51.9	53.6	52.5			
Russia	Men	76.9	77.9	77.6	77.7	77.8	78.1	78.1	78.6	79.1	79.8
	Women	69.2	68.9	68.8	68.0	68.1	68.2	67.9	68.1	68.2	68.9
South Africa	Men	64.3	67.1	65.2	63.3	62.8	63.3	63.4	63.7	65.1	65.4
	Women	50.8	51.9	50.2	48.4	49.0	49.4	50.4	50.7	52.1	52.2

Source: Data extracted from OECDStat

(52.5%), Costa Rica (34.5%) and Indonesia (33.5%). On the other hand, the minimum difference between the labor force participation rates among non-OECD countries was found to be in Russia with 7.7%.

When we look at the OECD countries for the year 2016, the countries with the highest difference in labor force participation rate are respectively Turkey (41.4%), Mexico (34.8%), Chile (21.3%), Korea (20.5%) and Italy (19.6%). However, in 2016, the countries with the least difference between men and women's labor force participation rates were Lithuania (3.2%), Sweden (3.7%), Finland (3.8%), Norway (4.4%), and Latvia (4.8%). Apart from these, the countries with a labor force participation rate difference of less than 10% in 2016 were found to be Denmark, Iceland, Slovenia, Portugal, Israel, Canada, France, Germany, Estonia, Switzerland, Austria, Belgium and the Netherlands. For non-OECD countries in 2016, the countries with the highest labor force participation rate difference were Costa Rica with 28.8%, Colombia with 21.8% and South Africa with 13.2%. It is seen in the table that the data from other countries in this group between 2007 and 2016 is not complete.

When we look at the change in 2006–2016, Latvia was the country with the highest rate of positive change with 52.5% in terms of women. Later, in Lithuania, the difference between women's and men's labor force participation rate decreased by 50%. Similarly, this unequal situation also decreased by about 48% in Spain. This unequal situation in labor force participation for Israel, Portugal, Slovenia, Luxembourg, Switzerland, Greece, Chile, Germany, Austria and Iceland has decreased by at least 30% or more. The least change in inequality was in Estonia (1.15%), while the positive change for women in Hungary, the United States, Mexico and Canada was less than 10%. When we look at Turkey between 2006 and 2016, the inequality in labor force participation has decreased by about 15% for women. However, female labor force participation rates are 2.14 times less than for men. The decrease in this inequality, which means taking part in labor markets for women, has not applied for all countries. Inequalities in female labor force participation in Finland increased by 8.57%. With this increase, there can be no significant inequality in labor force participation rates in Finland. When we ignore the change over the years, the situation in Finland is still below 4% and very good compared to many other countries.

Women's Equality Index of Education in Turkey

One of the main reasons for the feminization of poverty is access to educational opportunities. As education has a direct effective on income, it also indirectly plays a role in women's impoverishment. Table 10.3 shows the gender equality index of those enrolled at primary, secondary and higher education levels in Turkey between 2007 and 2016. The student gender equality index is the comparison of the gross enrolment rate of female students in a given academic year with respect to the enrolment rate of male students (TUIK, 2018b). The index is calculated by comparing the gross

Table 10.3 Gender parity index of the gross enrolment ratio in primary, secondary and tertiary education, 2007–2016

Year	Primary education	Secondary education	Tertiary education
2007	0.964	0.858	0.880
2008	0.979	0.890	0.801
2009	0.989	0.886	0.834
2010	1.004	0.897	0.862
2011	1.004	0.933	0.874
2012	1.018	0.942	0.881
2013	1.023	0.946	0.892
2014	1.018	0.954	0.902
2015	1.019	0.956	0.905
2016	1.009	0.943	0.964

Source: Turkey Ministry of National Education

enrolment rates of female and male students. If the value of the index is equal to "1", this figure is interpreted as a situation in which the male and female students are equal in terms of education. If the gender equality index is smaller than 1, there is inequality in favour of male students. On the other hand, if the index has a value greater than 1, then there will be inequality in terms of gross schooling in favour of female students.

In terms of primary education in 2007, the equality index value in education is 0.964. In this case, the index reveals the existence of inequality in favour of male students. This unequal situation for male students continued in 2008 (0.979) and in 2009 (0.989). However, in 2010, the equality index in education became more uneven in terms of girls, and in 2016 the index was approximately 1.1. In terms of secondary education, the index value, which was 0.858 in 2007, came closer to 1 and reached 0.943 in 2016. In terms of higher education, the index value was found to be less than 1 in 2007–2016. In 2016, the index received a value of 0.964 and reached a value of "1" indicating that gender equality for higher education was achieved.

In Turkey, it is seen that there are positive results for girls in the gender equality index in education. This will undoubtedly support women's participation in labor markets, opportunities to obtain higher income, participate more in social life and become free individuals in their decisions. Together with access to education opportunities, increasing education level will raise the wage income of women. Table 10.4 shows the difference in wages between the genders for the years 2010 and 2014 in Turkey. The difference between the genders in wages, which was 1.1 in 2010, was 0.4 in 2014. Therefore, it can be said that the difference between wages in terms of gender decreased in the four year period.

Table 10.4 Gender gap in wages, 2010, 2014

Year	Gender gap in wages %
2010	-1.1
2014	-0.4

Indicators of Violence against Women in Turkey

Women in Turkey and in the world are exposed to economic, sexual and physical violence in and out of the family. This situation restricts the presence of women in social and economic areas and sometimes causes them not to take part in these areas. Women experience most violence from their husbands or people they live with. Apart from husbands, it is known that women are exposed to violence from other individuals in the family as well. Violence against women should not only be reduced but it should be eliminated. Only then will women be able to live in a way worthy of human dignity.

The rates of violence experienced by women in Table 10.5 from their husbands or their partners in any period of their lives are physical, sexual and economic. These violence rates are classified separately according to the place, education level and employment status. When we look at the table, it is seen that women across Turkey face physical violence the most with 39.3% in any period of their lives. The second most common violence in general is economic violence with 23.4%. The third and last one is sexual violence with a 15.3% exposure rate.

Considering the distribution of women who are subjected to violence by their husbands or people they live with, the overall rate of women living in urban areas is around 80% while it is around 75% in rural areas. Similarly, the

Table 10.5 Physical/sexual/economic violence on women by husbands or intimate partners in Turkey (percentage)

Preventing them from working or causing them to quit their job (in any period lifetime)		economic	sexual	physical
Settlement	urban	26.6	14.3	38
	rural	13.9	18.3	43.2
Education	less than primary	19.7	22.2	52.2
	primary	24.5	15.2	39.9
	secondary	29.6	13.1	34.9
	higher	21.7	8.7	25
Employment status	not working	25	14.6	38.7
	working	19.1	17	40.7
Turkey		23.4	15.3	39.3

Source: TurkStat, Domestic violence statistics against women (2008)

distribution of economic, sexual and physical violence for urban areas does not change across the country. But for women living in rural areas, the situation is different. Women in rural areas experience sexual violence at a rate of 18.3% after physical violence. Women living in rural areas experience physical and sexual violence more than women living in urban areas. On the other hand, the rate of economic violence among women in urban areas is higher than that of women in rural areas. There are no significant differences in exposure to violence among women living in urban areas and those living in rural areas. Therefore, violence against women is not only a situation specific to rural areas, but the level of encountering violence across the country is 77.5%.

Considering the rate of violence according to the education level, those with a lower education level than primary education with the ratio of 80% are in the first rank. When we look at the rankings of types of violence against women with this level of education, physical violence again takes first place with 52.2%. One noteworthy point for women with lower levels of education than primary education is that they are exposed to sexual violence in second place, similar to women in rural areas. The rate of sexual violence is 22.2%, which is higher than the national average, and comes after physical violence for these women. Women whose education level is lower than primary education are exposed to sexual violence more than economic violence, whereas sexual violence is the least in the country. As the level of education increases, the rate of violence in all forms decreases. However, when we collect all forms of violence, the rate of violence is 55% even for women with higher education.

When we consider violence rates according to women's employment status, physical violence takes the first place in both groups. However, with 40.7%, working women are exposed to physical violence 2% more than women who do not work. For both groups of women, economic violence is the second and the sexual violence is the last. Unemployed women are less likely to suffer from physical and sexual violence than women who are employed, but they are more likely to experience economic violence.

It is highly anticipated that unemployed women experience more economic violence, because the unemployed woman is deprived of income and will be in need of someone. In addition, this is an inevitable result because the basis of economic violence is to prevent women from working and cause women to quit. What should be noted here is that working women have more sexual and physical violence. It is extremely upsetting that women experience physical violence and sexual harassment from their homes or workplaces. This situation will further reduce the labor force participation rate of women which is two times lower than for men.

Table 10.6 shows the rates of violence among women in Turkey from people other than their husbands. Women across the country face physical violence the most with a rate of 17.8%. There is a difference of not more than 1% between the rates of sexual or physical violence in terms of settlement. Similarly, there is no significant difference in the rate of sexual or physical

Table 10.6 Physical/sexual violence by other people in Turkey (percentage)

		Sexual	Physical
Settlement	urban	3.6	18
	rural	2.3	17.1
Education	less than primary	2	19.2
	primary	2.1	15.5
	secondary	3.8	19.6
	higher	6.4	19.6
Employment status	not working	3.1	17.5
	working	4.1	18.7
Turkey		3.3	17.8

Source: TurkStat, Domestic violence statistics against women (2008)

violence in terms of employment. However, according to the level of education, it is seen that the rate of sexual violence is sometimes two times and sometimes three times higher than the other education levels.

Women's Happiness Rates and Participation in Social Activities in Turkey

Participation in social life is one of the basic indicators of the feminization of poverty and social exclusion. The distribution of activities in the last four weeks by gender for the years 2014–2015 is given in Table 10.6. A number of social activities in which women and men participated or performed personally in the relevant period were included. The activity in which men and women participated the most with more than 90% was watching TV. Visiting relatives is the second most common activity with a participation rate of 71.4% for women and 68.3% for men. The third activity is visiting friends with a women's participation rate of 56.4%. Similarly, the rate of men's participation in the activity of visiting friends is quite high with 55.1%.

The rate of going to entertainment and socialization places (patisserie, coffee shop, cafe, bar, tavern, etc.) is 38.6% for men and 19.2% for women. In this case, it is seen that men have more than two times more time to spend in social areas than women. The rate of going to the internet cafe for men is seven times higher than that of women. It can be said that this situation is the result of the continuation of the habits of men in early ages and the fact that these places are mostly addressed to men. In terms of the time spent on social media, the rate of men is approximately 42%, while it is around 26% for women. It is seen that men spend twice or more time than women on social media.

Men are more involved than women in activities such as going to shopping centers (48.8%), listening to the radio (43.2%), reading newspapers/magazines (48.8%), having picnics (13.6%), solving puzzles (15.5%) and participating in

Table 10.7 The distribution of activities done or participated during the last four weeks by sex, 2014–2015 [10+age] (percentage)

Activity name	Total	Male	Female
Going to cinema	9.8	10.8	8.8
Going to theatre	1.7	1.6	1.8
Going to concert	2.2	2.3	2.1
Going to art exhibition, museum etc.	1.4	1.3	1.4
Going to library	3.1	2.8	3.3
Participating in sports activities as a spectator	3.5	5.9	1.2
Visiting relatives	69.9	68.3	71.4
Visiting friends	55.7	55.1	56.4
Going to kermis, fair, festival etc.	3.5	3.2	3.8
Picnic	12.8	13.6	12.1
Reading book	34.2	30.2	38.2
Reading newspaper, magazine etc.	39.4	48.8	30.1
Watching TV	94.6	95.6	93.6
Listening to radio	39.6	43.2	36.1
Going to places of entertainment and socializing (bakeries, coffee shops, cafes, bars, taverns, etc.)	28.8	38.6	19.2
Going to internet cafe	4.0	7.1	1.0
Going around shopping mall	40.5	42.8	38.3
Daily tours, participating in nature walks	2.1	2.3	1.9
Spending time on social media	33.9	41.7	26.2
Solving puzzles, sudoku etc.	13.0	15.5	10.6
Knitting, patchwork, sewing, embroidery, wood painting	12.7	0.4	24.8
Other	0.2	0.3	0.2

Source: TurkStat, *Time Use Survey*, 2014–2015

sports activities as spectators (5.9%). In contrast, it is observed that women are more involved than men in activities such as reading books (38.2%), going to theatre (1.8%), going to art exhibition (1.4%), going to the library (3.3%), visiting friends (56.4%), visiting relatives (71.4%) and knitting, patchwork, sewing, embroidery, wood painting (24.8%).

With the effect of the role imposed on women by society, it is seen that women are more involved in household chores, sewing and embroidery. As a similar result, the time spent outside and in social areas is not equal with men as a result of women's responsibilities in daily life. The absence of social exclusion requires not only being present in social areas, but also being happy by feeling comfortable in these areas. Therefore, loneliness in the community can be interpreted as a different form of social exclusion and inequality. The extent to which people in the community are happy can give us an idea about many issues. the distribution of general happiness levels in Turkey in 2014–2017 according to gender is given in Table 10.8. The table shows the proportions of the two levels, which are happy and very happy, for the genders.

While the total number of happy and very happy men was approximately 52% in 2014, the rate of women was around 60%. In 2015, the rate of happiness of men increased by 1% and the happiness rate of women remained unchanged. In 2016, the overall happiness of men and women increased by approximately 5%. In 2017, the overall happiness of men decreased by 5% and returned to its former value, while the rate of happiness of women decreased by 2.5%. The overall level of happiness among women and men is around 60% between the years 2014–2017. In other words, 60 out of every 100 people in the society consider themselves happy. In addition, it is observed that women are happier than men despite all the negativities and responsibilities they have in the society.

The details of the level of happiness approaching an average of 60% in the relevant period are also important. Table 10.9 shows the distribution of the source of happiness by gender. The greatest source of happiness among women and men is to be healthy. While over 70% of women express that health is a source of happiness, the figures for men is over 60%. Similarly, it is the work variable that has the least effect on happiness in both sexes. In this case, we can conclude that men and women do not enjoy their work, and therefore it does not contribute to their happiness. After health, the variable stated as the source of happiness with the highest rate is love. It is seen that women care about love 3% more than men. For both sexes, success and money were two sources of happiness following love. However, it is seen that men care about success three times more and money two times more than women.

Application on the Role of Gender in Terms of Income Inequality and Education

The effects of gender inequality on income and education level in Turkey were studied with two different models. The binary logistic regression was chosen as the analysis method.

Table 10.8 General happiness level, percentage (2014–2017)

		2014	2015	2016	2017
Male	Very happy	7.61	6.96	6.9	6.08
	Happy	44.35	45.94	51.16	47.54
Female	Very happy	8.53	8.9	8.2	8.35
	Happy	51.91	51.27	56.32	54

Source: TurkStat survey, 2014–2017

Table 10.9 Source of happiness (percentage)

		2014	2015	2016	2017
Male	Success	12.21	11.59	9.09	12.02
	Business	2.91	2.82	3.48	2.47
	Health	63.91	64.85	69.04	64.12
	Love	13.89	14.28	13.17	15.21
	Money	5.76	5.04	4.18	5.34
	Other	1.32	1.42	1.05	0.84
Female	Success	4.96	5.62	4.95	6
	Business	1.45	1.26	1.15	1.34
	Health	73.45	72.54	75.15	71.82
	Love	16.84	17.21	15.98	17.89
	Money	2.76	2.75	2.18	2.51
	Other	0.55	0.63	0.59	0.44

Source: TurkStat Survey, 2014–2017

Method

The provision of a multivariate normality condition is violated in the case of categorical or continuous variables. The problem can be solved by logistic regression which does not make any assumptions about the distribution of independent variables when such violation occurs. Therefore, it is appropriate to use logistic regression where independent variables violate normality assumption (Sharma, 1996). Logistic regression, which was used only in the fields of science such as medicine and biology, has been more frequently used in social sciences in recent years. In addition to the use in social sciences and marketing, logistic regression is also used in genetic research. Logistic regression is the most important type of analysis for modelling of categorical structure variables with widespread usage area. The use of logistic regression is also increasing in the business world. It is important in terms of ensuring the credibility of loans through different variables in Credit Ratings (Agresti, 2002).

Multiple conditions may apply for situations such as whether a student is a high school graduate or not, whether a person is working or not, and whether a patient under observation is responding to a treatment or not. In such a case, it is seen that a dependent variable in social sciences takes two possible values. If the expected outputs are successful, it is coded as 1, and 0 if unsuccessful. In this way, these variables which can take two possible values, such as 1 and 0, are defined as binary data. In studies involving the use of such data, an estimate of the probability of success or failure depending on a conditional dataset consisting of independent variables is carried out (Powers and Yu, 1999).

The other regression analysis, in which the logistic regression analysis is used, examines the relationship between one dependent variable and one or more independent variables. Logistic regression, which is based on the basic principles of linear regression, is actually different in terms of application and calculation methods. The most important difference between linear regression and logistic regression is that the dependent variable takes binary values. This difference due to the binary value is directly effective on the structure and basic assumptions of the logistic regression model (Hosmer et al., 2013). Logistic regression, whose coefficients are very easy to interpret, also does not require the assumptions of linear regression. Not looking for a number of conditions such as normal distribution, linearity and constant variance between the variables may be among the reasons for preferring logistic regression.

The logistic model is established by taking the natural logarithm of the odds ratio of the success and failure to be estimated. The equation 1 below shows the logistic $Gini = \dfrac{\sum^{i-1} n \sum^{j-1} n |x_i - x_j|}{2n \sum^{i-1} n x_i}$ transformation of the probability of success. From the equation 1, the Logit model, where x represents independent variables, will be obtained in equation 2. In logistic regression model:

- $logit\left(p_1\right)$ logistic transformation of probability p
- p_i; probability of the dependent variable to obtain 1 value
- $1 - p_i$; probability of the dependent variable to obtain 0 value
- x_i; Shows independent variables and k shows the number of independent variables.

$$logit\left(p_1\right) = log\left(\frac{p_i}{1 - p_i}\right) \tag{1.1}$$

$$Log\left(\frac{p_i}{1 - p_i}\right) = Z_i = \sum_{k=0}^{p} \beta_k x_{ik} \tag{1.2}$$

It is seen that there is more than one kind of logistic regression analysis in application. The status of dependent and independent variables will decide which method will be preferred here. Binominal (binary) logistic regression is preferred if the category number of the dependent variable is 2, the number of independent variables is 1, and the category number of independent variables is 2. Binominal (binary) logistic regression is preferred if the category number of dependent variable is 2, the number of independent variables is 1 and the category number of independent variable is more than 2. Multivariate logistic regression is preferred if the category number of the dependent variable is 2, the number of independent variables is 2 and more, and the category number of independent variable is 2 and more. Multinomial logistic regression is preferred, if the category number of dependent variables is at least 3 (more than 2) and if it is unordered; even if the number and category of independent variables is 1 or more. Ordinal logistic regression is preferred if the category number of dependent variable is more than 2 and the categorization is ordered, regardless of the number and category of independent variable.

Data Set and Variables

For the application related to the determination of the effect of gender inequality on income and education in Turkey, 2013 "Life Satisfaction Survey" data obtained from TUIK was used. The variables used in the models are given in Table 10.10. In the first model, income was chosen as the dependent variable and education in the second model. Both dependent variables are given binary values. The income level of 1550₺ (Turkish Lira) and above has the value of 1, and the lower income level has the value of "0". For the education variable, being at least high school graduate has a value of "1" and having a lower education level than high school has the value of "0".

The independent variables in the model are given a value of "1" for their probability of occurrence and "0" for the probability of non-occurrence. The age variable is between 15 and 99. If the marital status is married "1", if not "0" value is given; if the work status is public "1", if private sector "0"; if gender is female "1" and if male "0"; if there is insurance "1", if there is no insurance "0"; if experienced gender discrimination (repression) "1", if not "0", if working at her/his own business "1", if not "0"; and if happy "1", if not "0" value is given.

Table 10.11 provides summary information about the households used in the analysis. The total number of observations is 196,203 and the average age is 44 years. The percentage of those who are married is 77% and the rate of non-married is 33%. The percentage of those having the highest level of secondary education is 30%, while the ratio of those with a higher education level is 30%. While 57% of individuals are women, 43% are men. In terms of

Table 10.10 Variables and data descriptions

Type	Code	Explanation
Dependent variables	Income	At least 1550 Turkish Lira 1, not 0.
	Education	At least high school 1, not 0.
Independent variables	Age	15–99.
	Marital status	Married 1, not married 0.
	Employment status	Public sector 1, private sector 0.
	Wage-worker	Wage-worker 1, others 0.
	Gender	Male 1, female 0.
	Insurance	Yes 1, no 0.
	Gender discrimination	Yes 1, no 0.
	Own business	Yes 1, no 0.
	Happy	Yes 1, no 0.

Table 10.11 Summary information

Age	average (15 +) (%)	44
Marital status	married (%)	77
	not married (%)	23
Education	high school (%)	30
	secondary education (%)	70
Gender	female (%)	57
	male (%)	43
Employment status	public sector (%)	8
	private sector (%)	92
Home ownership	hirer (%)	22
	homeowner (%)	78
Average income	net monthly income at least 1550 ₺(Turkish Lira) (%)	33
	net monthly income less 1550 ₺ (Turkish Lira) (%)	67
Car ownership	yes (%)	3
	no (%)	97

work status, 8% are public sector employees and 92% work in private sector. The home ownership rate is 78%, while the tenancy rate is 22%. The percentage of those with a monthly net income of more than 1550₺ is 33%, while the proportion of those with less than 1550₺ is 67%. The rate of those who own a car is 3%, while the rate of those without a car is 97%. As a value between net minimum wage and absolute poverty line in Turkey in 2017, 1550₺ was preferred as the limit value for income.

Empirical Results

The reliability of the models and the analysis was provided by using the ROC (Receiver Operating Characteristic) Analysis, classification table, tests such as Pearson-chi2 and Hosmer-Lemoshow. All other independent variables in the model are given values categorically, especially binary values. The general significance of the logistic regression model is Wald-chi2 (Chi-Square) and measures the probability value. As seen in Table 10.12 and Table 10.13, the Wald-chi2 probability values for both models are significant at 5%. The total classification table related to the explanatory power of the models is also used. The classification table values are 85% for Model-1 and 79% for Model-2. The result of the ROC analysis was 87% for the first model and 85% for the second model. The Pearson-chi2 test results showed that the probability value ($p > 0.05$) was greater than 5% for both models. In addition, it is determined that there is no multiple linear connection problem which causes deviation in estimation by calculating the variance-covariance values for regression models.

Table 10.12 Estimation of factors on education

	Odds ratio	Standard error	z	P>z
Gender	0.148	0.00263	-107.83	0.000
Income	2.449	0.04305	50.97	0.000
Age	0.931	0.00046	-142.15	0.000
Gender discrimination	0.822	0.02393	-6.73	0.000
Marital status	0.952	0.01629	-2.82	0.005
Own business	1.511	0.18407	143.05	0.001
Insurance	5.237	0.0889	97.54	0.000
Wage-worker	2.34	0.07797	25.52	0.000
Constant	815.718	4.526	120.81	0.000
Number of observations	196,203			
Pseudo R^2	0.34			
Wald chi^2 – (p)	61317.30	Prob>chi^2	0.000	
ROC			87%	
Correctly classified			85%	

Table 10.13 Estimation of factors on income

	Odds ratio	Standard error	z	P>z
Education	1.021	0.00046	47.10	0.000
Age	0.993	0.00036	-17.41	0.000
Employment status	1.015	0.31669	74.34	0.000
Gender discrimination	0.778	0.01595	-12.19	0.000
Marital status	0.994	0.01256	-0.45	0.652
Own business	2.586	0.16668	14.74	0.000
Insurance	5.042	0.09185	88.81	0.000
Wage-worker	1.529	0.02084	31.20	0.000
Happy	1.652	0.03104	26.74	0.000
Constant	0.0987	0.00333	-68.64	0.000
Number of observations	196,203			
Pseudo R^2	0.27			
Wald chi^2 – (p)	39097.41	Prob>chi^2	0.000	
ROC			85%	
Correctly classified			79%	

The results of the Model-1 analysis, which was established to determine the effect of gender inequality and other factors on education level, are given in Table10.12. According to the results of the analysis, all the independent variables in the model were statistically significant at 1% (p <0.01). But the direction of the effect of all variables is not the same. Gender, age, gender discrimination, marital status variables have negative effects on education. On the other hand, the effect of income, being self-employed, being a wage employee and having insurance on education is positive.

It is seen that the increasing age decreases the probability of having a high school or above education by 0.93 times. The presence of gender discrimination (or gender repression) reduces the probability of having a high school or above education by 0.82 times compared to its absence. Similarly, it is seen that in gender being a woman has decreased the probability of having a high school or above education by 0.14 times. It has been found that being married has decreased the probability of having a high school or above education by 0.95 times compared to being single.

The fact that the income is above 1550₺ or higher increases the probability of having a high school or above education by 2.4 times compared to having a lower income. Working at a waged job increases the probability of having a high school or above education by 2.3 times compared to working in a temporary or daily job. It is seen that being self-employed instead of working in another job increases the probability of having a high school or above education by 1.5 times, and working with insurance increases it by 5.2 compared to working without insurance.

The analysis results of the Model-2, which was established for the determination of the effect of gender inequality and other factors on the income level, are given in Table 10.13. When we look at the details of the analysis results, it is seen that all the variables except the marital status in the model were statistically significant at 1% (p <0.01).

The effect of marital status, age and gender discrimination on income level is negative. On the other hand, it has been determined that education, working status, self-employment, wage earning, having insurance and happiness variables have positive effects on income level. Being employed in the public sector increases the probability of having an income level of 1550₺ or more by 1 time compared to the private sector, and similarly the probability of having a high school or above education increases the probability of having an income level of 1550₺ or more by 1 time compared to a lower education level. It is seen that working in an insured job increases the probability of having an income level of 1550₺ and more by 5 times than a non-insured job. It was found that working in paid work compared to a temporary job and being happy compared to being unhappy increases the probability of having an income level of 1550₺ and more by 1.6 times. Being self-employed increases the probability of having an income level of 1550₺ and more by 2.6 times compared to working at another job.

Conclusion and Evaluation

Countries have been carrying out a number of studies and policies to ensure that women are more active in economic and social life. In order for these policies to be successful, it is important to determine what are the factors that remove women from economic and social life. In this respect, it was observed that the female labor force participation rate increased relatively in Turkey between 2007–2017. However, the labor force participation rate of men is still two times higher than that of women. When we look at the gender equality index in education, it is observed that there has been an improvement in favor of female students in 2007–2016. When we look at the participation of individuals in social activities in terms of gender, men are more likely to go to shopping centers, spend time on social media, and engage in sports competitions than women. However, women are more likely to attend activities such as reading books, visiting relatives, sewing, embroidery and wood painting.

Women are subjected to physical, sexual and economic violence in Turkey. The reason for this violence can be the husband or someone else from the woman's environment, and physical violence is at the top of the list.Sexual violence is more prevalent among women who live in rural areas and have low levels of education. An important result here is that the rate of exposure to violence in general, even among women's groups with a high level of education, is around 55%.

The findings obtained from the established models also support the information mentioned above. Being female, the presence of gender discrimination and being married has a negative effect on the education level of high school and above. Whereas a high income level and being self-employed has a positive effect. The effect of age and gender discrimination on the high level of income is negative, but the effect of education level, working in the public sector, being happy and working in a paid job is positive. Both the high level of education and the high income have a negative effect on gender repression and discrimination faced by women. The lower the level of education, the more likely women are to become weak in the social and economic sphere. On the other hand, it is seen that there is an increase in education level with increasing income.

Women's employment in daily cleaning jobs, weekly or seasonal jobs will increase women's poverty. Not having a temporary or daily job has a positive effect on income. In this case, women are required to be employed in jobs where regular wages, i.e. monthly wages, are obtained in order to get high income. At the same time, women's high levels of income, health and education, which are indicative of the improvement in welfare, will also prevent women from being excluded from the social sphere. Otherwise, if women are temporarily employed in uninsured, informal jobs, poverty will be an inevitable result. It should not be forgotten that women's poverty does not only concern women. Women's poverty triggers child poverty and sometimes even family poverty. The fact that women are treated only individually means to ignore many roles such as mothers, wives, labourers, employers, household heads that they undertake in society.

There are many programs and policies implemented by the state and non-governmental organizations for women's poverty prevention and women's empowerment in Turkey. Of course, although women's labor force participation rates in Turkey have increased relatively in recent years, they still have the lowest participation rate among OECD countries. Similarly, it is seen that female students have a good level of gender equality index in education. However, these numerical improvements should be actively reflected in the role of women in economic life. Therefore, increasing female employment is important for preventing the feminization of poverty and eliminating social exclusion. The fact that women do not have gender discrimination in both family and working life and that they are not exposed to sexual and physical violence will increase female employment. In addition, the contribution of being happy on the income level of individuals was found to be positive. This situation is due to the fact that people like to do their job and they are happy in business life. It is therefore necessary to ensure that women are not only empowered in terms of income, but also in terms of social inclusion.

References

Agresti, A. (2002). *Categorical Data Analysis*. Canada: John Wily & Sons Inc.

Aktan, C.C. & Vural, I.Y. (2002). *Terminology, Concepts and Measurement Methods*. Ankara: HAK-IS Confederation Publication.

Bhalla, A.S. & Lapeyre, F. (2016). *Poverty and Exclusion in a Global World*. Springer.

Bradshaw, S. & Linneker, B. (2003). *Challenging Women's Poverty. Perspectives on Gender and Poverty Reduction Strategies from Nicaragua and Honduras*. London: Catholic Institute for International Relations.

Buvinić, M. (1997). Women in Poverty: A New Global Underclass. *Foreign Policy*, 38–53.

Chen, M., Vanek, J., Lund, F., Heintz, J., Jhabvala, R. & Bonner, C. (2005). *Progress of the World's Women 2005: Women, Work and Poverty*. New York: United Nations Development Fund for Women (UNIFEM).

Dixon, J. & Macarov, D. (Eds.). (2002). *Poverty: A Persistent Global Reality*. Routledge.

Foster, J.E. (1998). Absolute versus Relative Poverty. *The American Economic Review*, 88(2), 335–341.

Goldberg, G.S. & Kremen, E. (1990). *The Feminization of Poverty: Only in America?* (No. 117). ABC-CLIO.

Haughton, J. & Khandker, S.R. (2009). *Handbook on Poverty & Inequality*. World Bank Publications.

Hosmer, D.W., Lemeshow, S. & Sturdivant, R.X. (2013). *Applied Logistic Regression*. New Jersey: Wiley İnterscience.

Khusro, A. (1999). *The Poverty of Nations*. Springer.

McLanahan, S.S. & Kelly, E.L. (2006). The Feminization of Poverty. In *Handbook of the Sociology of Gender* (pp. 127–145). Boston, MA: Springer.

Narayan, D., Stern, N., Nankani, G., Page, J. & Jorgensen, S. (2002*). Empowerment and Poverty Reduction; A Source Book*. PREM Washington: The World Bank.

Pearce, D. (1978). The Feminization of Poverty: Women, Work, and Welfare. *Urban and Social Change Review*, 11(1), 28–36.

Powers, D.A. & Yu, X. (1999). *Statistical Methods for Categorical Data Analysis.* Academic Press İnc.

Şenses, F. (2001). *The Other Face of Globalisation: Poverty.* Istanbul: Dergâh.

Sharma, S. (1996). *Applied Multivariate Techniques.* Canada: John Wily & Sons Inc.

Silver, H. (1994). Social Exclusion and Social Solidarity: Three Paradigms. *International Labour Review,* 133, 531.

Turkish Statistical Institute (2018a). Retrieved from http://www.tuik.gov.tr/MicroVeri/ GYKA_2011/turkce/metaveri/tanim/yoksullukla-ilgili-taniimlar/index.html

Turkish Statistical Institute (2018b). Retrieved from http://www.tuik.gov.tr/PreTablo. do?alt_id=1068

UNDP (2004). *Human Development Report 2004-Turkey: Information and Communication Technologies.* Ankara: UNDP.

11 A Women Friendly Workplace

Can it be a Tool for Economic Empowerment of Women in Turkey?

Çağla ÜNLÜTÜRK ULUTAŞ

Introduction

There is a growing literature that shows a close link between female employment and women's economic empowerment. Economic empowerment can be described as the "capacity to participate in, contribute to and benefit from growth processes in ways that recognise the value of their contributions, respect their dignity and make it possible to negotiate a fairer distribution of the benefits of growth" (OECD, 2011: 6). Empowerment through working depends upon various factors including the relative income of women and men in the family, whether women's income is sufficient to cover care expenses, and employment status of women and men in the household (Elson, 1999).

Although women's role within Turkey's workforce has improved over the years in terms of both quality and quantity, the female employment rate is still far below the EU and OECD average. The rate of employment is 67.3% for men and 29.7% for women and the rate of unemployment is 9.2% for men and 15.1% for women (TURKSTAT, 2018). According to the Global Gender Gap Report of the World Economic Forum (2017), Turkey is ranked 128th among 144 countries, on the global economic participation and opportunity index. Most studies on women's entry into the labour market in Turkey show that one of the biggest obstacles to women's participation in work life is gender-based division of labour. In this context, this can mean being married, having young children, a care burden, spouses' or families' control over the decisions about employment of women, and dominance of a male breadwinner model (Eyüpoğlu et al. 1998; İlkkaracan, 1998; Karadeniz & Yılmaz, 2007; Ecevit et al., 2008; Çarkoğlu & Kalayıoğlu, 2013). Besides, being a woman increases the likelihood of being employed in bad jobs (Kumaş & Çağlar, 2017). The employment status of women in the Turkish labour market is marked by low trends, high rates of informal employment and unemployment and women's concentration in low-paid and low-status jobs. Gender based discrimination in the work life and male oriented workplaces exacerbate these conditions. Gender wage gap and representation gap in management and leadership roles are still important problems in Turkey. According to Aktaş and Uysal's study (2017: 17) when education, potential labour market experience, and tenure are taken into account, women earn about 8% less than men at the median. Tekgüç et al. (2017: 360) found that "the gender wage gap is 24% for less educated women and 9% for women with tertiary education in full-time formal employment".

It does not seem possible to reverse this trend without developing macro solutions by creating new and better jobs through macro economic policies, coping with discrimination in the labour market, and transforming patriarchal social norms. Gender mainstreaming is a *sine qua non* key to any achievement in this field. Meanwhile, in our present day circumstances where the means of organization and struggle of the working class are weaker, the global labour market generates negative outcomes for workers of both genders. Nevertheless, suggestions of longer-term macro policies should not be considered as fore-going micro and short-term solutions that may create better working environments for women at their workplaces. Indeed, while small-scale initiatives at workplace level may be influential in women's decisions to work and maintain their work after marriage and children, they are also very important in com-batting discrimination in recruitment and promotion. The present study focuses on women friendly workplace (WFW) practices as a micro-scale suggestion to increase women's employment in decent work that will ensure their economic empowerment and seeks answers to the question whether WFW practices in Turkey contribute to women's access to more and better jobs. "Women friendly workplace" is a concept that refers to a set of institutional policies that seek to provide women with the opportunity to successfully integrate their roles in the workplace, at home, and in their families (Cattaneo et al., 1994: 23). Improving childcare facilities in the workplace, interview and promotion policies sensitive to gender roles, parental leave, flexible work practices, coaching programmes directed at female workers, holding meetings during work hours, and alter-native career paths are all examples of women friendly workplace practices (Wooten, 2001: 227).

The first part of this chapter examines the definition and context of the WFW, which have found a place in the early 2000s, especially in human resources literature. The second part of the chapter presents the methodology of this study. The third part investigates the WFW programmes, projects, certificates and awards in Turkey. International organizations play a leading role in the dissemination of these practices. Some NGOs and trade unions also have initiatives on this issue. Finally, the fourth part analyses well-known companies' WFW practices.

Context: Women Friendly Workplace

Presently, while labour market conditions are changing, the composition of labour force and workplace are also in a rapid process of transformation as a result of socio-economic, technological and demographic factors. Along with an increase in women's employment, we observe an increase in the number of elderly workers, the collapse of traditional care regime, proliferation of models of double-earner and single parent families and the spread of women-friendly practices at workplaces with increasing work concentration and means of communication (Honeycutt and Rosen, 1997). Factors leading to the spread of such practices include without any doubt the rising women's movement, women workers' increased visibility in traditional men's jobs and women's demands for spatial and cultural changes in male dominated workplaces. Meanwhile, the reputation of trans-national companies (TNC) is tarnished by increasing human dignity violations and gender-based discrimination suffered by young women workers in TNC supply chains in the process of globalization. WFW practices are therefore seen as a way of image correction and increasing productivity. Hence, starting from the early 2000s WFW practices were first included in TNC policies and then in human resources policies of large domestic companies. The concept started to become an agenda item in Turkey starting from 2010. However, relevant practices in Turkey have as yet found no place in the growing literature on women's employment.

Women-friendly workplace policies have three basic components. The first includes policies geared to reconciling work and family life. Since care responsibilities mostly fall upon women as a result of traditional gender roles, family-friendly workplace policies and women-friendly workplace practices have many points of intersection. Family-friendly workplace supports provided by companies include policies such as flexible work arrangements; services such as resource and referral information about dependent care options and care subsidies (Neal et. al. 1993, cited in Hammer et. al., 2005: 799). The second component is equal treatment in the workplace and prevention of gender-based discrimination in recruitment and promotion processes. In this regard, a women-friendly workplace is defined as

> a place where all staff are being treated with equal respect; women are enjoying the benefits of affirmative action in a real sense; workers' needs and voices are equally valued at all levels of decision-making, planning and implementation, and all employees feel encouraged to give their maximum efforts to increase their potential without devaluing each other in any respect.
>
> (Ali, 2012: 4)

Finally, developing preventative mechanisms against all kinds of discrimination women face at the workplace is an indispensable element of women friendly workplace practices. To this end, fighting against sexual harassment at the workplace and prejudices regarding women's problems related to their performance, skills, contributions to work, absenteeism and attendance is very important (Sands & Scherr, 2001). Through mentorship programmes, which are important in WFW practices, solidarity can be ensured among women employees in different steps of hierarchy and at different levels of seniority. The third component in WFW practices is related to mechanisms of complaint that women can use in reporting cases of discrimination, violation of rights and harassment they experience, and establishment of boards to prevent such cases.

These three components, however, cannot be conceived as separate from each other; they must be taken together to ensure equality at work.

There is a list of musts for a workplace to be women-friendly including the following: flexible working hours; paid leave, parental leave, sick and elderly care leave; training programmes in gender equality; counselling services for women employees to build career; practices of positive discrimination for women; special units to handle complaints about gender discrimination and sexual harassment; wage policies observing gender equality; counselling services to help employees in balancing work and family life; childcare and nursing facilities at the workplace; subsidies for family members in need of care; monitoring of the number of rank and file women employees and women in managing positions in each unit; presence of a quota system to ensure a specific proportion of women at medium and top management levels; transparent and detailed job and promotion qualifications; and practices like mentoring (Zeitz & Dusky, 1988; Chiu and Ng, 1999). Being a WFW requires that ensuring a work–life balance and responding to the needs of women employees are made a part of attitudes, values and culture at all levels of institutional hierarchy. In short, in a truly women-friendly culture, reconciliation of work and family life should not be an issue related only to working hours or day-care centres, but coming in as a result of dialogue, guidance and counselling and conscious, continuous and collective efforts of all employees (Srinivasan, 2015).

Methodology

In this study, a multiple case study technique was applied as a research strategy. "The distinguishing characteristic of the case study is that it attempts to examine: (a) a contemporary phenomenon in its real-life context, especially when (b) the boundaries between phenomenon and context are not clearly evident" (Yin, 1981: 59). Case study is a method that enables us to grasp and deeply analyse social phenomena in the natural environment of a single case by taking due account of its complexity and context and protecting its integrity. The case may be an individual, a role, group, organization, a nation, process, policy and many other things (Punch, 2005: 144). There is no single data collection tool used in case studies. Case studies can be done by using fieldwork, archival records, verbal reports, observations, or any combination of these (Yin, 1981: 58). In the present study, I referred to secondary sources such as newspapers, websites of companies, reports and booklets and manuals related to certification and awarding processes. Following a detailed literature survey on WFW, I went over all WFW related documents of international organizations active in this issue. I conducted in-depth interviews with staff from UNDP, UNWOMEN and ILO-Turkey. Then I contacted companies in Turkey that had been awarded or certificated as WFW and examined these companies' codes of conduct, activity and strategy reports. I also examined relevant documents and statistics of trade union confederations and the

Ministry of Family, Labour and Social Services as parties relevant to the issue, and conducted semi-structured interviews with the three largest trade union confederations, one employers' organization and two staff from the Ministry of Family, Labour and Social Services.

While representation is important in quantitative sampling, the sample is selected purposefully in qualitative surveys to reach richer information (Meyer, 2001: 333). So I conducted in-depth interviews with HR or Communication representatives of three workplaces certified as WFW by at least one organization in order to obtain richer information on WFW practices. While evaluating data obtained through the examination of documents and in-depth interviews, I tried to use them together as a whole. I coded the names of interviews and companies since many of them preferred anonymity.

Programmes and Certificates related to Women-Friendly Workplaces in Turkey

Initiatives in Turkey to guide and document WFW practices were launched first by international agencies under the United Nations and then followed by a few governmental and non-governmental initiatives. In this study all initiatives geared to WFW practices in Turkey were examined but not all are included in the analysis. Only continuous and sustainable programmes and applications focusing on WFW are discussed. This part will first deal with initiatives geared to guidance and documentation in the field of WFW. The overall framework in this regard is drawn from the activities of the UN and its agencies in Turkey. It must be noted, however, that these activities are not coordinated and carried out as a part of an integrated scheme.

International Organizations and WFW Practices

The projects and programmes launched under the leadership of the UN and in cooperation with states, companies and non-governmental organizations to include women and increase investment in women are coined as "transnational business feminism" (TBF) by Roberts (2014). Gender equality is the leading theme in almost all projects carried out by UN agencies within the last ten years. However, the argument having its imprint on mentioned projects is "while investments in women contribute to gender equality they will also enhance companies in terms of profitability and competitive power." Roberts (2014) criticizes transnational business feminism spread by UN agencies for omitting historical and structural causes of poverty and gender-based inequality while they may be contributing to women's employment. The most outright criticism of "transnational business feminism" is that it helps legitimizing and reproducing the neoliberal macroeconomic framework that feeds gender inequality. Turning to Turkey, we observe that major outstanding initiatives in women's employment are either launched by UN agencies or realized with their contribution. It cannot be denied that these activities contribute to the creation of new and better jobs for women and increased gender equality awareness in the world of work. Still, in a way to confirm Roberts (2014) these activities yield no outcomes for many women who cannot participate in the labour force, are unemployed or employed in very low quality jobs since they do not envisage any programme which can alter economic and political conditions.

Women Empowerment Principles

Women Empowerment Principles (WEPs) were launched in 2010 by the UN Women and the UN Global Compact, as a means of guiding the business world for empowering women in the workplace and community (Roberts, 2014: 212). In this context each firm is called upon for proactive leadership to protect women against sexual harassment, violence and other violations in its sphere of influence (Kilgour, 2012: 119). The WEPs aim to ensure that enterprises examine and analyse their current practices, performance indicators and reporting practices by using a gender lens. For this purpose, the leaders of the business world are required to commit explicitly to the following seven principles for corporate policies geared to promoting gender equality (WEPs–Global Compact Türkiye, 2018).

- Establish high-level corporate leadership for gender equality
- Treat all women and men fairly at work – respect and support human rights and non-discrimination
- Ensure the health, safety and well-being of all women and men workers
- Promote education, training and professional development for women
- Implement enterprise development, supply chain and marketing practices that empower women
- Promote equality through community initiatives and advocacy
- Measure and publicly report on progress to achieve gender equality.

(Global Compact, 2018)

In the scope of Women Empowerment Principles, which were launched with the motto of "Equality Means Business", "equality is broadly understood as expanding the opportunities for women's inclusion and professional development in a safe, gender aware and violence-free workplace" (Gregoratti, 2018: 214). While these principles are essential for improving the conditions of women at the workplace, they are leaving aside the question of degradation of working conditions and devaluing of work traditionally carried out by women in the globalized economy (Prügl & True, 2014: 1152).

Leaders undersigning the CEO support statement commit themselves to impart Women's Empowerment Principles in all points from the executive board to supply chain and to translate them into life. Turkey ranks as the third country with the highest number of signatories (WEPs–Global Compact Turkiye, 2018). It is rather astonishing that Turkey remains at the bottom of all global indexes related to gender equality, as it is one of the leading countries in the number of signatories. One reason may be the formation of a strong initiative to eliminate this rather deep problem of inequality in the country. Meanwhile this high number of signatories may also be associated with the fact that an online signature and CEO support statement is sufficient for being a WEPs signatory in the absence of a monitoring and supervision process afterwards. Indeed the WEP is based on voluntary reporting and information sharing processes rather than examinations and sanctions. Its aim is to learn from each other through learning tools such as webinars, articles and best practices provided by pioneering TNCs (Gregoratti, 2018: 215).

One of our expert participants stated that companies in Turkey undersign WEP mainly for three reasons:

> In the first group there are big firms that have already been observing gender equality criteria in company practices for many years. These firms were also the first ones in signing WEPs in Turkey in 2011. The second group comprises TNCs and banks joining in with the expectation that this will increase their prestige. And the third group consists of small and medium size enterprises (SMEs) owning women who want to turn their workplaces into WFW. This last group constitutes a smaller part among signatories.
>
> (Participant A)

Another participant asserts that while WEP put forward some strong principles it is actually emptied for not having any supervision or sanctioning afterwards:

> WEPs have turned into something that confers unjust prestige to some companies that actually take no step to promote gender equality. This intention keeps such companies away from gender equality certification schemes or programmes that require efforts and fees. For example, to be prestigious in the eyes of individual or corporate clients procuring goods/services from them they say they are WEPs signatory.
>
> (Participant B)

World Bank and the Women Entrepreneurs Association of Turkey

Equal Opportunities Model

The Gender Equity Model (GEM) was first put into implementation by the World Bank (WB) has been implemented since 2010 by the Women Entrepreneurs Association of Turkey (KAGIDER) under the name "Equal Opportunities Model" (FEM)[1] with the technical support of WB. Either private sector companies or government agencies can adopt GEM. The GEM was in fact constructed as a model based on public–private partnership. It is, however, led in Turkey by a non-governmental organization (NGO) working on women's entrepreneurship. Companies such as PwC and Ernst &Young manage evaluation processes. Auditing companies have no place in the model in WB practices in other countries of the world.

FEM criteria include seven steps to promote equity:

- The CEO Declaration and Commitment to Equal Opportunities
- Equal Opportunities in Job Recruitment and Selection
- Equality in Access to Trainings and Self-Improvement Activities
- Equality in Promotions and Career Development Opportunities
- Career Support Procedures for Employees with Children
- Procedures for Harassment and Claim Management in the Workplace
- Communications Language and Corporate Advertisements.

(KAGIDER, 2018)

The name "Equal Opportunities Model" instead of "Gender Equality Model" was not randomly selected. In all interviews with both employers' organization and company, the response "workplace initiatives to ensure equal opportunities" was common when they were asked what the concept of a women-friendly workplace meant to them. It can be noted that recently the government as well as women's and workers' organizations sharing the same political line with the government refuse the term "gender equality" and promote the alternative "gender justice."

The FEM is the most common and well-known certificate that firms in Turkey apply to be recognized as WFW. Taking a look at companies with FEM certification, however, we see that most of them are TNCs and the remaining are the leading holdings in Turkey. Several FEM certified companies also received the Gender Equality Award of the Ministry of Labour and Social Affairs.

UNDP: The Gender Equality Seal

The Gender Equality Seal (GES) Certification developed by the UNDP in 2009 was applied as a model by both UNDP country offices and public and private sectors throughout the world. As in the case of GEM, its pilot work was carried out in Latin American countries. The most important characteristic of GEM is that some of its elements may vary as a result of different institutional and economic structures in countries where it is taking place. In the context of GES the UNDP extends technical support to public and private companies who want to develop and implement their own Gender Equality Management Systems. A state institution undertakes responsibility in giving a start to the programme. This institution identifies necessary steps to be taken to guarantee the effective implementation of the system, its reliability, and the programme's overall success (Gusta, 2012: 19).

Participating organizations can benefit from UNDP support in all processes related to internal assessment and analysis, identifying strength and weaknesses, firm's gender equality policy, and developing gender-sensitive external communication strategies. The UNDP also delivers training in gender equality (UNDP, 2016a).

According to information supplied by a UNDP representative, following the certification programme and inspection process to encourage gender equality and empower women at workplaces, a company is awarded GES in 18 or 24 months. However, the process does not end with certification, and monitoring of gender equality at the workplace continues. The GES guide serves as a roadmap not only in order to get a GES certificate but also to keep going as a workplace where gender equality is constantly observed. The scheme is planned to be implemented by the UNDP in Turkey starting from 2019 in cooperation with the public sector. A pilot scheme has already been launched with a leading firm in Turkey. The GEM developed by the WB and the GES developed by the UNDP have very similar steps, objectives and content. The common points of the WEP and GEM can be seen by looking at six fundamental areas given below:

- Correct gender based imbalances in decision-making positions.
- Detecting and eliminating gender-based pay gaps.
- Policies to improve work-life balance.
- Insertion of women into occupational areas that are traditionally male-dominated.
- Inclusive and non-sexist corporate communication.
- Promoting zero tolerance of sexual harassment in the workplace.

ILO: Programme for Gender Equality in SMEs

Sustaining Competitive and Responsible Enterprises (SCORE) is an International Labour Organization (ILO) global programme, which includes a modular training and in-factory counselling programme in small and medium enterprises (SMEs) (ILO, 2015: 55). The "Gender Equality Model in SMEs" (MIG[2-]SCORE) emerged upon the addition of a new gender module to the SCORE Programme in June. The pilot implementation of the programme was first launched in Turkey on 22 October 2018. Under the MIGSCORE programme, training activities are organized and one-to-one counselling services are delivered to encourage institutions to impart gender equality into organizational culture and their mode of operating. The programme focuses on five fundamental areas of gender equality in the world of work (ILO, 2018):

- work–private life balance,
- voice equality,
- equal pay for equal work,
- inclusive employment,
- work environment
- good treatment.

A member of staff from ILO expresses the main orientation of enterprises taking part in a pilot scheme as follows: "We started our pilot work with four enterprises. One important factor leading SMEs to ask for the implementation of the model is the expectation that contract manufacturers will build prestige in the eyes of global employers." Negative effects of extremely competitive production in global value chains on working conditions significantly damaged the reputation of buyers in the eyes of consumers (Béthoux et al., 2007; Harpor and Peetz, 2011). As a result, global companies had to ask SMEs producing for them to regulate social conditions at their workplaces through established documents and standards. Gender equality at the workplace is one of the important components of these social conditions.

Earlier UN documents of relevance were used while designing the MIGSCORE. The main feature of the MIGSCORE that distinguishes it from FEM and GES, however, is that it targets SMEs. In fact, SMEs constitute 99.9% of all enterprises in Turkey (KSEP, 2015: 28). The way to increase women's employment and ensure gender equality at workplaces thus requires gender mainstreaming in SMEs. Secondly, its system of management related to gender equality is not an auditable standard, a document and/or a seal. The MIGSCORE is not an ILO document pertaining to working conditions in enterprises and organizations applying it. The FEM and GES processes, on the other hand, end up with a document that is subject to supervision.

WFW Practices in Enterprises

Issues that used to be regarded as under the responsibility of the government are now making themselves on to the agenda of the world of business. This change derives from privatizations that followed neoliberal economic policies and the state's new course in fulfilling its responsibilities that has shifted from rowing to steering only. While increasing the share of the private sector in GDP and employment, this transformation also led to companies assuming more important roles in policy issues that were earlier considered as "politics" (Grosser, 2009: 293). Also under the impact of transnational business feminism spread under the lead of the UN, the private sector started to appear at the centre of an important part of policies related to gender equality. Starting from the early 2000s, companies in Turkey began approaching their gender equality agenda in the context of social sustainability, social accountability and social responsibility. The worldwide discussion emerging on the issue of social responsibility has its significant share in this. An important role in this context is also played by international studies stressing women's contribution to economic growth and efforts of TNCs engaged in export-oriented production to comply with social responsibility standards. Companies started to seek to achieve a competitive advantage through their Corporate Social Responsibility (CSR) policies. Therefore, they are more willing to adopt equality practices.

Almost all firms in Turkey coming to the fore with their WFW practices are institutionalized big enterprises of which many are TNCs. In the study, I selected as cases a holding active in the sectors of iron-steel, energy and logistics, a textile company producing for export, and a transnational cosmetics company. Earlier, I had applied for my study to those firms that were awarded or certificated as WFW and were known in the public for their gender equality policies. Of those firms agreeing to take part in the research, I selected the firms mentioned above that had different characteristics and operating in different sectors. All mentioned firms are WEPs signatories. Upon the request of firms, their actual names are not used and given the code names of A Textile, B Holding and C Cosmetics. This study focuses on practices within the company, which are less visible.

A Textile

Producing for many international brands, the A Textile is one of the companies in Turkey employing the highest number of women under one roof. The common belief that textile manufacture is a woman's job doubtlessly has its share in this rather high number. Indeed, about 48–50% of employees are women at A Textile.

The communication officer of the firm describes the women-friendly workplace as one at which all employees, women and men, have equal access to all relevant rights and opportunities. The company has developed a gender equality policy document. Besides the principle of non-discrimination, this document brings to the fore the rights of employees who are victims of domestic violence. Further, progress reports of the company have a separate section about women employees and its report card in gender equality can be followed in this section. Employees are given training in domestic violence and gender equality. The company received the SA 8000 certification in 2014.[3] Under the project that the company is implementing jointly with a women's organization, awareness-building activities are organized for all women employees in health, law, and family/personal development. There is also awareness building in "Combating Domestic Violence" and employees can benefit from free counselling services delivered by lawyers in related issues. The company psychologist who delivers free counselling services also supports women psychologically. The company has no board specially formed to deal with cases of sexual harassment and no specialist or organ for gender equality. However, the institutional communication director is in charge of overseeing all issues and activities related to gender equality. There is cooperation with women's organizations in specific issues. There is no practice of quota in jobs or management positions traditionally dominated by males.

Some 70% of employees of A Textile are unionized and covered by a collective agreement. The company committed to have its sub-contracting firms observe SA 8000 criteria as well. The company representative states that buyers too are inspected with respect to social accountability including gender discrimination.

The firm comes to the fore as women-friendly mainly for its crèche facility. It was established in 1986 with a capacity of 1,000 children. Presently 218 children from working families benefit from this facility free of charge. Service periods in the facility are fine-tuned according to shifts applied in the workplace as 07:00–15:00 and 15:00–23:00. The crèche gives priority to the children of employees in the workplace. Still, when capacity allows, children of male workers whose wives are covered by social security can also benefit from its services. Women workers who leave their children at the crèche after the expiration of their maternity leave can also take them to nursing rooms for breastfeeding. Women's access to nursing and childcare services after giving birth kept labour turnover at quite a low level. Indeed, 50% of working-women have their seniority for over ten years. The representative of the firm explains this by saying "worker's happiness and ease finds reflection in your products. Practices like this enhance motivation and a sense of belonging." Children can enjoy the free transportation facilities that their mothers also use. Working families sending their children to the crèche are given training as "parents" which also includes training in gender equality.

B Holding

The B Holding is active in traditionally male dominant sectors such as iron and steel, energy and logistics. Following general trends in Turkey, the proportion of women in both blue and white-collar jobs is very low in works related to technology, engineering and management. The proportion of women workers in white-collar jobs is 24.6% while it is only 1.13% in blue-collar jobs. The proportion of women managers is 18.48% at higher levels and 25.49% at middle level. With its FEM certificate, the B Holding established a Social Equality platform to tackle this problem. The priorities of this non-hierarchical and open platform are: working to maintain full support of all management levels; challenge, impact and develop company and HR policies; play an active role in commissioning national and international treaties and principles; develop suggestions to change discriminatory statement, practice and actions.

The document "Management Concept and Practices of B Holding Group" states that no gender discrimination shall be made in recruitment and promotion, in working conditions, and in relations with clients, buyers and their partners. Sustainability documents of the holding include gender equality as well.

There is a Board of Ethics in the B Holding and violations such as harassment are enquired into and resolved by this board. The Board of Ethics responds to all questions and information received by its Information and Counselling Desk via e-mails or phone calls.

The holding does not directly provide crèche services in its companies but ensures discounts in fees of various child-care services. To each blue-collar male worker in one of its companies whose wife is formally employed, the company pays a monthly subsidy of $57 to ensure crèche attendance of a child from age 0 to 6. Under a project carried out by the holding in cooperation with the relevant ministry, crèches bearing the name of the holding have been constructed in organized industrial zones in ten provinces. However, it is worth noting that the holding does not provide free crèche services in all workplaces under its companies. The B Holding follows the rates of return to work of women employees after maternity. For the last year 66% of women in maternity leave returned to their jobs. B is also granting working mothers and fathers additional leave to attend school meetings.

The company provided a guide on how to avoid discriminatory discourses and acts in working life. Some 6,500 employees of the holding received training on this issue. Further, one of the companies within the group delivered training in coding to daughters of employees in the age group 7–14.

Employees in companies of the holding are unionized and these companies are engaged in collective bargaining. However, since it is not a part of the agenda of trade unions organized particularly in metal works and transportation, there is to date no strong demand for crèches.

Women employees are provided mothers' rooms to breastfeed their children. Gender equality is one of the strategic issues addressed by the B Holding. Recently, it has become an agenda of the holding to recruit women technical personnel to blue-collar positions traditionally dominated by men. The B Holding representative says "At workplaces where there is balanced distribution of women and men there are more democratic, respectful and productive environments" and goes on "However, relevant departments of technical high schools and vocational colleges which are the sources of labour force are all attended by male students only. Moreover, women do not want to remain in shifts and work while there are so many men around; they don't want to work in male jobs and outdoors... We are trying to bring in transformation in these issues."

Meanwhile, the fact that almost all blue collar workers were men led to male domination at workplaces within the B Holding in spatial terms as well. The holding then reviewed its facilities such as showers, toilets, nursing rooms and other services. The first initiative took place in 2016 to employ women in male dominant works in the logistics sector. "In logistics we recruited some women as crane sling operators at the port and they were quite successful." While earlier there was no woman employed in blue-collar jobs in the company of the holding engaged in steel production, such traditional male jobs as crane operation were opened to women as of 2018 under the slogan "No job is difficult for women." They met some resistance before starting the practice: "We want to train and employ women as crane operators. But the operator who is expected to give this training tells me, 'I train the man sitting next to me in the cabin in an applied way by holding his hand in some cases. Now how would I do it with a woman?'". In spite of this resistance 2,500 women applied to job posting for women in early 2018 and 26 of these applicants were taken in for training. Having an average score of 99.5 in all trainings, women then started working as crane, scale and entry operators.

C Cosmetics

The C Cosmetics is a multinational company in cosmetics active since the 19th century. The company markets its products through its distributors almost all of whom are women on the basis of a network marketing system. In almost all company documents it is stated that empowerment of women through their employment is the underlying philosophy shaping their working models. Women make up 60% of 33,200 company employees around the world. While 7 of its 11 executive board members are women, women occupy 455 of top management positions.

In Turkey, 80% of 400 tenured employees of the C Cosmetics are women and women constitute 78% of positions like directors and higher positions. Women also have their share of 64% in company's management board. The C Cosmetics representative underlines the importance they attach to gender equality as follows: "Our working environment is completely equal with respect to gender. There is equal access to all processes related to training, promotion and recruitment. We are engaged in a range of practices to closely support our women employees in such fields as career building, maternity and personal development. Pregnant employees in the company with FEM certificate receive coaching one hour a day before and after delivery." They explain the motive behind certification with their desire to strengthen and document existing inner company practices. The representative of the company explains the benefit of WFW as "ensuring diversified, efficient and productive working environment by merging the power of women and men." Since a significant number of employees are women there has as yet been no reporting of any case of sexual harassment. There are no specific policies and procedures to combat cases like harassment and workplace bullying It is stated that law and IC departments and compliance communication line can be used in case a complaint is to be lodged relating to such events. There are nursing rooms at workplaces, but no crèche services. As stated earlier, however, employees may benefit from discounted rates in crèches with which the company has a contract.

> "Since the number of our women workers is high, so is the rate of maternity leave. Women employees can exercise all their rights related to maternity as prescribed by legislation in effect. Although they have their maternity benefits from the Social Security Agency (SGK) we keep paying their salaries in full. Under our private health insurance scheme, we send infant nurses to homes after birth. Since it is difficult in Istanbul to use nursing leave as 1.5 hours, mothers can use this leave collectively if they wish so. We also provide opportunities of flexible work. The daily working hours is actually from 7:45 to 16:45, they can have it as from 10:00 to 18:00 and they can also leave at 15:30 by keeping their lunch breaks shorter. Finally they have the opportunity to work at home for one day."

While coming to the fore in the media with its women-friendly practices, C Cosmetics has also made some news about heavy working conditions of women employees in warehouse and dismissals upon unionization. In the period concerned, women warehouse workers waged a long resistance in front of C Cosmetics. While workers asserted that the primary employer is C Cosmetics, the representative of the company claimed that warehouse works were outsourced, C Cosmetics was not the employer but only a client receiving warehouse services and therefore it had no responsibility related to the issue. When asked whether they oversee working conditions and violations of equality at workplaces to which they supply services they replied that they had no such overseeing. Regardless of the existence of a prearranged outsourcing contract as asserted by the union, it is important that primary employers oversee conditions in their suppliers and expect them to fulfil the same principles in relation to the employment of women in decent conditions. As a matter of fact, while many TNCs today offer decent work conditions to their mostly white-collar, educated and high-paid employees, there are young women humiliated and paid low wages despite their long working hours at the other end of global value chains.

Attitudes of Trade Unions towards WFW Practices

All the documents of trade unions concerning gender and interviews were conducted with the representatives of the three biggest trade union confederations as a part of the research. The evaluation of gender policies of trade unions exceeds the limits of this chapter. However, the attitudes of trade unions towards WFW practices are briefly evaluated.

With the exception of HAK-IS Confederation, trade unions have no work on the promotion of women-friendly practices at workplaces in which they are organized. However, it is doubtless that trade unions constitute the party that should have their say at least as much as employers and act as advocates to ensure equality at workplaces where they are organized.

Interviews show that the TURK-IS, which is the largest and oldest trade union confederation in Turkey, has no focus on gender equality in its agenda. The DISK, the only trade union confederation in Turkey with a woman president holds the opinion that micro solutions at workplace level will yield no meaningful results unless the government's conservative and unequal gender policy changes. The HAK-IS, on the other hand, stands against the idea that women and men are equal and avoids using the term gender equality. Still, this confederation characterized by extremely conservative attitudes, has its women's committees down at its lowest levels and delivered training in gender justice to all. The confederation having a close affinity to the government pursues a policy for women's employment that is at peace with the existing conservative and neoliberal socio-economic structure. In this context, it conducted the "Project on the Certification of Women-Friendly Workplaces through Social Dialogue." At 80 workplaces where trade unions affiliated to HAK-IS are organized, Women-Friendly Workplace certifications were issued in line with SA 8000 Social Accountability Standards. Under the project, workplaces satisfying required criteria were awarded their certificates.

Concluding Remarks

Empowerment can be ensured by access to decent and egalitarian working conditions and by observing the work–life balance. Increases in women's employment is not enough by itself to empower women. The present study focuses on the question whether WFW practices can be a part of an empowerment strategy of this type. Our work shows that the backbone of WFW practices in Turkey basically concentrate on the projects of international organizations. Further, it became possible at some workplaces to reconcile work and family life and to give effect to transformation of traditionally gendered occupations in others. In addition, some NGOs and business people have their initiatives to the same effect. However, with the exception of a project implemented by HAK-IS, the issue is not raised as a request from employers by the workers' movement. Given this, the demand for WFW mainly stands on the discourse that women constitute a category that enhances profitability and diversity in production processes. It will not be sufficient if trade union and women's movements remain as parties to macro policies only. They also need to be parties to local-level employment, care and family policies, and guide gender equality policies of workplaces.

There are many WFW applications implemented by large and corporate companies. However, the small and medium sized enterprises constitute the majority of enterprises in Turkey. It is difficult to encounter SMEs that come up with WFW applications. The new project, which focuses only on SMEs by the ILO, has the potential to change this trend. However, awareness-raising on gender equality in SMEs should be supported by economic policies to change the labour-intensive mode of production pattern based on cheap labour. It is observed that WFW applications, focus on highly skilled, white-collar workers in Turkey. Many companies that stand out with their practices in this field operate in the banking and insurance sector. Some companies, such as C Cosmetics, have outsourced their manufacturing and production activities which are performed by blue-collar workers. While some of the high-skilled women are employed in the women friendly workplaces, there are women workers who are condemned to inferior jobs at the other end of the chain. The fact that B Holding, which has the most prominent of WFW applications, has less than 2% of blue-collar women employment supports this argument. The higher the level of education of women, the higher the employment opportunities and better working conditions in Turkey. The fact that WFW applications focus on the white-collar women's workforce reinforces this dualist structure. The way to break this trend is the struggle of the organizations which may be the voice of the unskilled female labour force. Certainly, these policies require a radical transformation in the economy and gender policies carried out by the government in order to produce significant results.

Notes

1 FEM is the abbreviation of *Fırsat Eşitliği Modeli*.
2 Modele deigualdad de genero.
3 SA 8000 is the most widely recognized international standard for social accountability of enterprises.

References

Ali, R. (2012). Brac as a Workplace: Is It Women-Friendly? *Brac Research Report*. Retrieved from: http://research.brac.net/reports/BRAC%20as%20work%20place.pdf.
Aktaş, A. & Uysal, G. (2016). The Gender Wage Gap in Turkey. *Marmara Üniversitesi İktisadi ve İdari Bilimler Dergisi*, 38(2), 1–19.
Béthoux, É., Didry, C. & Mias, A. (2007). What Codes of Conduct Tell Us: Corporate Social Responsibility and the Nature of the Multinational Corporation? *Corporate Governance: An International Review*, 15(1), 77–90.
Cattaneo, J. R., Reavley, M. & Templer, A. (1994). Women in Management as a Strategic HR Initiative. *Women in Management Review*, 9(2), 23–28.
Çarkoglu, A. & Kalaycıoğu E. (2013). *Türkiye'de Aile, Is ve Toplumsal Cinsiyet*. Istanbul Politikalar Merkezi. Retrieved from: http://ipc.sabanciuniv.edu/wp-content/uploads/2013/11/Aile-2012-ISSP-Family-Survey-final.pdf.
Chiu, W.C.K. & Ng, C.W. (1999). Women-Friendly Harm and Organizational Commitment: A Study among Women and Men of Organizations in Hong Kong. *Journal of Occupational and Organizational Psychology*, 72, 485–502.
Ecevit, Y., Tan, M., Sancar, S. & Acuner, S. (2008). *Turkiye'de Toplumsal Cinsiyet Esitsizligi: Sorunlar, Oncelikler ve Cozum Onerileri*. İstanbul: TUSIAD.
Elson, D. (1999). Labor Markets as Gendered Institutions: Equality, Efficiency and Empowerment Issues. *World Development*, 27(3), 611–627.
Eyüpoğlu, A., Özar, Ş. & Tanrıöver, H. (1988). Kentli Kadinlarin Calışma Kosullari ve Calisma Yasamini Terk Nedenleri. In O. Citci, *20. Yüzyılın Sonunda Kadınlar ve Gelecek*. Ankara: TODAİE.
Global Compact. (2018). Retrieved from: https://www.unglobalcompact.org/take-action/action/womens-principles.
Gregoratti, C. (2018). Feminist Perspectives on the UN Women's Empowerment Principles. In J. Elias and A. Roberts, *Handbook on the International Political Economy of Gender*. Cheltenham, UK; Northampton, USA: Edward Elgar Publishing, pp. 211–224.
Grosser, K. (2009). Corporate Social Responsibility and Gender Equality: Women as Stakeholders and the European Union Sustainability Strategy. *Business Ethics: A European Review*, 18(3), 290–307. doi:10.1111/j.1467-8608.2009.01564.x.
Gusta, A. (2012). *Gender Equality in the Workplace. How to make progress with a Certification Programme for Gender Equality Management Systems*. UNDP-RBLAC. Retrieved from: http://www.americalatinagenera.org/es/documentos/Gender-Equality-in-the-Workplace.pdf.
Hammer, L.B., Neal, N.B., Newsom, J.T., Brockwood, K.J. & Colton, C.L. (2005). A Longitudinal Study of the Effects of Dual-Earner Couples' Utilization of Family-Friendly Workplace Supports on Work and Family Outcomes. *Journal of Applied Psychology*, 90(4), 799–810.

Harpur, P. & Peetz, D. (2011). *Is Corporate Social Responsibility in Labour Standards an Oxymoron?* Association of Industrial Relations Academics in Australia and New Zealand Conference. Retrieved from: https://ssrn.com/abstract=1804795.

Honeycutt, T. & Rosen, B. (1997). Family Friendly Human Resource Policies, Salary Levels, and Salient Identity as Predictors of Organizational Attraction. *Journal of Vocational Behavior*, 50(2), 271–290. doi:10.1006/jvbe.1996.1554

ILO. (2015). *Small and Medium-sized Enterprises and Decent and Productive Employment Creation.* International Labour Conference, 104th Session, 2015 Report IV. Geneva: ILO. Retrieved from: https://www.ilo.org/wcmsp5/groups/public/@ed_norm/@relconf/documents/meetingdocument/wcms_358294.pdf.

ILO. (2018). ILO Office for Turkey Launches "Gender Equality Model in SMEs" in Turkey for Gender Equality at Work. Retrieved from: https://www.ilo.org/ankara/news/WCMS_648267/lang–en/index.htm.

İlkkaracan, İ. (1998). Kentli Kadinlar ve Calisma Yasami. In A. Hacımirzaoğlu, *75 Yılda Kadınlar ve Erkekler.* İstanbul: Tarih Vakfi Yayınlari.

KAGIDER. (2018). Retrieved from: http://www.kagider.org/en/corporate/projects-and-activities/projects/lists/projects/equal-opportunities-model-(fem)-a-gender-equality-certification.

Karadeniz, O. & Yılmaz, H. (2007). Kadinin Isgucune Katilimini Etkileyen Faktorler. *Is Dunyasinda Kadin.* Istanbul: TURKONFED.

Kilgour, M. (2012). The Global Compact and Gender Inequality. *Business & Society,* 52(1), 105–134. doi:10.1177/0007650312459918.

KSEP. (2015). *KOBI Strateji ve Eylem Plani 2015–2018.* Retrieved from: https://www.kosgeb.gov.tr/Content/Upload/Dosya/Mali%20Tablolar/KSEP/Kobi_Stratejisi_ve_Eylem_Plani_(2015-2018).pdf.

Kumaş, H. & Çağlar, A. (2017). Tabakali Isgucu Piyasasi Teorisine gore Turkiye'de Ozel-Hizmet Sektorunde Istihdamin Kalitesi. *ISGUC The Journal of Industrial Relations and Human Resources*, 19(1), 49–86. doi:10.4026/isguc.346258.

Meyer, C. B. (2001). A Case in Case Study Methodology. *Field Methods*, 13(4), 329–352. https://doi.org/10.1177/1525822X0101300402.

OECD. (2011). *Women's Economic Empowerment.* Retrieved from: https://www.oecd.org/dac/gender-development/47561694.pdf.

Prügl, E. & True, J. (2014). Equality Means Business? Governing Gender through Transnational Public-Private Partnerships. *Review of International Political Economy, 21*(6), 1137–1169. doi:10.1080/09692290.2013.849277.

Punch, K. (2005). *Introduction to Social Research: Quantitative & Qualitative Approaches.* Los Angeles: Sage.

Roberts, A. (2014). The Political Economy of "Transnational Business Feminism". *International Feminist Journal of Politics*, 17(2), 209–231.

Sands, D.M. & Scherr, S.J. (2001). *Center Self-Assessment for a Woman-Friendly Workplace.* CGIAR Gender and Diversity Program Working Paper, No.29. Retrieved from: https://cgspace.cgiar.org/bitstream/handle/10947/2730/29_Centre%20Self-Assessment%20for%20a%20Woman-Friendly%20Workplace_genderdiversity_WP.pdf?sequence=1.

Srinivasan, M.S. (2015). Building a Woman Friendly Workplace. *The XIMB Journal of Management*, 12(2), 119–126.

Tekgüç, H., Eryar, D. & Cindoğlu, D. (2017). Women's Tertiary Education Masks the Gender Wage Gap in Turkey. *Journal of Labor Research*, 38(3), 360–386.

TURKSTAT. (2018). Isgücü Istatistikleri. No. 27690. Retrieved from: http://www.tuik. gov.tr/PreHaberBultenleri.do?id=27690.

UNDP. (2016a). *The Gender Equality Seal: A Certification Programme for Public and Private Enterprises*. Panama: UNDP. Retrieved from: http://www.undp.org/content/ dam/undp/library/gender/gender%20and%20governance/2%20Gender%20Equality %20Seal%20Certification%20for%20Public%20and%20Private%20Enterprises% 20-%20LAC%20Pioneers.pdf.

UNDP. (2016b). *The Gender Equality Seal Certification Programme for Public and Private Enterprises: Putting Principles into Practice*. Panama: UNDP. Retrieved from: http://www.undp.org/content/dam/undp/library/gender/gender%20and%20gov ernance/3%20Gender%20Equality%20Seal%20Certification%20for%20Public%20a nd%20Private%20Enterprises%20Summary.pdf.

WEPs–Global Compact Turkiye. (2018). Retrieved from: http://www.globalcompa ctturkiye.org/global-compact-turkiye/kadinin-guclenmesi/weps-nedir.

Wooten, L. P. (2001). What Makes Women-Friendly Public Accounting Firms Tick? The Diffusion of Human Resource Management Knowledge through Institutional and Resource Pressures. *Sex Roles*, 45(5–6), 277–297. doi:10.1023/A: 1014353413496.

World Economic Forum. (2017), *The Global Gender Gap Report*. Retrieved from: http://www3.weforum.org/docs/WEF_GGGR_2017.pdf.

Yin, R. (1981). The Case Study Crisis: Some Answers. *Administrative Science Quarterly, 26*(1), 58. doi:10.2307/2392599.

Zeitz, B. & Dusky, L. (1988). *The Best Companies for Women*. New York: Simon and Schuster.

12 Constructing Female Entrepreneurial Identity in Turkey

Murat Şakir EROĞUL

Introduction

Mainstream, more traditional, literature on entrepreneurship is portrayed as gender neutral; although feminist scholars have noted that it is nevertheless a gendered process (Ahl, 2006; Bruni et al., 2004a and b; Lewis, 2006; Gherardi, 2015) that institutionalizes gender norms and roles of men and women. For instance, professional sex typing, that is "think/manager (i.e. entrepreneur), think male" still persists as a global theme today (Schein, 2001; Schein et al., 1996). We continue to find that the consensus is that normative, cognitive and regulative pillars play competing roles in entrepreneurship (Slotte-Kock & Coviello 2010; Naguib & Jamali, 2015) in both providing opportunities and imposing challenges.

From the outside, Turkey tends to be viewed as an essentially paternalistic environment where women adhere to traditional roles. While this perspective may be valid in certain contexts, Turkey also sets a model for the region in relation to connecting religious and traditional values to standards of modern economical-social-cultural-political complexity. Women in Turkey are seen in all facets of professional life, engaged as citizens in the economic and social development of this rapidly changing country. Within this complexity, Turkey offers an interesting vantage point for studying attitudes towards women professionals as it brings together both a cultural as well as a geographical "bridge" between the "East" and "West" (Aycan et al., 2012). Emphasizing women's role in the modernization process, Ataturk is known to have declared that "Our women must be even more enlightened, more virtuous, and more knowledgeable than our men!" (cited in Inan, 1967: 118). Yet, several studies conducted in Turkey in the 1970s, 1980s, and 1990s indicate that the ratio of women senior executives does not exceed 4% in the private sector or 7.6% in the public sector (Kabasakal et al., 2011). Furthermore, within the Organization of Eastern Caribbean States (OECS) and European countries Turkey has the greatest gender gap among efficiency-driven economies, presenting difficulties that women must face when starting up and continuing their business. The institutional and sociocultural context of Turkey makes it an apt representative of the "majority world" (Kağıtçıbaşı, 2007) that is economically "developing" and culturally "traditional" (Aycan et al., 2012).

Persistent patriarchal social values and associated traditional gender roles, together with limited access to education and training opportunities, lack of experience in business life, lack of role models and limited access to informal and formal networks deter women from entrepreneurship in Turkey (Karataş-Özkan et al., 2010). Furthermore, the lack of feminist psychology along with historical, political, intellectual, and cultural factors affect feminism's influence on psychology (Boratav, 2011)

I aim to review this "gap" with an anti-essentialist view of gender identity (Alvesson et al., 2008; Cerulo, 1997) to untangle the social construction of gender utilizing institutional logic of societal norms (DiMaggio & Powell, 1983) exploring the plethora of women's approaches on becoming an entrepreneur (Patriotta, 2011; Gherardi & Perrotta, 2016). Institutional theory provides a sharper focus to unravel the context, which may foster and inhibit female activity. By drawing on institutional framework of competing logics, incorporating an anti-essentialist view on gender identity, and utilizing intersectionality enables examining the interplay between multiple categories of identity, which work to construct particular experiences. My use of intersectionality takes economic, social, cultural, political and historical contexts into account, offering a more tangible analysis of the lived experiences of Turkish women.

The chapter is organized as follows. I begin by describing institutional theory and contextualizing. Next, I discuss the concept of competing logics in gender identity and provide insight into the essentialist and non-essentialist view making way into exploring competing logics in becoming a female entrepreneur. From here, I move into contextualizing competing logics within the Turkish context where we enter into utilizing institutional theory to contextualize the current state of Turkish female entrepreneurship. I then provide a brief overview of the competing logics in the sameness and difference feminist conceptual framework. This framework allows us to understand institutional competing forces that present the need for a multiple-identities approach in shaping and conditioning the process of becoming empowered. I discuss how individual discursive practices in relation to influences of formal and informal cultural templates and structural arrangements may act as a source of empowerment (Barragan et al., 2018; Eroğul et al., 2016; Essers et al., 2013; Pio, 2005). Here, I note that entrepreneurship and context is intertwined with gender identity and is constructed in fragmented ways in narration (Czarniawska, 2004; Gherardi & Perrotta, 2014), where sense-making processes are embedded within the discursive practices of Turkish female entrepreneurs, and the cultural and structural templates that inhibit and foster their entrepreneurial identity. I end by presenting a new approach that captures all of the above by not only recognizing female entrepreneur's experiences but by facilitating them to engage in bottom-up approaches to empower agency over their environment.

Institutional Theory and Contextualizing

Institutional theory captures the influence of formal and informal institutions on particular phenomena (Naguib & Jamali, 2015) by focusing on normative, cognitive and regulative pillars affecting and constraining organizational behavior (Scott, 2008). The regulative pillar comprises institutions such as codified rules and laws enforced by state machinery (Scott, 2008). The normative pillar refers to institutions in the form of moral beliefs and norms, obligations or standards of behavior that provide a basis for social meaning and social order (Scott, 2008). Individuals in this respect are strongly influenced by collective norms, values, representations or normative frameworks that impose social obligations on them, constraining their choices and behaviors. Lastly, the cultural-cognitive pillar refers to institutions that take the form of cognitive social constructions and internalized interpretations of the culture, customs and traditions (Markus & Zajonc, 1985). In other words, cultural-cognitive institutions influence behavior by controlling conceptions of what the world is and the types of actions that are considered appropriate/suitable based on those conceptions (Scott, 2008). Consequently, different institutional logics from different social contexts may then contradict each other or even compete against each other (Thornton et al., 2012). Accordingly, becoming an entrepreneur and being one happens in a context where formal and informal institutions enable, obstruct or condition this process in terms of gender norms and expectations.

Competing Logics in Gender Identities

The study of identities, as well as the process of constructing them, have occupied many pages in psychology, sociology, gender studies, and organizational studies fields of research, and have been approached by different perspectives and ontological and methodological traditions. (For a review, see: Alvesson et al., 2008; Brown, 2001, 2008; Cerulo, 1997; Thomas et al., 2004.) In all these works, identity has been defined in more or less similar terms, implying "a form of subjectivity" ranging from "coherent and enduring" characteristics to more "dynamic", "temporary, and "fragmented" character (Alvesson et al., 2008: 6). I discuss two competing perspective on (gender) identities, the essentialist view and the anti-essentialist view (Alvesson et al., 2008; Cerulo, 1997), departing from different schools of thought.

Essentialist View – Functionalist Approach

In Cerulo's (1997: 386) review, the essentialist view on identity endorses the ontological perspective that "reality" is out there; therefore, natural attributes provide the "essential" characteristics of identity, such as "physiological traits, psychological predispositions, regional features, or the property of structural locations" (Cerulo, 1997). Psychologists have seen identity as something stable and fixed, as pointed out by Potter & Wetherell (1987: 95–96): "the self is an entity and, like any other entity or natural physical object, it can be described definitively...given proper investigative methods, the true veridical description of the [self] will ultimately emerge." Biological sex has been used to attribute characteristics to each of these groups, assuming essentialist identities and behaviors (West & Zimmerman, 1987). Many studies in entrepreneurship have approached the study of male/female differences by ascribing specific and fixed characteristics to each sex in relation to aspirations, abilities, barriers, and type of companies (Ahl, 2006; Calás & Smircich, 2009). However, this essentialist view of identity, based on gender as a dichotomous variable, has been contested in entrepreneurship studies (see: Bruni et al., 2004a; Bruni et al., 2004b; Lewis, 2006, 2013).

Anti-Essentialist View – Interpretive Approach

Other studies have departed from "destabilized accounts of the identifying processes, considering the 'symbolic, rhetorical and/or discursive process' (Alvesson et al., 2008: 14). In Modernity, 'the self, like the broader institutional contexts in which it exists, has to be reflexively made'. This reflexive process termed 'identity work' refers to 'people being engaged in forming, repairing, maintaining, strengthening or revising the constructions that are productive of a sense of coherence and distinctiveness' (Sveningsson & Alvesson, 2003: 1165). Yet this task has to be accomplished amid a puzzling diversity of options and possibilities" (Giddens, 1991: 3), although, the next view on identity contends that those possibilities are limited. In studies with the interpretive approach, the emphasis is placed on how individuals engage in a "discursive struggle over meaning" (Alvesson et al., 2008: 14) and this is an ongoing process involving anxiety, uncertainty, and self-doubt (Knights & Willmott, 1989). Cerulo (1997: 387) contends that social constructionist researchers "reject any category that sets forward essential or core features as the unique property of a collective's members". In particular, some feminist scholars do not consider identity as an essential collection of unique traits of an individual. Rather, it is conceptualized as a social construction and a relational concept (Kärreman & Alvesson, 2009).

Here, I present the construction of identity as a discursive process dependent on place, time and context (Haraway, 1991). Within the tradition of the social constructionist perspective on identity, McAdams (1997: 61) conceptualizes multiple identity construction as a reflexive project that people "work on", situated within time and context, and in dialogue with their relevant others (Watson, 2009). Thus, to better understand entrepreneurship, we need to analyze the socially accomplished and culturally constructed identities of entrepreneurs (Essers et al., 2010: 322).

Competing Logics in Becoming a Female Entrepreneur

To understand the process of becoming an entrepreneur, we have to attend to the competing contextual and relational aspects of identity construction (e.g. Adib &

Guerrier, 2003; Alvesson & Willmott, 2002; Gherardi & Poggio, 2007). The context is where individuals' identities are regulated (Alvesson & Willmott, 2002: 629). In this regard, Bruni et al., (2004b: 257) contend that "being an entrepreneur and the nature of entrepreneurial practice" is determined and reinforced through gendered "stereotypical script[s]" (Down & Warren, 2008), including the masculinized norm (i.e. image) of the entrepreneur (Lewis, 2006, 2013). Gherardi & Poggio (2001), drawing on Alcoff's (1988: 434) notion of "positionality", offer that women construct their identities and are construed within a context with a particular "symbolic order of gender" (p. 190).

The other characteristic of constructing identity is the relational aspect. Individuals (i.e. entrepreneurs) "define [themselves] directly" and "by defining others" (Alvesson & Willmott, 2002: 629). Adib & Guerrier (2003), drawing on Said's (1979) Orientalism, argue that the process of engaging in othering, as the constitutive other, is presented as different from the self. In the context of entrepreneurship, the notion of entrepreneurial activity is enacted as having masculine characteristics (Ogbor, 2000), and therefore, an entrepreneur can be equated with a male figure (Ahl, 2006; Bruni et al., 2004a). Similarly, Lewis (2006: 455) labels this normative entrepreneur as the "invisible (masculine) entrepreneur", who is (as is his behavior) considered as the norm of which female entrepreneurs are compared to (as is their behavior) as "a universal norm". Moreover, when female entrepreneurs deviate and compete away from "the normative standard of serious, professional business, women experience an 'othering' as the non-male" (Lewis, 2006).

In Fournier's (2002) case, women entrepreneurs from Italy reject the idea of being cast by their otherness when they portray fragmented identities by both accepting and resisting those categorizations. The process of "competing logics" can also occur when women construct their "self as other", to deal with the pressures to conform to traditional roles, and therefore, they "the self as other" in relation to this dominant position (Sawicki, 1994; cited in Thomas & Davies, 2005: 725) of the private realm.

Contextualizing Competing Logics within the Turkish Context

In the beginning of the 1980s, there was a shift in the perceptions of Turkish people towards commerce. People started to get familiar with concepts like markets, competition and quality. In this period, many structural reforms (e.g. the liberalization of foreign trade, currency and investments, free floating exchange rates, elimination of price controls, new interest rate policy to enhance savings, strictly controlled public expenditures and finally an open and flexible foreign investment policy) had been introduced in the general framework of the Turkish economy (Demirci, 2013). However, a shift in the perception of women in commerce is much more complicated. With the influence of religious cultural norms on Turkish culture (Karataş-Özkan et al., 2011) women began to lose their status in society and still struggle today. There has been many attempts to change deeply rooted patriarchal values in traditional Turkish society (Wasti, 1998). Those struggles began largely in the second half of the nineteenth century, as women started to regain their social status. Yet again, despite the structural changes that have taken place, Turkish women still today often have to cope with certain problems originating from the duality between secularism on the one hand, and religiousness and patriarchal Middle Eastern values on the other (Kabasakal et al., 2011). The analysis of women in society reveals the simultaneous impact of Eastern and Western cultures in the Turkish context (Kabasakal et al., 2011).

Women's participation in the marketplace and social attitudes toward working women have changed drastically in recent years. In addition, women are becoming more educated and they are getting married at a later age; and fertility rates are declining (Dildar, 2015). Even though these changes are taking place, Turkey has a unique sociocultural structure, which is visible in relation to gender inequality that exists in many areas of work. Still, work outside of the home is dominated primarily by patriarchy and masculine rationality (Yetim, 2008; Özturk, 2011; Arat, 2010), and the social roles of women as defined by the norms of patriarchal society play an influential role in shaping women's decisions in everything they do. It is this patriarchal social structure, which is the cause of gender discrimination (Hisrick & Özturk, 1999; Maden, 2015).

Many women in Turkey stay engaged in personal conflict between domestic and work life. Women are expected to embody social roles as mother and housewife, which puts extra pressure on them (Maden, 2015), on top of the significant gender-based barriers when pursuing certain careers (see Özar, 2007; Kancı & Altinay, 2007). Regardless, many women in Turkey have succeeded and excelled as managers, entrepreneurs, academics, engineers, doctors, lawyers and soldiers, among many other newly accessible jobs, specialties and skills. Yet again, these same women continue to face stereotypes about who they are and how capably they perform their duties.

Contextualizing the Current State of Turkish Female Entrepreneurship

In recent years, many institutions, nations and organizations across the globe have begun to promote the benefits of women-focused entrepreneurship programs as a means to achieve gender equality and national economic development (Özkazanç-Pan, 2014). Demirci (2013) states that identical to the growing worldwide interest in entrepreneurship, Turkey is also facing a paradigm shift towards the understanding of the importance of entrepreneurship. In accordance with the evolution of entrepreneurship in Turkey, as a major step in developing the entrepreneurial mindset in the country, KOSGEB (Small and Medium Industry Development Organization), a governmental agency to support the operations of small and medium-sized enterprises, was founded in 1990. A little over a decade later, in 2002 the Women Entrepreneurs Association of Turkey (KAGIDER) was founded. Since then steady interest towards entrepreneurship prevails among government, business, NGOs, public authorities and the academic community among many others. Both KOSGEB and KAGIDER play an important role in increasing entrepreneurial activity, attitude and aspiration in Turkey. There contributions have been significant not only with their ongoing government policies encouraging female labor force participation but the modifications they have taken out towards positive discrimination for female entrepreneurs. Along with the financial support they provide through grants and interest free loans, the training, coaching and mentorship programs are a significant part of the entrepreneurial ecosystem.

Despite the growing interest and development of the entrepreneurial ecosystem there are still many problems that remain unsolved. Although there are a limited number of studies that have focused on female entrepreneurship, these studies have provided a recognition system in which the inhibiting and fostering factors entrepreneurs come across are understood. In addition, some studies provide top-down policy recommendations and/or implications, and a few explore coping strategies at the individual level (see Bedük & Eryeşil, 2013; Benzing et al., 2009; Çetindamar, 2005; Karataş-Özkan et al. (2011); Maden, 2015; Nayir, 2008; Ökten, 2015; Özdemir, 2010; Özkazanç-Pan, 2014; Tuzun & Takay, 2017; Ufuk and Özgen 2001a, 2001b; Yılmaz et al., 2015). We now begin surveying the literature to contextualize the current state of female entrepreneurship in Turkey.

Karataş-Özkan et al. (2010) argue that the recent developments in Turkey, particularly the rise of religious conservatism and patriarchal norms, have affected the segregation of women's roles to motherhood and home making. They state that these changes in social mores present women entrepreneurs with challenges in reconciling the competing expectations of work and private life. The impact of these changes are seen within the sociocultural structure, which is especially visible in business. For instance, within OECS and European countries, Turkey has the lowest rate of female entrepreneurs (GEM, 2012). In Turkey, women are less likely than men to engage in entrepreneurial activities, and the ratio of male to female entrepreneurs is one of the highest among efficiency-driven economies (i.e. Bosnia-Herzegovina, Croatia, Russia, Estonia, Hungary, Georgia, Kosovo, Latvia, Lithuania, Turkey, Romania, Poland, Macedonia). According to the GEM (2015) special reports on female entrepreneurship, male total entrepreneurial activity rates (from the TEA (Total Early-Stage Entrepreneurial Activity) index) were 2.43 times greater than women's TEA rates. Karataş-Özkan et al., (2011) mention that women are deterred from entrepreneurship due to persistent patriarchal social values and associated traditional gender roles. They also list the limited access to education and training opportunities, as well as lack of experience in employment and business among having relatively little access to role models, and limited financial and social capital (i.e. limited access to informal and formal support networks: Karataş-Özkan et al., 2010).

Similar challenges have been cited by others. For instance, issues related to government bureaucracy, lack of financing, a weak economy, traditional views against business ownership by women (Benzing et al., 2009), community's view on women's place in society (Ufuk & Özgen 2001b), gender role conflicts in relation to home and child care (Bedük & Eryeşil, 2013), and unsupportive husbands contributing to work–family conflict (Maden, 2015). Thus, Turkey has the greatest gender gap among efficiency-driven economies, which presents difficulties (like the ones mentioned above) that women must face when starting up and continuing their business in Turkey (Tuzun & Takay, 2017).

In a recent study, Tuzun & Takay (2017) set out to understand how women define motivational factors, challenges and future needs of their entrepreneurial experience in urban and rural areas of Ankara, the Capital of Turkey. Their findings indicate that female entrepreneurs are mostly intrinsically motivated and achievement is the most important motive for them, particularly in rural areas. However, the desire to be independent is a crucial motivation factor regardless of location. For their other objective, Tuzun & Takay (2017) investigate the challenges identified by women during their entrepreneurial activity. Here, they found that social roles pose a major challenge to both rural and urban women and the primary challenge was in gender-related areas. Overall, they conclude that female entrepreneurs in Turkey face gender barriers to starting and growing their businesses, including an unequal share of family and household responsibilities (Tuzun & Takay, 2017). These factors, combined with social exclusion based on gender, mean that female entrepreneurs are in a less favorable position than their male counterparts in Turkey. Although Tuzun & Takay provide useful insight into female entrepreneurship in Turkey, their study focuses on a descriptive nature of the motivational factors, obstacles and future needs of female entrepreneurs and no relationship among these factors is assessed (Tuzun & Takay, 2017). Testing the relationships between those variables, would be very useful for both researchers and practitioners.

Relying on secular and Islamic feminist perspectives, Özkazanç-Pan (2014) examines whether promoting and fostering women's entrepreneurship as part of the economic development agenda can potentially achieve gender equality. She states that the critical issue is how, in an era of globalization, neo-liberal development ideologies and practices may perpetuate gender inequality in Turkey and whether individual entrepreneurship activities guided by secular or Islamic feminist principles serve to change or challenge existing patriarchal structures, institutions and norms in Turkish society. Özkazanç-Pan (2014) states that gender equality remains elusive in Turkey, a nation where secular and Islamic ideologies compete and produce different solutions to ongoing economic, socio-cultural and political issues. She continues by saying, women's entrepreneurship has emerged as an important solution toward gender equality and economic development. In her study, Özkazanç-Pan uses two women's organizations that exemplify secular and Islamic feminist ideologies; she examines whether the entrepreneurship activities they promote give way to challenging patriarchal norms, values and practices widespread in Turkish society. She found that through their distinct practices and engagement with entrepreneurship, both secular and Islamic feminist positions allowed for praxis and represented an ethico-political commitment to dismantling neo-liberal development ideologies in the Turkish context that perpetuate gender inequality. Secular and Islamic feminist practices and entrepreneurship practices have different implications for achieving gender equality including changes in gender norms, economic development policies and women's empowerment in a Muslim-majority country (Özkazanç-Pan, 2014).

In their 2011 study, Karataş-Özkan and her co-authors focus on the role of women in the context of Turkish family businesses examining the drivers for, and the contributions and challenges of, Turkish women in family business settings. In their research, they highlight the importance of rapidly changing cultural values and changing views in regards to what roles women should hold in the public sphere in Turkey. They find that gender-based inequalities are underpinned by societal and family perceptions of women. Karataş-Özkan et al., (2011) claim that careful examination of the challenges and issues that Turkish women face in family businesses can be an important step in addressing problems such as "invisibility", lack of role models and mentors, and that of support frameworks, such as tailored education and training.

In efforts to contextualize Turkish female entrepreneur's experiences, in connection to the notion of entrepreneurship as women's empowerment requires recognizing institutional norms and values. To achieve this, a review of the current state of female entrepreneurship in Turkey and the challenges these women come across helps understand the process shaped by prescriptive gender roles that are composed of behaviors, values, and attitudes that a society considers appropriate for both males and females. These essentialist approaches tend to initiate shortages in facilitating social reforms to transform entrepreneurial initiatives and support mechanisms due to their stereotypical gender role perceptions among decision-making bodies. Keeping in mind that biological sex is determined formatting physiologically, gender is considered a social construction (Reskin & Padavic, 1994), women can and do draw on "masculine" or "feminine" repertoires to construct a "masculinize[d]" identity or engage in an identity process of "femalization" (Lewis, 2013). What is important to note is how identities are fragmented and that there is room to create alternative positions (see Barragan et al., 2018; Bourne and Calás 2013; Bruni et al. 2004a; Eroğul et al., 2016; Essers & Benschop 2007). Therefore, it is important for future research to adopt an anti-essentialist view of gender identity (Alvesson et al., 2008; Cerulo, 1997; West & Zimmerman, 1987) that considers gender identity as a performative action discursively constituted rather than fixed (Harding et al., 2013).

Overview of Feminist Conceptual Frameworks

Different feminist conceptual frameworks (Benschop & Verloo, 2011; Calás & Smircich, 2006; Harding, 1987; Thomas & Davies, 2005) have been used in management and organization studies, to explain how different feminist theories conceptualize gender in relation to the context of entrepreneurship. However, we find that their outcomes may lead to further confusion and discrimination legislatively and at the level of society's views.

The first group considers men and women as essentially the same. In this notion, women and men are considered the same in terms of essential traits. The idea of equality is rooted in the "sameness" or "equal opportunities" perspective (Nentwich, 2006; Thomas & Davies, 2005; van den Brink et al., 2010), which is based on "liberal individualism" and "liberal structuralism" theories. On the one hand, these scholars proposed that women are disadvantaged, in comparison to men, because they have been socialized differently. On the other hand, different social structures produce asymmetries of power in favor of men (Calás & Smircich, 2006; Kanter, 1977; Nentwich, 2006). Accordingly, women have to learn "fitting the norm" of the masculinized ideal entrepreneur (Lewis, 2006, 2013). They have to overcome their femininity to compete in a men's world. In this view, society has to create "opportunity structures" for women (Benschop & Verloo, 2011: 282) to make their womanhood responsibilities easier, such as childcare, and access to financial opportunities for them. These two strategies can level the field for women entrepreneurs. However, it has been noted that treating men and women as equals will work only if they are the same (Nentwich, 2006). There is always the risk of trying to "normalize" women according to the male norm (Martin, 2003), and this has implications not only for women, who might display a variety of complex and contradictory identities, but also for men, due to the assumption of a "hegemonic masculinity" rather than a variety of "masculinities" (Hearn, 2004). For example, it can create stereotypes that women prefer small and stable businesses in order to have a work–life balance for their womanhood roles (Lee-Gosselin & Grisé, 1990). Moreover, this may affect the creation of policies that promote growth, and constrain access to resources needed to start-up these types of businesses. Similarly, it underestimates that many males are owners of small businesses (Bridge et al., 1998; cited in Lewis, 2006).

In the second framework, women are considered essentially different (and possibly superior) than men. According to this view, female entrepreneurs have different and valuable characteristics to satisfy specific needs. Working from this tradition, one can expect that by making visible the differences between men and women, in particular, the feminine entrepreneurial advantage, women can be empowered as entrepreneurs. Nevertheless, this position may reinforce the traditional stereotypes and dichotomies of masculinity and femininity attached to men and to women (Knights & Kerfoot, 2004; Martin, 2003). Similarly, Bruni et al., (2004b) contend that women can draw on more than one repertoire when constructing their entrepreneurial identities. In addition, the "feminine way" view can accentuate the gender segregation of women in specific sectors, where nurturing and caring traits are important.

These two essentialist views present the "sameness–difference" dilemma as whether women and men have a same or different nature. These views leave us with the dilemma between considering women as either disadvantaged or in a superior position to men. In this chapter, we draw from a conceptualization that eliminates the sameness–difference dilemma by considering multiple identities.

The third group proposes to solve this dilemma by arguing that these similarities and differences are socially constructed and require contextualization (see Welter, 2011). We borrow Calas & Smircich's (2006) question: "women's condition: same or different"? In a simplistic way, they answer this by stating that "these theoretical tendencies have been charged with 'essentialism'" (Ibid.: 300). The notion of men and women as equal or different reproduces "a gender binary steeped in hierarchy" (Knights & Kerfoot, 2004: 432). Therefore, even if women try to adopt a specific notion of gender to construct their identities, they draw on antagonistic discourses and/or face existential struggles to achieve a true authentic self (Costas & Fleming, 2009; Ybema et al., 2009). Multiplicity of alternativee identities for men and women rest on social constructionist feminism and poststructuralist feminist theorizing (Butler, 1990; Weedon, 1987; West & Zimmerman, 1987). While reproductive organs determine biological sex, gender is considered a social construction (Reskin & Padavic, 1994). This process of constructing differences occurs through gender practices such as the use of accepted forms of language and expressions (West & Zimmerman, 1987). Individuals' identities (including their entrepreneurial identifications) and the characteristics associated with them are considered to be discursive constructions (Foucault, 1977), which are historically and culturally produced (Weedon, 1987, 1999).

These social constructions of gender have to be exposed to empower women's entrepreneurial activities. By drawing on this tradition, it is possible to see how women's identity constructions (and those of others) struggle between "masculine" and "feminine" discourses that "challenges, changes and yet sustains the dominant gender order" (Bruni et al., 2004b). For example, in Essers & Benschop's (2009) study on Muslim women entrepreneurs in the Netherlands, these women demonstrate how they negotiate between multiple categories of identification when narrating their identities and experiences. In particular, they struggle around essentialisms attached to those categories by re-defining them through alternative provisional selves (Davies & Harré, 1990). In a different study, Eroğul et al. (2016) investigate the cultural and structural challenges within the Arab context found to constrain women's opportunities towards entrepreneurial development and activity. They bring together gender, identity and networking into the subjective experiences of Emirati female entrepreneurs through antenarrative perspectives to demonstrate that developing cooperation with men is a viable and complementary means to addressing contextual challenges and achieving empowerment. They show that Emirati female entrepreneurs employ a multi-layered identity work process which manifests in a relational manner via efforts to strategically construct opportunity by means of engaging in discursive relationships with men.

Lastly, in a more recent study, Barragan et al. (2018) adopt a more comprehensive view of entrepreneurship, as a form of emancipation and social change for women by considering micro-emancipation at the level of both agency and identity of women entrepreneurs in patriarchal and Islamic societies. In their study, they draw on the notions of the dynamic and ongoing process between dominators (i.e., men of the patriarchal family) and the dominated (i.e., women entrepreneurs) (Ibid.). In this process, micro-emancipation and active obedience are intertwined. Barragan et al., (2018) show how adopting an interpretive approach, provided the means to analyze the narratives of female entrepreneurs in their early stages of becoming an entrepreneur who engage in strategic (dis)obedience and confirmed that micro-emancipation is always "tailored" (Ashcraft, 2005: 86) to specific societies in the case of women.

Social science disciplines in Turkey, especially psychology are said to be the least influenced by feminism (Boratav, 2011). Some of the main reasons include:

the relatively recent expansion of the discipline in terms of numbers of academic programs, the structure of the professions in Turkey in general which favored an elite recruitment pattern, the force of the Republican ideology which has failed to challenge a primarily familial definition of women's roles and a familial definition of "self" in general, the political propagation in the past decade of conservative religious values, as well as the changing priorities of social psychological research in Turkey away from a social issue focus.

(Ibid.: 32)

The unified message from all the sections of this chapter is that *the influence of institutional competing logics, notions of gender and feminist perspectives, the importance of contextualization and the Turkish context, the current state of Turkish female entrepreneurs* put forward the necessary leap to propose an alternative approach to studying female entrepreneurship in Turkey. This approach goes beyond identifying the economic, social, cultural, political, religious, and psychological contextual features of Turkey. Current research on female entrepreneurship in Turkey provides models on how to change this external environment of the entrepreneur. The difficulty of this approach is that "being an entrepreneur" will depend on the context of the female. I propose reducing the effect of external disturbances by developing joint actions and activities, so that a collective and eventually a support system may be developed, to facilitate survival in its environment.

An Alternative Approach to Studying Female Entrepreneurship Identity Work

Without the progress made in understanding the current state of Turkish female entrepreneurship through past research, and without the evolution of feminist theory, we would not be able to step out and beyond into new models of female entrepreneurship that can resonate with the 21st century complex social and competitive environment.

There is a need to move from solely conceptualizing the current state of female entrepreneurship to a new phase of deeper engagement in understanding and solving how individual Turkish female entrepreneurs experience becoming entrepreneurs within the contextual patterns and arrangements that may enable or inhibit justifying their entrepreneurial identity. One way would be through employing the multiple-identities approach and engaging women entrepreneurs not as participants of research but as research partners and designers of bottom-up approaches. Here, solutions or models for female entrepreneurs are developed through the application of theories to identify notions that may be useful in practice. In other words, the aim is to stabilize activities in practice within their current contextual state. This type of engaged research approach would not only help (aspiring) entrepreneurs anticipate the means to cooperate, coordinate and collaborate but it would empower women to have greater agency in developing their own process of becoming empowered, which in return may facilitate empowering women in their entrepreneurial activities. For researchers, this provides the means to conceptualize the social construction of higher quality experiences and activities that have been stabilized within practice, and allow testing and developing contributions to knowing how to change female entrepreneur's experiences. With this said, indeed, more work is needed to apply intersectionality to structural levels.

Conclusion and Recommendations for Future Research

There is certainly need for more work drawing on an anti-essentialist view of gender identity through intersectionality to understand the process of becoming a female entrepreneur in Turkey. Towards this path, I recommend exploring the particular discourses on empowering Turkish women as entrepreneurs by employing a socially constructed conceptualization of gender identity to facilitate further understanding of how Turkish female entrepreneurs experience challenges of institutional "competing logics" and do "identity work" in corroboration of becoming entrepreneurs; this may in return enable women in their activities.

The concept of competing logics and identity work will allow examining the individual discursive practices that the Turkish female entrepreneur uses in relation to institutionalized influences of formal and informal cultural templates and structural arrangements, to construct and legitimize her identity as a business owner. Employing a theoretical framework that enables capturing the regulative, normative and cultural-cognitive challenges through these women's narratives will provide the means to examine the constructions of discursive practices developed by the entrepreneurs, and identify how they engage in the identity work against or with institutional competing logics they confront. Furthermore, intersectionality enables gender, politics, religion, culture, social structure, economics and location to come together at varying intersections to construct "Turkish woman's experience" in becoming and being an entrepreneur in Turkey. This could foster more engaged-based research approaches (i.e. collaborative process between the researcher and the participant/community) prescribing models for facilitating female entrepreneurial activity rather than solely describing the female entrepreneurial environment and its impact.

These lines of study will then contribute to understanding the competing discourses on empowering women as entrepreneurs, which in return may facilitate empowering more women to collectively greater understanding and control over institutional templates and the support systems needed within them. This chapter ends with a call towards new models of study to help empower female entrepreneurs through engaged research at the experiential and structural level.

References

Adib, A. & Guerrier, Y. (2003). The Interlocking of Gender with Nationality, Race, Ethnicity and Class: the Narratives of Women in Hotel Work. *Gender, Work & Organization*, 10(4), 413–432.

Ahl, H. (2006). Why Research on Women Entrepreneurs Needs New Directions. *Entrepreneurship: Theory & Practice*, 30(5), 595–621.

Alcoff, L. (1988). Cultural Feminism versus Post-Structuralism: The Identity Crisis in Feminist Theory. *Signs*, 13(3), 405–436.

Alvesson, M. & Willmott, H. (2002). Identity Regulation as Organizational Control: Producing the Appropriate Individual. *Journal of Management Studies*, 39(5), 619–644.

Alvesson, M., Lee Ashcraft, K. & Thomas, R. (2008). Identity Matters: Reflections on the Construction of Identity Scholarship in Organization Studies. *Organization*, 15 (1), 5–28. Arat, Y. (2010). Religion, Politics, and Gender Equality in Turkey: Implications of a Democratic Paradox? *Third World Quarterly*, 31(6), 869–884.

Ashcraft, K.L. (2005). Resistance through Consent? *Management Communication Quarterly*, 19, 67–90.

Aycan, Z., Bayazit, M., Berkman, Y. & Boratav, H.B. (2012). Attitudes towards Women Managers: Development and Validation of a New Measure with Turkish Samples. *European Journal of Work and Organizational Psychology*, 21(3), 426–455.

Barragan, S., Eroğul, M.Ş, & Essers, C. (2018). Strategic (Dis)obedience: Female Entrepreneurs Reflecting on and Acting upon Patriarchal Practices. *Gender, Work and Organization*, 25(5): 575–592.

Bedük, A. & Eryeşil, K. (2013). Women Entrepreneurship & Problems in Turkey. *World Academy of Science, Engineering and Technology*, 77, 568–572.

Benschop, Y. & Verloo, M. (2011). Gender Change Organizational Change and Gender Equality Strategies. In E.L. Jeanes, D. Knights, and P.Y. Martin (Eds.), *Handbook of Gender Work and Organization*, 277–290. UK: John Wiley and Sons Ltd.

Benzing, C., Chu, H.M. & Kara, O. (2009). Entrepreneurs in Turkey: A Factor Analysis of Motivations, Success Factors, and Problems. *Journal of Small Business Management*, 47(1), 58–91.

Boratav, H.B. (2011). Searching for Feminism in Psychology in Turkey. In A. Rutherford et al. (Eds.), *Handbook of International Feminisms: Perspectives on Psychology, Women, Culture and Rights*. Springer.

Bourne, K.A. & Calás, M.B. (2013). Becoming "Real" Entrepreneurs: Women and the Gendered Normalization of Work. *Gender, Work and Organization*, 204, 425–438.

Bridge, S., O'Neill, K. & Cromie, S. (1998). *Understanding Enterprise, Entrepreneurship and Small Business.* London: Macmillan Business.

Brown, A.D. (2001). Organization Studies and Identity: Towards a Research Agenda. *Human Relations,* 54(1), 113.

Brown, A.D. (2008). *Organizational Identity.* In S. Clegg & C.L. Cooper (Eds.), *The Sage Handbook of Organizational Behavior.* Vol. 2: *Macro Approaches,* pp. 175–191. Sage.

Bruni, A., Gherardi, S. & Poggio, B. (2004a). Doing Gender, Doing Entrepreneurship: An Ethnographic Account of Intertwined Practices. *Gender, Work & Organization,* 11(4), 406–429.

Bruni, A., Gherardi, S. & Poggio, B. (2004b). Entrepreneur-Mentality, Gender and the Study of Women Entrepreneurs. *Journal of Organizational Change Management,* 17(3), 256–268.

Butler, J. (1990). *Gender Trouble: Feminism and the Subversion of Identity.* New York: Routledge.

Calás, M.B. & Smircich, L. (2009). Feminist Perspective on Gender in Organizational Research: What is and is yet to be. In D. Buchan & A. Bryman (Eds.), *Handbook of Organizational Research Methods.* London: Sage.

Calas, M.B. & Smircich, L. (2006). From the Women's Point of View Ten Years Later: Towards A Feminist Organization Studies. In: Clegg, S., Hardy, C. and Nord, W. (Eds.) *Handbook of Organization Studies.* London: Sage, pp. 284–328.

Cerulo, K.A. (1997). Identity Construction: New Issues, New Directions. *Annual Review of Sociology,* 23(1), 385–409.

Çetindamar, D. (2005). Policy Issues for Turkish Entrepreneurs. *International Journal of Entrepreneurship and Innovation Management,* 5(3/4), 187–205.

Costas, J. & Fleming, P. (2009). Beyond Dis-identification: A Discursive Approach to Self Alienation in Contemporary Organizations. *Human Relations,* 623, 353–378.

Czarniawska, B. 2004. *Narratives in Social Science Research.* London: Sage.

Davies, B. & Harré, R. (1990). Positioning: the Discursive Production of Selves. *Journal of Theory of Social Behavior,* 1: 43–63.

Demirci, A.E. (2013). Cross-Cultural Differences in Entrepreneurial Tendencies: An Exploratory View in Turkey and Canada. *International Journal of Entrepreneurship,* 17, 21–40.

Dildar, Y. (2015). *Structural Transformation, Culture, and Women's Labor Force Participation in Turkey.* Doctoral Dissertations, 468. University of Massachusetts Amherst. https://scholarworks.umass.edu/dissertations_2/468

DiMaggio, P. & Powell, W.W. (1983). The Iron Cage Revisited: Institutional Isomorphism and Collective Rationality in Organizational Fields. *American Sociological Review,* 48, 147–160.

Down, S. & Warren, L. (2008). Constructing Narratives of Enterprise: Clichés and Entrepreneurial Self-Identity. *International Journal of Entrepreneurial Behaviour & Research,* 14(1), 4–23.

Eroğul, M.Ş., Michel, R. & Barragan, S. (2016). Contextualizing Arab Female Entrepreneurship in the United Arab Emirates. *Culture and Organization.* Published online: 24 October.

Essers, C. & Benschop, Y. (2007). Enterprising Identities: Female Entrepreneurs of Moroccan or Turkish Origin in the Netherlands. *Organization Studies,* 281: 49–69.

Essers, C. & Benschop, Y. (2009). Muslim Businesswomen Doing Boundary Work: The Negotiation of Islam, Gender and Ethnicity within Entrepreneurial Contexts. *Human Relations,* 623: 403–423.

Essers, C., Benschop, Y. & Doorewaard, H. (2010). Female Ethnicity: Understanding Muslim Immigrant Businesswomen in The Netherlands. *Gender, Work & Organization*, 17(3), 320–339.

Essers, C., Doorewaard, H. & Benschop, Y. (2013). Family Ties: Migrant Female Business Owners Doing Identity Work on the Public–Private Divide. *Human Relations*, 66(12), 1645–1665.

Foucault, M. (1977). *Discipline and Punish: The Birth of the Prison*. New York: Vintage.

Fournier, V. (2002). Keeping the Veil of Otherness: Practising Disconnection. In B. Czarniawska & H. Höpfl (Eds.), *Casting the Other: The Production and Maintenance of Inequalities in Work Organizations* (pp. 68–88). London: Routledge.

GEM (2012). *Global Entrepreneurship Monitor 2012 Report*. London: GEM.

GEM (2015). *Global Entrepreneurship Monitor 2015 Report*. London: GEM.

Giddens, A. (1991). *Modernity and Self-Identity: Self and Society in the Late Modern Age*. Stanford, CA: Stanford University Press.

Gherardi, S. (2015). Authoring the Female Entrepreneur While Talking the Discourse of Work-Family Life Balance. *International Small Business Journal*, 33(6), 649–666.

Gherardi, S. & Perrotta, M. (2016). Daughters Taking Over the Family Business. *International Journal of Gender and Entrepreneurship*, 8(1), 28–47.

Gherardi, S. & Perrotta, M. (2014). Gender Ethnicity and Social Entrepreneurship: Qualitative Approaches to the Study of Entrepreneuring. In E. Chell and M. Karataş-Özkan (Eds.) *Handbook of Research in Small Business and Entrepreneurship* (pp. 130–147). Cheltenham: Edward Elgar.

Gherardi, S. & Poggio, B. (2001). The Maintenance of the Glass Ceiling as a Cultural Practice. *Journal of World Business*, 36(3), 245–259.

Gherardi, S. & Poggio, B. (2007). *Gendertelling in Organizations: Narratives from Male Dominated Environments (Vol. 23)*. Copenhagen: Copenhagen Business School Press.

Haraway, D. (1991) *Simians, Cyborgs and Women: The Reinvention of Nature*. London: Free Associations Books.

Harding, S. (1987). Introduction: Is There a Feminist Method? In: S. Harding (ed.) *Feminism and Methodology*. Bloomington: Indiana University Press, 1–14.

Harding, N., Ford, J. & Fotaki, M. (2013). Is the "F"-word Still Dirty? A Past, Present and Future of/for Feminist and Gender Studies in Organization. *Organization*, 20, 51–65.

Hearn, J. (2004). From Hegemonic Masculinity to the Hegemony of Men. *Feminist Theory*, 51: 49–72.

Hisrich, R.D. and Ozturk, S.A. (1999). Women Entrepreneurs in a Developing Economy. *Journal of Management Development*, 18(2), 114–125.

Inan, A. (1967). *Kadinin Sosyal Hayatini Tetkik Kurumu: Aylik Konferanslar* [Studying Women Life]. Ankara, Turkey: Ayyildiz Press.

Kabasakal, H., Aycan, Z., Karakas,, F. & Maden, C. (2011). Women in Management in Turkey. In M.J. Davidson & R. Burke (Eds.), *Women in Management Worldwide: Progress and Prospects* (pp. 317–338). Surrey: Gower Publishing Limited.

Kağıtçıbaşı, C. (2007). *Family, Self and Human Development across Cultures: Theory and Applications*. UK: Lawrence Erlbaum Associates Ltd.

Kancı, T. & Altınay, A.G. (2007). Educating Little Soldiers and Little Ayses: Militarized and Gendered Citizenship in Turkish Textbooks. In M. Carlson, A. Rabo, & F. Gok (Eds.), *Education in Multicultural Societies – Turkish and Swedish Perspectives* (pp. 51–70). London: I.B. Tauris.

Karataş-Özkan, M. & Chell, E. (2010). *Nascent Entrepreneurship and Learning*. Cheltenham: Edward Elgar Publishing.

Karataş-Özkan, M., Erdogan, A. and Nicolopoulou, K. (2011). Women in Turkish Family Businesses: Drivers, Contributions, and Challenges. *International Journal of Cross Cultural Management*, 11(2), 203–219.

Kanter, R.M. (1977). *Men and Women of the Corporation*. New York: Basic Books.

Kärreman, D. & Alvesson, M. (2009). Resisting Resistance: Counter-resistance, Consent and Compliance in a Consultancy Firm. *Human Relations*, 62(8), 1115–1144.

Knights, D. & Kerfoot, D. (2004). Between Representations and Subjectivity: Gender Binaries And the Politics of Organizational Transformation. *Gender, Work and Organization*, 114: 430–454.

Knights, D. & Willmott, H. (1989). Power and Subjectivity at Work: From Degradation to Subjugation in Social Relations. *Sociology*, 23(4), 535–558.

Lee-Gosselin, H. & Grisé, J. (1990). Are Women Owner-managers Challenging our Definitions of Entrepreneurship? An In-depth Survey. *Journal of Business Ethics*, 94(5), 423–433.

Lewis, P. (2006). The Quest for Invisibility: Female Entrepreneurs and the Masculine Norm of Entrepreneurship. *Gender, Work & Organization*, 13(5), 453–469.

Lewis, P. (2013). The Search for an Authentic Entrepreneurial Identity: Difference and Professionalism among Women Business Owners. *Gender, Work and Organization*, 20(3), 252–266.

Maden, C. (2015). A Gendered Lens on Entrepreneurship: Women Entrepreneurship in Turkey. *Gender in Management: An International Journal*, 30(4), 312–331.

Markus, H. & Zajonc, R. (1985). The Cognitive Perspective in Social Psychology. In G. Lindzey & E. Aronson (Eds.), *Handbook of Social Psychology* (pp. 137–230). New York: Random House.

Martin, J. (2003). Feminist Theory and Critical Theory: Unexplored Synergies. In M. Alvesson and H. Willmott (Eds.) *Studying Management Critically* (pp. 66–91). London: Sage Publications.

McAdams, D.P. (1997). The Case for Unity in the (post)Modern Self: A Modest Proposal. In R. Ashmore & L. Jussim (Eds.). *Self and Identity: Fundamental Issues* (pp. 46–78). Oxford: Oxford University Press.

Naguib, R. & Jamali, D. (2015). Female Entrepreneurship in the UAE: A Multi-level Integrative Lens. *Gender in Management: An International Journal*, 30(2), 135–161.

Nayir, D.Z. (2008). Women between Work and Family: Work-Family Conflict Management Strategies of Female Entrepreneurs in the Textile and IT Industries. *Ege Academic Review*, 8(2), 631–650.

Nentwich, J.C. (2006). Changing Gender: The Discursive Construction of Equal Opportunities. *Gender Work and Organization*, 136: 499–521.

Ogbor, J.O. (2000). Mythicizing and Reification in Entrepreneurial Discourse: Ideology Critique of Entrepreneurial Studies. *Journal of Management Studies*, 37(5), 605–635.

Ökten, C. (2015). *Female Entrepreneurship in Turkey: Patterns, Characteristics, and Trends*. Washington, DC: World Bank. https://openknowledge.worldbank.org/handle/10986/25410

Özar, S. (2007). Women Entrepreneurs in Turkey: Obstacles, Potentials and Future Prospects. In N. Chamlou & M. Karshenas (Eds.), *Women, Work and Welfare in the Middle East and North Africa: The Role of Socio-demographics, Entrepreneurship and Public Policies* (pp. 235–262). UK: Imperial College Press.

Özdemir, A.A. (2010). Motivation Factors of Potential Entrepreneurs and a Research Study in Eskisehir. *Ege Akademik Bakis*, 10(1), 117–139.

Özkazanç-Pan, B. (2014). Secular and Islamic Feminist Entrepreneurship in Turkey. *International Journal of Gender and Entrepreneurship*, 7(1), 45–65.

Özturk, M.B. (2011). Sexual Orientation Discrimination: Exploring the Experiences of Lesbian, Gay and Bisexual Employees in Turkey. *Human Relations*, 64(8), 1099–1118.

Patriotta, G., Gond, J.-P. & Schultz, F. (2011). Maintaining Legitimacy: Controversies, Orders of Worth and Public Justifications . *Journal of Management Studies*, 48(8), 1804–1836.

Pio, E. (2005). Knotted Strands: Working Lives of Indian Women Migrants in New Zealand. *Human Relations*, 58(10): 1277–1300.

Potter, J. & Wetherell, M. (1987). *Discourse and Social Psychology: Beyond Attitudes and Behaviour*. London: Sage.

Reskin, B. & Padavic, I. (1994). *Women and Men at Work*. Thousand Oaks, CA: Pine Forge Press.

Said, E.W. (1979). *Orientalism*. New York: Random House Inc.

Sawicki, J. (1994). Foucault, Feminism, and Questions of Identity. In G. Gutting (Ed.) *The Cambridge Companion to Foucault* (pp. 286–313). Cambridge: Cambridge University Press.

Scott, R. (2008). *Institutions and Organizations*. Thousand Oaks, CA: Sage.

Schein, V.E. (2001). A Global Look at Psychological Barriers to Women's Progress in Management. *Journal of Social Issues*, 57(4), 675–688.

Schein, V.E., Mueller, R., Lituchy, T. & Liu, J. (1996). Think Manager–Think Male: A Global Phenomenon? *Journal of Organizational Behavior*, 17(1), 33–41.

Slotte-Kock, S. & Coviello, N. (2010). Entrepreneurship Research on Network Processes: A Review and Ways Forward. *Entrepreneurship Theory and Practice*, 34(1), 31–57.

Sveningsson, S. & Alvesson, M. (2003). Managing Managerial Identities: Organizational Fragmentation, Discourse and Identity Struggle. *Human Relations*, 56(10), 1163.

Thomas, R. & Davies, A. (2005). What Have the Feminists Done for Us? Feminist Theory and Organizational Resistance. *Organization*, 12(5), 711–740.

Thomas, R., Mills, A.J. & Helms Mills, J. (Eds.). (2004). *Identity Politics at Work* [electronic resource]: *Resisting Gender, Gendering Resistance* (Vol. 331.4/01 22). London: Routledge.

Thornton, P.H., Ocasio, W. & Lounsbury, M. (2012). *The Institutional Logics Perspective: A New Approach to Culture, Structure, and Process*. Oxford, UK: Oxford University Press.

Tuzun, I.K. & Takay, B.A. (2017). Patterns of Female Entrepreneurial Activities in Turkey. *Gender in Management: An International Journal*, 32(3), 166–182.

Ufuk, H. & Özgen, O. (2001a). Interaction between the Business and Family Lives of Women Entrepreneurs in Turkey. *Journal of Business Ethics*, 31(2), 95–106.

Ufuk, H. & Özgen, O. (2001b). The Profile of Women Entrepreneurs: A Sample from Turkey. *International Journal of Consumer Studies*, 25(4), 299–308.

Van den Brink, M. & Stobbe, L. 2009. Doing Gender in Academic Education: The Paradox of Visibility. *Gender, Work and Organization*, 16(4), 451–470.

Wasti, S.A. (1998). Cultural Barriers in the Transferability of Japanese and American Human Resources Practices to Developing Countries: the Turkish Case. *The International Journal of Human Resource Management*, 9(4), 608–631.

Watson, T. (2009). Entrepreneurial Action, Identity Work and the Use of Multiple Discursive Resources. The Case of a Rapidly Changing Family Business. *International Small Business Journal*, 27(3), 251–274.

Weedon, C. (1987). *Feminist Practice and Poststructural Theory.* Oxford: Basil Blackwell.

Weedon, C. (1999). *Feminism Theory and the Politics of Difference.* Oxford: Blackwell.

Welter, F. (2011). Contextualizing Entrepreneurship: Conceptual Challenges and Ways Forward. *Entrepreneurship Theory and Practice,* 351, 165–178.

West, C. & Zimmerman, D. (1987). Doing Gender. *Gender Society,* 1, 125–151.

Ybema, S., Keenoy, T., Oswick, C., Beverungen, A., Ellis, N. & Sabelis, I. (2009). Articulating Identities. *Human Relations,* 623, 299–322.

Yetim, N. (2008). Social Capital in Female Entrepreneurship. *International Sociology,* 23(6), 864–885.

Yılmaz, E., Özdemir, G. & Oraman, Y. (2015). Women Entrepreneurs: Their Problems and Entrepreneurial Ideas. *African Journal of Business Management,* 6(26), 7896–7904.

13 Women Empowerment through Political Participation in Rising Powers

Comparison of Turkey and Nigeria

Özgür TÜFEKÇİ and Mohammed HASHIRU

Introduction

Feminists have always argued that the world has had enough of men dominating in major human endeavours. According to Randall (2006: 3) activities of women and their achievements in leadership positions has made women's representation or political participation a topic for discussion. Arguments about participation were a significant part of international debates about democracy. It is argued that women are equal citizens and therefore should share equally with men in policy-making process. Without women's participation in political institutions, it is not possible to build sustainable democracies. In this sense, Madeleine Albright puts this approach into words as follows: "success without democracy is improbable and democracy without women is impossible" (National Democratic Institute for International Affairs (NDI), 2010: 12).

To prevent all forms of discrimination against women the United Nations (UN) General Assembly adopted "The Convention on the Elimination of All Forms of Discrimination against Women (CEDAW)" in 1979, which is often described as an international bill of rights for women. By accepting the Convention, states commit themselves to undertake a series of measures to end discrimination against women in all forms, including:

- to incorporate the principle of equality of men and women in their legal system, abolish all discriminatory laws and adopt appropriate ones prohibiting discrimination against women;
- to establish tribunals and other public institutions to ensure the effective protection of women against discrimination; and
- to ensure elimination of all acts of discrimination against women by persons, organizations or enterprises. (www.un.org)

Yet, despite deliberate attempt to increase women's activity in politics, the fact remains that even in developed states women are less represented.

The countries, which aim to solidify democracy, have put in place measures in order to ensure the empowerment of women. This is because women empowerment has been recognised as a prerequisite for women's advancement and the underpinning in society of gender equality. The political empowerment of women is founded on the equality between men and women, rights of women to fully develop their potentials and the right of women to self-determination and self-representation (Fadia, 2014: 539). Since politics is all about influence and power and it remains a struggle of competing viewpoints about resources apportionment and distribution, political struggle has largely been in the domain of men. In this context, the marginalization of women in spheres of politics is as a result of this limited conception of the relevance of women in politics (Ajogbeje, 2016: 71).

Rising powers have also shown some level of concern about women empowerment. For instance, the BRICS countries (Brazil, Russia, India, China, South Africa) did not only create BRICS Feminist Watch but has also organized an 8th BRICS summit in Goa, India under the theme "Building Responsive, Inclusive, Collective Solution" in 2016. In July 2018, at the 10th BRICS Summit Johannesburg Declaration, preambles 32, 99 and 100 reiterate the rising states' commitment to ensuring women empowerment and political participation in member states. Preamble 99 for instance states "… including of women parliamentarians, we look forward to further strengthening of BRICS exchanges in this regard" (BRICS, 2018). Two emerging powers, Turkey and Nigeria, which are considered by Goldman Sachs to constitute the next tier called MINT countries (Mexico, Indonesia, Nigeria and Turkey) are under investigation in this chapter.

The goal of this chapter is to look at the women empowerment capacities through political participation in Turkey and Nigeria. In addition, this chapter aims to contribute to the theoretical literature of rising powers a new determining factor, "strengthened democracy through women's political participation". In the first part, the women empowerment and rising powers concepts will be introduced. The second part will analyse the current situation in the BRICS countries and regarding women's political participation. And then, Turkey and Nigeria are discussed and compared with each other through the determining factor "strengthened democracy through women's political participation".

Women Empowerment and Rising Powers

Power in international relations is explained in various ways. For instance, Machiavelli uses the term "power" as an ultimate goal for mankind and the state. In his book, *The Prince*, he examines the means and methods of gaining and keeping power. For ages, humans have built their relationships with others on power politics. In this regard, the international system has recently introduced a new type of dialogue by experts who want to draw a certain line between powers (Kınık & Tüfekçi, 2018). The aim is to categorize powers in order to make each of them remember what their role is in the system. By doing so, the status quo is preserved and the leadership of the US continues, at least in the mind of the people. Through this new type of dialogue, several acronyms have been produced, such as BRICS, MINT, MIST, PINE and MIKT.

In addition, through these acronyms, new powers such as China, Russia, Brazil, India, South Africa, Indonesia, Mexico, Turkey and Nigeria came to the forefront in order to seek a global political role with strong powers. Since the concept "rising power" is quite volatile, it is a prerequisite to determine several criteria to make a thorough categorization. In this sense, democratic development, population, geographic location, economic development, military capability, technological development, and soft power are the main criteria (Tüfekçi, 2016: 103–104). It is a fact that these states penetrated global politics with their expanding political and cultural influence and rapid economic development (Yavuzçehre & Öztepe, 2016: 211). Here we look at the various activities of these states and their endeavour to ensure women empowerment and political participation and aim to compare Turkey and Nigeria through the lens of a new determining factor, "strengthened democracy through women's political participation" under the democratic development criteria.

The BRICS and Women Empowerment

At the club level and individual state levels the BRICS continue to put measures to ensure female empowerment leads to massive or equal participation of women in political portfolios. At the club level, the BRICS demonstrated its commitment to women empowerment when it declared at its 8th Summit that

> we reiterate the commitments to gender equality and empowerment of all women and girls as contained in the 2030 Agenda. We recognise that women play a vital role as agents of development and acknowledge that their equal and inclusive participation and contribution is crucial to making progress across all Sustainable Development Goals and Targets.
> (BRICS, 2016)

It is necessary to act based on the declaration to booster the inflow of women contribution in politics.

Despite the economic strides made by China in recent times, the situation of women empowerment and political participation is not encouraging. This is because the international ranking of female deputies in the People's Congress dwindled from 12th in 1994 to 52nd in 2012. Again, the gap between women participation in diverse structures of political power in the country has widened (Zeng, 2014: 136). This can be blamed on the ineffective and discouraging proactive policy for women's participation implemented by the government of China, which has not brought about a broader participation of women in politics. Over time, the drawing back of women from waged production becomes mirrored at the political level in their falling participation in party and government leadership. (Howell, 2002: 44). The situation is not the same in India. Fadia (2014: 542) mentions that women's participation in the political sphere has been encouraging. The increment in participation rather empowers women, boosts their level confidence, changes perceptions about their contribution as well as improves their societal status. The 73rd and 74th amendment of the constitution were responsible for the strengthening of grassroots democracy and political participation in India. The 110th amendment of the constitution in 2009 elevates female representation to 50 percent from 33 percent.

The case of Brazil is even better because the state has witnessed the increase in women's participation in legislative positions since 1998. The adoption of legislation, which provides quotas for female candidates, is a major contributing factor to this improvement. However, despite this being a remarkable breakthrough, the number of elected women in the political sphere has remained stable over time. The stunted growth of women in political representation in Brazil is largely blamed on electoral financing that influences state election (Moisés & Sanchez, 2016: 27). Despite the finance hurdles, 2018 witnessed the highest number of women seeking presidential tickets in the history of Brazil. Senator Ana Amelia reiterates that the more women participate the more the state gains. With the exception of Jair Bolsonaro and Marina Silva all major presidential candidates have selected female running mates. Moreover, recent polling in the country reveals that 80 percent of the electorates in the country think that Brazilian democracy would improve if women were elected into public offices (Shook & Harden, 2018).

In Mexico, the existence and the activities of NGOs have been critical in ensuring women's political participation and human rights. According to the 2000 World Values Survey, 42 per cent of Mexicans in the year 2000 believed that women were second to men in effective political leadership (Inglehart, 2004). This showed a backward thinking in a rising state like Mexico. Zapatistas, a groups formed to cater for victims of earthquake in 1985, and the Partido de la Revolucion Democratica (Democratic Revolution Party–PRD) formed in 1989, are instrumental in ensuring female political participation in Mexico. The PRD for instance availed 30 percent quotas for women, which got extended to other political parties (Randall, 2006: 12). Fernanda (2014: 5), employing data from the Federal Electoral Institute and the National Survey on Citizens and Political Culture of Mexico suggests that a series of social factors constrains political participation of women in Mexico. These social factors are embedded in organizations, which are structured to satisfy the male oriented practices. Religion and biased cultural value have negatively affected the number of women in political positions. Randall (2006) notes that the failure to integrate women and other sectors into the political process breeds doubts on the capacity of the political system when women are given the sole responsibility of representing the needs of women.

Women Empowerment Capacities through Political Participation in Turkey

Mustafa Kemal Ataturk emphasised the need for gender balance when he said "If a society does not wage a common struggle to attain a common goal with its women and men, scientifically there is no way for it to get civilized". In 1934, the right to vote and be elected was given to women in Turkey. This breakthrough in Turkish politics came at the time when same rights were not given to women in many European states. Though a breakthrough, there is a wide gap between women in active politics and other women who consider it a distant reality. (Çelik & Lukuslu, 2012: 31). The participation of women at the initial stages was largely in issues of equality regarding domestic violence, labour force and restricted participation in education. A turnaround of events was witnessed when these issues were politicized by the organization of women. This led to the essential changes and development in the Turkish state. Ayata and Tutuncu (2008: 365) indicate that in the last decade feminists movements have played a critical role within the Turkish political landscape by both their demands and infiltration into political movements and parties. The trends had positive effects on the key legal changes, which affect the political, social and economic status of women. Despite the historical struggle, women continue to be under represented in Turkish politics. Stefan Fule (EU Commissioner for Enlargement and Neighbourhood Policy) once remarked that there is a need for Turkey to make reforms that will see an increase in women in political activities. This is because Turkey compared to the EU average appears to lag behind in its effort to increase women political representation. Some 80 years after the introduction of women rights, less than 15% of women have made it to the Turkish parliament, to date.

A recent report published by the Global Gender Gap Report (GGGR) (2017) puts Turkey 131st on the list of 144 countries and 8th amongst the 17 Middle East and North African States. This report benchmarks national gender gaps on education, economic health and political criteria (GGGR, 2017: 3). The report explains that though Turkey sits on 131st position, it is progressing towards closing the gender gap in its legislator, senior official and manager positions. The only place where the gap keeps on widening is political empowerment (GGGR, 2017: 21). Among the G20 group of countries, Turkey falls behind France, Germany, United Kingdom, Canada, South Africa and Argentina.

Previous research on women's political participation in Turkey has lamented the scanty number of women in the game. However after the local election of 2014 the following distribution was witnessed across metropolitan municipality mayors, municipal councillors, village head positions: 3 out of 30 elected metropolitan municipality mayors, 37 out of 1,366 municipality mayors, 2,198 out of 20,498 municipal councillors and 58 out of 18,143 heads of village positions were held by women (TUIK, 2014: 137). It is also the case that women fall behind men with regard to political representation. The rate of women deputies in the state is 14.73 as of February 2016 (TBMM, 2016) and only two of the 16 ministers of state are women. Many studies have tried to outline some reasons for women remaining in the shadow of men. Data from 2014 revealed that 30.3% represents the participation of women in the workforce. The main reason for the low percentage is household chores (TUIK, 2014: 78–79).

Women representation in politics, political parties, government and among political leaders is limited despite the lack of sexist provisions concerning political rights. This is an indication that problems exist in the political rights implementation given to women to ensure equality with men (Caglar, 2011: 59). Various social, cultural, economic and political factors account for this. Factors preventing women from active participation in politics are low education levels in the rural areas especially, traditional patriarchal family relations, excessive political pressures of fathers, husbands, brother and other households, and most importantly financial constraints and lack of confidence (Doğramaci, 1997: 141 cited in Caglar, 2011: 65). Inadequate political parties' policies for women, their sexist methods and applications; their unwillingness to nominate a female candidate for the Turkish elections means that Tansu Ciller remains the only female to hold a prime minister position. Women who appear to have the potential for making female challenges heard in parliament are denied the chance of taking part in processes of making decisions. It is against this background that the Turkish state has made some assurance that it will develop policies as well as propose regulations and make them laws resulting from decisions, engagements and advices of the Convention on the Elimination of All Forms of Discrimination Against Women (CEDAW) and later establishments like Organization For Economic Cooperation and Development (OECD), International Labour Organization (ILO), European Social Charter and in accordance with the Action Plan of Cairo Conference on World Population Development (TUIK, 2014: XXIII). In some democracies, despite the constraints, women engage themselves with the women's wing of the political party they are affiliated to. However, studies on Turkish political parties have revealed that the effectiveness of women cannot be felt due to social and political reality in the branches of women that are not able to get an effective political activity (Altindal, 2007; Yaraman 1998). It is also mentioned that women appear to prioritize their party identities instead of their female identity without being mindful of the disparity between both ideologies. Again representatives working in the female branches find fulfilment in being seen in the political spectrum and so do not give attention to the issue of gender equality. They avoid being part of crucial political party decisions and only apply the decisions taken by the political party (Cakir, 2001: 407–408).

Alkan (2009: 35) also relates that the three main factors underlining the inadequate participation of women in Turkish politics are the existence of figurativeness in politics, the exclusion of locals from the political field of interest until recently, and the gross limitation of social mobility of women at the local community level. Spreading women's participation across all local politics and actively in the municipal, metropolitan, metropolitan municipal council, provincial council and village leadership level is a necessity for democratic consolidation, justice and vibrant governance. However, women are rarely seen in leadership positions after elections are held.

The most important significant indicator of women's participation in Turkish politics is their active involvement in province and metropolitan mayoral elections. Political parties more often only prefer that women join councillorship elections. Yavuzçehre and Öztepe (2016: 217) summarize that though recent involvement of women in national and party politics has increased especially in the last four elections, there is much room for improvement. The participation of women will add to efforts to bridge the wide gender gap in the country. More importantly the participation of women in the processes of making decisions actively and equally with men is a necessity for a democratic consolidation since the local governments are the basic units of the executive that are closest to the public and therefore carry out local resources and services for supervision. To ensure these goals are reached, the level of education of women must increase, NGOs and local governments and female politicians should apply more sensitivity to female problems and female politics, as they take responsibility in resolving them. Women should also be given a quota so as to check the predominated male politics at the party level as central government endeavours to make legal regulations in a way that female empowerment related issues are implemented.

The Turkish government reforms and proposed policies to close the gender gap by ensuring more women participation in politics can also be considered as a way of negotiating to become a EU member (Bozkurt, 2010: 6). Yet, the Turkey report of the European Commission in 2018 mentions that women's participation in Turkey needs to be improved since Turkey's number of women in politics is below EU average (European Commission, 2018).

Women Empowerment Capacities through Political Participation in Nigeria

Though lagging behind in terms of women political participation, Nigeria's case is different from that of Turkey. When President Buhari said that his wife's position is in the kitchen and in his bedroom as his response to the public criticism she made about his government, many women showed their dissatisfaction.[1] The comments of the Nigerian President came at a time when people are tirelessly working to empower women. Meanwhile decades of struggle by international bodies via several declarations and charters to eliminate discrimination against women are yet to materialize in the Nigerian political dispensations. Before elections scores of women dominate rally grounds in the bid to campaign for their various parties. The presence of women in political rallies adds more colour to the political forums with their attention seeking party dresses, singing and shouting of party slogans.

Table 13.1 illustrates the state of women's political participation in Nigeria. Despite the fact that 50% percent of the Nigerian population is made up of women, Nigeria has the lowest number of females in politics in sub-Saharan Africa (Orisadare, 2018: 3). The return of Nigeria to democratic rule since 1999 has been marked by scores of women contesting for a plethora of political positions throughout the five successful elections the state has had. Unfortunately, results after elections showed poor performance by the women. A study on why women do not appear in political positions reveals that many women go through party registration but refuse to regularly participate in party caucuses and meetings during which important decisions are taken. The frightening nature of party congresses sometimes discourages women from participation. For this reason some women think that only women who are willing to be "dirty" and irresponsible would have the guts to attend such party gatherings (Ajogbeje, 2016: 72). Many women have gone through traditional gender violence. Some women who came out to contest the elections were however flagbearers of the least popular parties in the country. This creates the assumption that the more competitive parties cannot accommodate them. Out of the three women who participated in the Nigerian general election in 2003, two women represented the least popular party. Though the 2015 elections witnessed a decrease of violence meted out to females, the reality of the Nigerian election in some regions is that it is violent prone. Despite the setbacks suffered by women in Nigeria, they still have the capacity to influence the voting pattern. In many cases however women do not even consider their fellow women as capable of leading the nation. They rather follow the trend of voting for men (Ajayi, 2005).

Moreover, the existence of a powerful class of male political pundits in the Nigerian political system who have run the state historically has grossly undermined their participation and reduced the chances of women in Nigerian politics. Unlike in Rwanda where women have more than 50% parliamentary representation, the political game in Nigeria is such that men have dominated. In South Africa and Rwanda women are allowed to contest winnable seats at the party level to allow equitable distribution (Orisadare, 2018). If quota systems were to be implemented at the party level in Nigeria, an equitable distribution would be achieved quite quicky. For instance, a 35% minimum quota for women representation could be implemented. Quotas, however, are not enough although

Table 13.1 Global comparison of percentage of women in national parliament as at 1st April 2018

Averages	Lower Houses	Upper Houses	Both Houses
World Average	23.8%	23.9%	23.8%
Sub-Saharan Africa	23.9%	23.1%	23.8%
Nigeria	5.6%	6.5%	6.1%

Source: Orisadare, 2018

they can provide an impetus for further gender policies. The Canadian President Justin Trudeau, for instance, ensured gender equity in his government by appointing an equal number of men and women. In the Buhari government cabinet in Nigeria only 16 percent were women despite a national gender policy that assigned women a minimum of 35 percent. Nevertheless only 14 out of 360 House of Representative and 7 out of the 109 Senate seats are occupied by women (Orisadare, 2018: 12).

In Nigeria women only make up 20% of the formal business sector due to limited access to finance. Men on the other hand are more likely to get finance compared to women despite research that women are twice more likely to repay loans. Their financial constraints have further crippled their ability to provide needed collateral for loans. Attempts to strengthen their property rights through the Land Administration Act could not be materialized since ownership of land is still dependent on the patrilineal inheritance system, which favours only male.

The rights of women in Nigeria were greatly in jeopardy during the period 1914–1960s. The British policy during those years of colonization was informed by the English culture and traditions of a single sex political system, which was against the indigenous dual-sex political system (Olugbemi, 2011). The colonial masters at that time did not put any relevance on the contribution of women in the society. They also refused to appreciate the significant contribution of women in education and the traditional participation of women in public society affairs. The interesting aspect of women empowerment trends in those times was that Nigerian men recognized the contribution in social, economic and politics and for that matter became polygamous whilst their British colonial masters considered their wives as weak vessels. During those times of colonialism, Nigerian women formed the National Council of Nigerian Citizens (NCNC) as the female political wing that rubbed shoulders with the political activities of men (Olugbemi, 2011). These are all indications that women were empowered during colonial periods and political spaces were available for their participation in national politics. They were less influenced by the western world in their efforts to participate in national politics as they contributed to nationalism and independence attainment.

After years of independence many Nigerian women still continue to play important roles in politics. The problem is not coming out or vying for position but winning it. To ensure women join with their male counterparts in government, many states continue to adopt a gender quota system for public elections. Half of the states in the world today use some electoral quota for parliaments (Dahlerup, 2005). The international recommendations are believed to influence the use of the quota system. To close the structural gap quota systems are critical though they do not completely solve the problem. In some other democracies, quotas are in relation to bridging the gap about ethnicity, region, linguistics, religion, and gender. Quotas for women stipulate that a certain number of women should make up a certain number in a group, club, association or even government. The French government has one of the strongest local level quotas of 50% (Dahlerup, 2005). There is no clear gender quota for the Nigerian state but the National Gender Policy (NGP) aims at empowering women through basic education and the abolishment of traditional practices harmful for women. The main objective is to reduce gender biases, which are found in the traditional customs of the country. The initiative aims to achieve women empowerment for political capacity of women (Olufunke, 2013: 28). Both a public and private sector gender sensitive framework has been established for that purpose. It looked at achieving 35% of elected positions to be occupied by female gender by 2015. Unfortunately, the goal has not been actualized, so far. There is also evidence that the Women Affairs and Social Development Ministry has received a lower if not the lowest ministerial budgetary allocation from the national budget when compared with other ministries (Orisadare, 2018: 10). That is why the situation of women is so deplorable in Nigeria since while the women's population is around 100 million, 60% of the 75 million poor Nigerians are women (Orisadare, 2018: 11).

Although Saudi Arabia is considered oppressive especially in relation to its women, surprisingly it is showing much willingness to address women related political challenges having issued a decree in 2013 to introduce a 20% percent quota for the 150-member Shura Council as well as appoint 30 women to join the consultative assembly whereas Nigeria, a democratic nation and the largest black state on earth appears to lack clear and ground breaking policies to solve its political challenges concerning women's representation. Rwanda, a country that suffered near extinction due to genocide has a record of electing up to 64 percent of its women in parliamentary elections (Adaji, 2017: 1). South Africa, Nigeria's economic rival in Africa is competing with established powers like Britain whilst Nigeria remains with other states at the bottom.

Conclusion and Final Remarks

The two states under discussion appear to underperforming in their endeavours to ensure equitable representation of women in the individual states. Political dynamics of these two states are not the same but the economic strides achieved by both means that when other tenets of democratic consolidation like equality in political representation are achieved more development could be witnessed in them. Table 13.2 indicates that Turkey has almost twice the GDP of Nigeria despite abundant resources including oil in Nigeria. Nigeria has however, a huge workforce and it has double the population of Turkey. The population growth rate also indicates that Nigeria's population grows faster than that of Turkey. Whereas Nigeria's population sex ratio stands at 1.03 Turkey's population sex ratio stands at 0.97. The Human Capital Index score difference in between the states is only 9.27.

Table 13.3 illustrates the economic, educational, health and political empowerment scores of both countries. Though very developed in all three sectors, economic, education, and health, scores given show very little difference between the two states. With a GDP twice that of Nigeria, Turkey could have done far better than Nigeria.

Table 13.2 Comparison of Turkey and Nigeria

	Turkey	Nigeria
GDP (US$ billions)	857.75	405.08
GDP per capita (constant '11, intl. $, PPP)	23,679.40	5,438.92
Total population (1,000s)	79,512.43	185,989.64
Population growth rate (%)	1.56	2.61
Population sex ratio (female/male)	0.97	1.03
Human Capital Index score	60.33	51.06

Source: The Global Gender Gap Report (GGGR) data

Table 13.3 Comparison of Turkey and Nigeria according to the country scores for the four subindexes

TURKEY (T)/ NIGERIA (N)	T	N	T	N	T	N	T	N
	2006				2017			
	Rank		Score		Rank		Score	
Global Gender Gap Score	105	94	0.585	0.610	131	122	0.625	0.641
Economic participation and opportunity	106	59	0.434	0.612	128	37	0.471	0.728
Educational attainment	92	104	0.885	0.816	101	135	0.965	0.813
Health and survival	85	99	0.969	0.966	59	94	0.977	0.972
Political empowerment	96	99	0.052	0.049	118	135	0.088	0.052

Source: The Global Gender Gap Report (GGGR) data

Table 13.4 is an illustration of the political empowerment of both states. Though the political history and dynamics of the two states would not allow us to make fair comparison between them, the table illustrations indicate that both states score below 100. The two states have setbacks in women empowerment endeavours. One main difference is that Turkey was under colonial rule but has witnessed a series of coups d'état. On the other hand, Nigeria has experienced both. The colonial legacy as mentioned before rather had negative effects on the female empowerment setting in the Nigerian state. This was due to the political and cultural orientation of the colonizers prior to independence. Now that the colonial masters have gone through the enlightenment period and have resolved to close the gender gap, Nigeria is lagging behind in its effort to catch up with the other states. Both South Africa and Rwanda were affexted by the same colonial legacies but have done enough to ensure they can catch up with the world. The Turkish state, although developed and more powerful in terms of global politics, appears to be constrained by the traditional belief that women belong to the home.

Table 13.4 Comparison of Turkey and Nigeria regarding political empowerment index.

TURKEY/NIGERIA	T	N	T	N	T	N	T	N
	2006				2017			
	Rank		Score		Rank		Score	
Political empowerment	106	84	0.067	0.096	118	135	0.088	0.062
Women in parliament	105	115	0.10	0.08	108	139	0.171	0.059
Women in ministerial positions	123	45	0.04	0.29	135	103	0.040	0.136
Years with female head of state (last 50)	21	40	0.06	0.00	38	69	0.057	0.000

Source: The Global Gender Gap Report (GGGR) data.

This chapter brought together information from previous studies done on female empowerment and political participation in emerging power states with much emphasis on Turkey and Nigeria. The chapter acknowledged several setbacks in both states impeding women's participation in national and local politics. In the case of Turkey, the lack of few women's will to engage and encourage other women to join politics, the societal defined job of a woman to do house chores, and financial constraints are among the impediments. Though Turkey has not satisfied the gender equity demand of the EU, this is one of the foreign factors pushing the political will of the Turkish state to resolve female related issues that currently restrict women's representation in the country. Nigeria on the other hand is characterized by violent elections in some areas, which discourages many females who want to actively join politics. This has resulted in some women thinking politics is dirty and reserved for only dishonourable people. The predomination of some men in the political game has also scared away women who are nursing political ambitions. In cases where women are allowed to contest, the seats are either difficult or even impossible to win. It is also observed that women are also constrained by finance. Though several different factors determine the level of finance needed to empower oneself for political representation it is evident that money is a problem. Both states have put measures in place but little significant progress has been made. The Nigerian government has reneged on the 35% minimum women representation whereas Turkey has done little to give a clear road map for women empowerment in the state. The other MINT members could come together, make the club a realistic one and try just like BRICS to make sure they progress economically as issues of women empowerment become paramount in doing so. Yet, currently neither Turkey nor Nigeria seem to be rising powers from the perspective of strengthened democracy through women's political participation under the democratic development criteria, given the fact that their political empowerment ranks are 118 and 135 out of the 144 countries, respectively.

Note

1 Nigerian President Muhammadu Buhari on a visit to Germany said: "I don't know which party my wife belongs to, but she belongs to my kitchen and my living room and the other room".

References

Adaji, S. (2017). Women and Non-passage of the 35% Affirmative Action Bill by Nigeria Parliamentarians. *Lawyers Alert* (https: //lawyersalert.wordpress.com)

Agishi, T. V. (2014). Women Participation in Party Politics in Nigeria: Challenges and the Way Forward. *Nigerian Chapter of Arabian Journal of Business and Management Review*, 2(4), 95–100. doi:10.12816/0011586

Ajayi, K. (2005). Women in Politics. A Paper Presented at the University of Ado Ekiti at the Symposium on the Role of Women in Politics, June 3–4, 2005.

Ajogbeje, O. O. (2016). Women Participation in Nigerian Politics and its challenges for Nigeria's Centenary. *Nigerian Journal of Social Studies*, XIX (2), 71–84.

Alkan, A. (2009). Gendered Structures of Local Politics in Turkey. *Digest of Middle East Studies*, 18(1), 31–56.

Altindal, Y. (2007). Kadının Siyasal Katılımı Bağlamında Partilerin Kadın Kollarının Sosyolojik Açıdan Değerlendirilmesi, *Yayımlanmamış Yüksek Lisans Tezi*, Adnan Menderes Üniversitesi Sosyal Bilimler Enstitüsü, Aydın.

Ayata, A. & Tutuncu, F. (2008). Party Politics of the AKP (2002–2007) and the Predicaments of Women at the Intersection of the Westernist, Islamist and Feminist Discourses in Turkey. *British Journal of Middle Eastern Studies*, 35(3), 363–384.

Beeson, M. & Zeng, J. (2018). The BRICS and Global Governance: China's Contradictory Role. *Third World Quarterly*, 1–17. doi:10.1080/01436597.2018.1438186

Bozkurt, E. (2010) Women's Human Rights: Turkey's Way to Europe. Retrieved from: http://www.esiweb.org/pdf/esi_turkey_tpq_id_84.pdf

BRICS. (2016). 8th Summit. Retrieved from: brics2016.gov.in/content/innerpage/8th-summit.php

BRICS. (2018). Full Text of the 10th BRICS Summit Johannesburg Declaration. Retrieved from: https://www.fmprc.gov.cn/mfa_eng/wjdt_665385/2649_665393/t1580853.shtml

Caglar, N. (2011). Kadının Siyasal Yaşama Katılımı ve Kota Uygulamaları. *Süleyman Demirel Üniversitesi Vizyoner Dergisi*, 3(4), 56–79.

Cakir, S. (2001). *Bir'in Nostaljisinden Kurtulmak: Siyaset Teorisine ve Pratiğine Cinsiyet Açısından Bakış*. In A. İlyasoğlu & N. Akgökçe (Eds.), *Yerli Bir Feminizme Doğru*, pp. 385–422. İstanbul: Sel Yayıncılık.

Çelik, K. & Lukuslu, D. (2012). Spotlighting a Silent Category of Young Females: The Life Experiences of 'Housegirls' in Turkey. *Youth and Society*, 44(1), 28–48.

Dahlerup, D. (2005). Increasing Women's Political Representation: New Trends in Gender Quotas. In J. Ballington and A. Karam (Eds.), *Women in Parliament: Beyond Numbers*. International IDEA.

Doğramacı, E. (1997). *Türkiye'de Kadının Dünü ve Bugünü*. Ankara: İş Bankası Yayınları.

Drude, D. (2005). Increasing Women's Political Representation: New Trends in Gender Quotas. In J. Ballington and A. Karam (Eds.), *Women in Parliament: Beyond Numbers*. International IDEA.

European Commission. (2018). *Commission Staff Working Document: Turkey 2018 Report*. https://ec.europa.eu/neighbourhood-enlargement/sites/near/files/20180417-tur key-report.pdf

Fadia, K. (2014). Women's Empowerment through Political Participation in India. *Indian Journal of Public Administration*, 60(3), 537–548. doi:10.1177/ 0019556120140313

Fernanda, V. (2014). Understanding Equality in Mexico: Women in Politics. *International Journal: Advances in Social Science and Humanities*, 2(2). 1–6. Retrieved from: http://www.academia.edu/6662360/Understanding_equality_in_Mexico_Wom en_in_politics

Gökçimen, S. (2008). Ülkemizde Kadınların Siyasal Hayata Katılım Mücadeleleri. *Yasama Dergisi, Sayı*, 10, 5–59.

Howell, J. (2002). Women's Political Participation in China: Struggling to Hold up Half the Sky. *Parliamentary Affairs*, 55, 43–56.

Inglehart, R. 2004). *Human Beliefs and Values: A Cross-cultural Sourcebook Based on the 1999–2002 Values Surveys*. Mexico: Siglo XXI.

Kınık, H. & Tüfekçi, Ö. (2018). Rising Powers and The Dynamics of Conflict and Cooperation within Eurasi. In O. Tufekci, H. Tabak, R. Dag (Eds.), *Politics of Conflict and Cooperation in Eurasia*. Newcastle upon Tyne: Cambridge Scholars Publishing.

Moisés, J. Á. & Sanchez, B. R. (2016). Women's Political Representation in Brazil. *Gender and Power*, 11–34. doi:10.1057/9781137514165_2

National Democratic Institute for International Affairs. (2010). *Democracy and the Challenge of Change: A Guide to Increasing Women's Political Participation*. Washington: National Democratic Institute.

Olufunke, J. (2013). Violence and Women Participation in Politics: A Case Study of Ekiti State, Nigeria. *International Journal of Sociology and Anthropology*, 5(1), 26–34.

Olugbemi, K. V. (2011). *Women and Political Development in Nigeria since 1960*. In A. A. Agagu & R. F. Ola (Eds.), *Development Agenda of the Nigerian State*. Akure: Lord Keynes.

Orisadare, M. A. (2018) The Role of Government in Women Political Empowerment in Nigeria: Challenges and Implications for Economic Growth, July 21–25. Retrieved from: http://wc2018.ipsa.org/events/congress/wc2018/paper/role-governm ent-women-political-empowerment-nigeria-challenges-and-0

Randall, L. (2006). *Changing Structure of Mexico Political, Social, and Economic Prospects*. Armonk, NY: M.E. Sharpe.

Shook, B. & Harden, C. (2018). Will Women Decide the Brazilian Election? The Potential Impact of Female Voters and Candidates, March 10. Retrieved from: http s://www.wilsoncenter.org/event/will-women-decide-the-brazilian-election-the-poten tial-impact-female-voters-and-candidates

The Global Gender Gap Report. (2017). World Economic Forum. Retrieved from: https://www.weforum.org/reports/the-global-gender-gap-report-2017

Tüfekçi, Ö. (2016). Yükselen Güçler ve Dış Politika Aracı Olarak Dış Yardımlar, Içinde Erman Akıllı (Ed.), pp. 101–119, *Türkiye'de ve Dünyada Dış Yardımlar*, Nobel Yayınevi: Ankara.

Türkiye Büyük Millet Meclisi (TBMM). (2016). Retrieved from: https://www.tbmm. gov.tr/develop/owa/milletvekillerimiz_sd.dagilim (October, 2018).

Türkiye İstatistik Kurumu (TUİK). (2014). *Toplumsal Cinsiyet İstatistikleri*, Ankara. Retrieved from: http://kasaum.ankara.edu.tr/files/2013/02/Toplumsal-Cinsiyet-İstatis tikleri-2013-TUİK.pdf

UN General Assembly. (2012). Resolutions, September 17. Retrieved from: http://www.un.org/en/ga/66/resolutions.shtml

Yaraman, A. (1998). *Üniversite Gençlerinin Kadınların Siyasal Katılımına Yönelik Tutumları, 4. Ulusal Kadın Çalışmaları Toplantısı, Kadın Sorunlarının Çözümüne Doğru Yöntem ve Politikalar*, pp. 97–101, İzmir: Ege Üniversitesi, Kadın Sorunları Araştırma Merkezi ve Ege Kadın Araştırma Derneği Yayınları.

Yavuzçehre, P. S. & Öztepe, M. C. (2016). The Representation of Women in Turkish Local Governments. *European Journal of Interdisciplinary Studies*, 4(2), 210–219.

Zeng, B. (2014). Women's Political Participation in China: Improved or Not? *Journal of International Women's Studies*, 15(1), 136–150.

Index

Note: Indicators in *italic* refer to figures; those in **bold** refer to tables.